THE PASSIONATE
SHEPHERDESS

Maureen Duffy was born in 1933 and, since the 1960s she has been prolific in fiction, poetry, drama, history and politics. Her work reflects her socialism and commitment to animal rights.

THE
PASSIONATE
SHEPHERDESS

The Life of Aphra Behn
1640–1689

Maureen Duffy

PHOENIX
PRESS

5 UPPER SAINT MARTIN'S LANE
LONDON
WC2H 9EA

A PHOENIX PRESS PAPERBACK

First published in Great Britain
by Jonathan Cape Ltd in 1977
This paperback edition published in 2000
by Phoenix Press,
a division of The Orion Publishing Group Ltd,
Orion House, 5 Upper St Martin's Lane,
London WC2H 9EA

A CIP catalogue record for this book
is available from the British Library.

Printed in Great Britain by
Butler & Tanner Ltd, Frome and London

ISBN 1 84212 166 9

'Does not my fortune sit triumphant on my brow? dost not see the little wanton god there all gay and smiling? have I not an air about my face and eyes, that distinguish me from the crowd of common lovers?'

The Rover

Contents

Illustrations

Plates

Figures

Preface

Since 1977 when this biography first appeared, Aphra Behn's reputation has grown until it now stands higher than at any time since her death in 1689. As a consequence much research has been done and many papers have been published and there is now more of her work in print than for over two hundred years. In reissuing this book I had to decide whether to update it completely with subsequent material or to let it stand substantially as it first appeared as one writer's appraisal of, and response to, the life and work of another.

Because I believe the original book to have a voice and structure of its own I decided to take the second course and to use this preface to indicate some of the areas of enquiry which will continue to attract the interest of readers and scholars for the foreseeable future. I have also updated the family tree which appears on page 28. With all the difficulties of seventeenth century biography where there are few original documents to go on, and such a large body of work to study and enjoy, the possibilities for Aphra Behn research and exploration seem almost limitless, and so they are proving.

I have continued to work from time to time on her biographical details and her writings, adding to my knowledge of both, and revising or fleshing out my original ideas. I originally believed for example that the name of the eponymous hero of *Oroonoko* was an invention by her based on the name of the South American river. A subsequent discovery by one of those lucky chances that sometimes happen in research showed me that this was wrong and that the name derives from the Yoruba god Oro whose symbol is the bullroarer. Simultaneously, although by a more systematic method, Professor Bernard Dhiucq of the Sorbonne had also realized that the names and words Behn uses in *Oroonoko* as part of the slave culture are indeed of genuine African origin and not mere inventions. Imoinda, for example, means 'little honeyed one' and is still in use today, as are at least two variations on Oro: Orcokunle and Oroowusi. These discoveries reinforce her claim to have personally witnessed the events she describes.

Professor Dhiucq has also made very valuable contributions to the study of *Love Letters Between a Nobleman and His Sister* and to the French writers who were her contemporaries and whose work she translated. In addition Mary Ann O'Donnell's *Annotated Bibliography of Primary and Secondary Sources* (Gorland Publishing Inc 1986) has provided much valuable information on the dating of individual works.

My own chief interest in publication has been in making her work available in a paperback format that might reach a wider public who wanted to know more about the earliest professional women writers. There are now several interesting studies of her contemporaries which help to place her in this feminist literary context, notably by Antonia Fraser, Elaine Hobby and Fidelis Morgan.

The Passionate Shepherdess was first conceived as a book for the general reader whom I felt it inappropriate to burden with too much genealogical detail when ignorance of Aphra Behn's life and work was almost universal. As a consequence the evidence for my identification of her birth and family was perhaps too lightly sketched in. Since then, and by yet another piece of serendipity, I have been able to fill in much more of the family history on her mother's side with its subsequent implications for her upbringing, education and connections.

The importance of her or his mother in a writer's development is a commonplace which includes writers as disparate as Colette and D. H. Lawrence. Behn's natural father, Bartholomew Johnson, remains a shadowy figure, although he was a substantial yeoman and freeman citizen of Canterbury, and as such a freeholder entitled to vote in parliamentary elections. He was an innholder and not the only one to have artistic connections in the seventeenth century, as Henry Purcell's father-in-law also kept a drinking establishment.

Both the Memoir that precedes her works and Colonel Thomas Culpepper in his *Adversaria* are agreed that her maiden name was Johnson and that she came from Canterbury. Furthermore, there seems no good reason to doubt the Colonel's assertion that Aphra Johnson-Behn was his foster sister and her mother his nurse. No other poet gets so much attention from him in his *Adverseria* which was, after all, meant for private, not public, consumption. Other poets, like Shadwell, have, as Behn has in another part of the work, under D for death, a mention of the date of their deaths. He not only describes her work, her appearance, burial spot and epitaph but also his relationship to her. Brilliant and eccentric as he undoubtedly was, he is, as befits a member of the Royal Society, accurate with those facts about her which we can check, and I see no point in rejecting his other assertions.

The baptism of Eafry (that is Aphra or Aphera or Afery as it might be variously spelt) Johnson in the next parish to the Colonel's childhood home, on the outskirts of Canterbury, (and at the time when the Colonel and his sister were infants and his mother sickly) is too close to his assertions to be coincidental. No other candidate has emerged after exhaustive researches of the Kent registers and records at the Society of Genealogists, (including the Salt Lake City microfiche catalogue, records in the Kent Record Office at Maidstone and at Canterbury Cathedral Record Office). There is no other approximation to the name Aphra Johnson, let alone one belonging to someone born in the right place and on the right date.

We should not make the mistake of believing that a wet nurse was necessarily a person held in low estimation, a kind of seventeenth century Sarah Gamp. The term 'foster sister' makes it clear that the provision of milk was held to set up a quasi familial bond. It was believed that both physical and mental characteristics might be sucked in with such nourishment. The Colonel's mother was the daughter of an earl, Robert Sydney of Leicester. Her first children by her first husband, Lord Strangford, had been baptized and buried with the Sydneys at Penshurst. On her first husband's death she had married Sir Thomas Colepepper, governor of Dover Castle, against the advice and wishes of her father. When she began to bear his children she would look for a young mother of good health and some refinement as provisioner for them. Elizabeth Denham Johnson, mother of Eafry (or Aphra as I shall now call her) was just such a person.

When *The Passionate Shepherdess* was first published, I already knew that Elizabeth Denham's father had described himself as 'gent' when he had married her mother in 1611. In the seventeenth century such descriptions were accurate guides to social status. I knew that there was at least one other child of their marriage: a son, George, born in 1620 in Smeeth, only a mile or two from Lady Barbara Strangford's home during her first marriage. My piece of luck was subsequently to find this son as a doctor practising in Stamford, Lincolnshire in 1666 when he registered his pedigree with the visiting herald of arms and thereby opened up the whole family background to study.

The entry which he signed specifies both his parents and grandparents and the family and seat from which they came. George Denham himself, as well as another brother, Samuel, of Spalding, Lincolnshire, were not only well known doctors (or chirurgeons) locally but engaged in extensive consultation by letter with 'persons of quality' including Lord Hatton and Sir Henry Sloane. George had taken his BA at Magdalen College, Oxford in 1642 and had then been licensed to practise medicine from St John's Cambridge in 1654. By then he had married Elizabeth, daughter of John Boughton, gentleman of Lenham and their first son, John, had been born, who was to follow his father to Magdalen and eventually take orders and become vicar of Rogate and Iping in Sussex.

This discovery of medical practitioners in the family fits in with Ann Finch's comment that she had heard from local people that Aphra Behn's father was a barber in Wye. Doctors were often barber-surgeons and could therefore be satirically described as merely barbers. Wye is contiguous with Mersham and Smeeth where Elizabeth Denham was living when she married. The rumour had as so often, elements of half-truth in it.

George names his grandparents as George Dynham, which is how he spells the family surname in his pedigree, and Lucy Potter. The elder George is described as coming from Milksted Kent and being 'younger brother of Sir Thomas Dynham of

Bostoll in com. Bucks, Kent'. Sir Thomas Dynham, alias Rowe, the first George's father, was the illegitimate son of Sir John Dynham, baron, knight of the garter and Under Treasurer of England. He had inherited the manors of Boarstall and Eythorpe in Buckinghamshire. Boarstall Hall still stands; in Aphra Johnson's childhood during the Civil War it was held for a time by Dame Penelope Dynham as a royalist stronghold. Dame Penelope, who was therefore a distant (though in seventeenth century terms not so distant) relative of Aphra Johnson, left a bequest to 'my niece Mrs Anna Wharton' in her will and was also related to Aphra Behn's friend and patron the Duke of Buckingham. This old connection of the Dynham family with Buckinghamshire ties in neatly with Aphra Behn's own links with William Scot and Sir Thomas Gower, as discussed in chapters III to IX.

Sir Thomas's eldest son John had died before he could inherit and the title and manor passed to another Sir Thomas, Chief Forester and Steward of Bernwoode. The third son, George, had moved to Kent some time in the sixteenth century where he married a daughter of Richard Potter of Wellstreet House, Westerham, Kent, one of the local gentry. By this marriage George Denham allied himself through his brothers and sisters-in-law with some of the most important families in Kent: the Seliyords, Titchbournes, Swannes and the Potters themselves, all described in their local registers as 'gent' or 'esquire'. Several children were born of the marriage, five of whom their uncle, Thomas Potter, included in his Visitation pedigree of 1574. His own son, Nisell, went to University College, Oxford and became one of Kent's earliest antiquaries. William Swanne, his nephew, was knighted by Charles II at Rochester on his return in 1660. Nicholas Seliyord, his uncle, was Principal of Cliffords Inn for nearly fifty years. This network of landed gentry, several of them university educated, including two Kent vicars, lawyers and doctors, with many links to London gives us the right social level at which to place a future Aphra Behn, and clearly fulfils the Memoir's claim 'of good family'.

On George Denham's death, circa 1598, his widow Lucy seems to have moved from Mil(k)stead to the next door parish of Murton, where a relative, Gavin Heard, from her home parish of Edenbridge, was now vicar and where her daughter Jane was married to Will Croft, yeoman, the licence having been witnessed by her son Francis, Aphra Johnson's grandfather. Lucy was still alive in 1604 as a 'widow generosa'. Meanwhile several of her siblings, their families and her own mother, Alice, were still living in Edenbridge. Francis himself was now living in Sturry, the other place suggested by Colonel Thomas Culpepper for Aphra Behn's birth, which is just to the south east of Canterbury.

Although they were technically gentry there was probably little money to go round among the numerous Denham children in each generation. By the Kentish custom of gavelkind, property was divided equally between the sons where there was no will or agreement to set the arrangement aside. The Denhams appear to have been the least well-off amongst their relatives, even though they were entitled to a crest and coat of arms. George, Aphra's doctor uncle, seems to have gone as a poor scholar to Magdalen, having free tuition from a tutor with the Kentish name of Knatchbull. Belonging to the impoverished gentility is a great spur to aspiration and this shows in George's vigorous assertion of his pedigree in Lincoln in 1666. Similarly his sister would have maintained her social position in spite of marriage to a yeoman and, through the contacts which her employment as nurse to a daughter of the nobility brought, would have been able to give her children an education 'above their station'.

The household of Sir Thomas Culpepper had links not only with the poet Edmund Waller through his dedication to Lady Barbara's sister, Sacharissa, but also with the cavalier poet Endimion Porter, a protegé of the first Duke of Buckingham, whose son George was a gentleman of the bedchamber to Charles II. George's daughter Mary married as his second wife, after the death of his first wife, his cousin Isabella Sydney, daughter of the then Earl, Lady Barbara's son by her first husband Philip Lord Strangford. Endimion's third son, Thomas Porter, married Lady Barbara's daughter by Sir Thomas Culpepper, Roberta Ann, 'the Colonel's sister'. Sir Nicholas Crispe, father of Aphra Behn's admirer Henry, was Sir Thomas Culpepper's executor and had the task in 1642 of asking the Duchess of Leicester to persuade her husband to take on the guardianship of the orphaned Philip, his nephew, which he finally agreed to do. Most tantalizing is the reference in the accounts of a Kent Commonwealth official to Mr Johnson as Lord Strangford's steward, a position occupied later by Colonel Thomas Culpepper himself.

Each new piece of information reinforces the likelihood that this is the right Aphra Johnson. Meanwhile there is more work to be done on the Kent branch of the Willoughby family who lived at Chiddingstone and Penshurst which might reveal some link with Aphra Behn's visit to Surinam 'that poor and sad colony' as Francis Willoughby called it on 23rd January 1664, in answer to a letter from Henry Adis in Tyrarica on the 10th of October, referring to the previous bad government, oaths and drunkenness among the settlers and to the 'person that your Lordship has lately honoured with the title and power of your Lieutenant General of this Continent of Guinah', a clear comment on the appointment of Aphra Behn's enemy Byam which seems to give weight to the claim that her father or stepfather had been intended for the post before him.

But whatever queries might remain about aspects of her life, in the end it is Aphra Behn's work that counts and by which she must be judged, and it is therefore most important that in the tercentenary year of her death we should have a greater opportunity to do that than at any time since she died, refusing to compromise her art and her loyalty.

London 1988

Author's Note

The difficulties which face a would-be biographer of Aphra Behn are daunting. I have, I believe, uncovered and extracted a great deal of new material, yet even so the reader may well feel cheated at the end by the sheer lack of the kind of intimate detail which biographies of more modern subjects, or more portentous ones, have led us to expect. Apart from her published work, there are only some twenty-odd assorted documents relating to or by her (which include all her extant letters) to cover a life of nearly fifty years, and even some of those have been through other hands and must therefore be biographically suspect. Where there is an authentic autograph letter, it speaks out so distinctively that the loss of the rest of what must have been an enormous correspondence is made even more bitter. If she had been a monarch or a member of a powerful family more might have survived. As it is we have about as much as for most of her literary contemporaries like Otway and Congreve but much less than for Rochester or Dryden.

However, the biographer's job isn't to complain but to make the best of what there is, and in the case of Aphra Behn there is a very great deal indeed in the enormous body of her published work. As with so many artists, her work was her life. Fortunately she embodied in it many of those things that concerned her most. Brought up in the post-Romantic tradition we may tend to think that private agony or ecstasy is all that matters to an artist, but there are dozens of examples in English literature alone, from Langland to Byron, that contradict this and in the seventeenth century literature was passionately public and political. Aphra Behn does reveal her private emotional life in her work, particularly in her poems, but she also reveals her political and intellectual life which has been either misunderstood or neglected by posterity except for some vague idea that she was a Tory.

This neglect isn't the fault of her two most important biographers, Montague Summers and George Woodcock, who in their different ways did their best to correct the false impression of her as a kind of literary harlot which nevertheless still persists. The edition of the Westminster Abbey Registers of 1875 in its note on her burial entry epitomizes this attitude. 'Of her social position and literary abilities it is unnecessary to speak. She has taken a certain place in history and seems likely to keep it. It must, however, always be a reflection upon the judgement and good taste of Bishop Sprat, then Dean of Westminster, first, that he permitted her interment in the Abbey ground at all, and, secondly that he gave his assent to the extravagant doggerel cut upon her gravestone.' Maurice Ashley, in his *England in the Seventeenth Century*, gives the modern version: 'In conclusion we should doff our hats to a lady who demands a passing reference. Mrs Aphra Behn, who also tried her hand at spying and compiling plays, was perhaps the first English novelist, a somewhat thin and feeble shadow of her French contemporaries who regaled the Court of King Louis XIV with their long romances. Her *Oroonoko*, set in Surinam, is said to be the great-grandmother of all the modern horrors that bespangle our bookstalls.'

To ask, then, as I do, that her work and life should be given serious consideration is almost as outrageous as her work and life have themselves long been considered. In reviewing her for a new generation which I think may now be ready to give her that consideration, I have been determined to be as unfictional and unemphatic as possible, given the sensational nature of many aspects of her life.

I have been helped by many people and to them I must now make my acknowledgments. The Arts Council gave me the vital assistance of a grant while the Public Record Office, the London Library, the Victoria and Albert Museum, the British Library, the Kensington and Chelsea Public Library and the Society of Genealogists all gave me the assistance of their invaluable collections. Miss Oakley and her staff at the Canterbury Record Office and Miss Revell at the Kent Record Office in Maidstone were particularly helpful in local enquiries and I am also grateful to the Reverend Cyril Monk who allowed me to inspect the Harbledown registers in St Michael's church. Miss Anderson of the Royal Commission on Historical Manuscripts answered several queries for me and Miss Morcom of the Staffordshire Record Office was immensely helpful in matters relating to the Gower family and in xeroxing documents. The Record Offices of Cumbria, Gloucestershire, Leicestershire and Lincolnshire also patiently answered my queries as did Mr Francis Steer, Archivist and Librarian to his Grace the Duke of Norfolk, and Major S. Codrington. The University of Nottingham supplied photostats from their collection of the Portland MS. All Souls, New College and the Bodleian Library, Oxford, were all helpful, and Brigadier Peter Young kindly gave me the benefit of his Civil War records. The vicars of Wye, Sturry, Halling, Westbere and Throwley, all in Kent, answered queries about their parish registers. Mr Richard Jeffree and Mr Christopher White of the Mellon Foundation gave me valuable assistance on the portraits of Aphra Behn and Mr John Harris supplied useful bibliographical advice. I am particularly grateful to Miss E. Evans of the National Portrait Gallery for her continuing help in tracing portraits of Aphra Behn.

I should like to thank the following for permission to reproduce illustrations: Mr Arthur Schlechter, for plate 1; the owner, the Earl of Haddington, the Scottish National Portrait Gallery, to whom the painting is on loan, and Tom Scott, who took the photograph, for plate 8; and the Controller of H. M. Stationery Office, for figures 3, 4 and 5 and the endpapers, which are Crown-copyright records in the Public Record Office.

Abroad I am indebted to Mr Douglas of the Surinam Museum and Miss Thea Doelwyt in Surinam; in the United States, to Dr Helen Yalof, the Huntingdon Library, California, the South Carolina Department of Archives and History, and especially, for plate 4, to the John Carter Brown Library; and to the National Library of Ireland. My enquiries in Holland were all abortive but all the same I must thank the following institutions who kindly answered them: Algemeen Rijksarchief, Universiteits-Bibliotheck Amsterdam, Rijksuniversiteit

Leiden, the Koninklijke Bibliotheck Den Haag and the Familie-archieven, Utrecht.

Above all I must thank Michael Levey who found for me the edition of Aphra Behn's works edited by Montague Summers without which this book could truly not have been written, and Mrs Grace Ginnis who so faithfully typed it.

1976   M.D.

I

Aphra Johnson

Literary survival is largely a matter of fashion and chance. No greater gods preside over it and we deceive ourselves if we think they do, that we have a just appraisal of what is excellent and worth preserving from the millions of words ever written. The work of a single writer, of a school or of a whole era can be dismissed to the dustheap where broken reputations lie about like discarded toys. If anyone disputes this I should remind him of just one instance: the resurrection job T. S. Eliot and others had to do on the metaphysicals, and in particular on one of the greatest of English writers, John Donne, earlier this century.

It's therefore no surprise that the woman on the Clapham bus should be unable to answer when asked the name of the first woman in England to earn her living as a professional writer[1] and even when prompted 'Aphra Behn', should be completely unresponsive. For Aphra Behn has suffered not only a personal eclipse which is almost unparalleled in literary history but the eclipse of her whole idiom, English baroque, in the company of as acknowledged a genius as Dryden, to whom we pay an examination paper lipservice without any real appreciation or much understanding. Where we have acknowledged her existence it has usually been to mock or abuse her apparently without even the justification of having read her work.

There have been honourable critical exceptions to this, whom I have acknowledged in the preface, but too often, even where intentions were of the best, a fictionalizing process has taken over to make nonsense or romance of the facts of her life. This does her no service. The facts themselves are astounding enough to need no embellishment, above all the fact of her reputation in her own day which caused men to consider seriously that there might be a 'female laureate', and I shall therefore try to stick to them or to make conjecture absolutely clear for what it is.

I hope to establish that she was born in 1640. This means she grew up during the Civil War and the interregnum and was a young woman of nineteen when Charles II was restored in 1660. In her early twenties she went to Surinam in South America, which provided her with the material for one of the most famous, popular and influential novels of the period, *Oroonoko*. After her return to England, she was sent by Charles II as a spy to Antwerp, where she was involved in the complex politics of the first Anglo-Dutch war and of the English republican exiles. Back in England again, she was imprisoned briefly for debt and then set about earning her living as a professional writer, as, indeed, one of the most successful dramatists of the Restoration theatre, and as poet and novelist. Many of her plays and poems were written in support of the Stuart cause, to which she was attached by personal as well as political loyalty. Her closest friends included 'the wits', Buckingham, Rochester and Etherege, and the dramatists Dryden and Otway. Appropriately to her political views, she died five days after the coronation of William and Mary. She was buried in Westminster Abbey but the moral climate was already undergoing the change that brought about her long eclipse.

Those are the facts. The fictions begin with her birth. The account which you will find in most works of reference, which is that she was born Aphra Amis in the town of Wye in July 1640, is quite untrue. As the present vicar very kindly pointed out to me when I wrote to him and as had already been noticed,[2] that Aphra died a few days after she was born. The whole Aphra Amis legend rested on a note by Anne Finch, Countess of Winchelsea, to one of her own poems where she described Apollo lamenting for Aphra Behn's death.

> And standing where sadly he now might descry
> From the banks of the Stoure the desolate Wye,
> He lamented for Behn, o'er that place of her birth,
> And said amongst women there was not on earth,
> Her superior in fancy, in language, or wit,
> Yet own'd that a little too loosely she writ.[3]

The note reads: 'Mrs Behn was daughter to a barber, who liv'd formerly in Wye, a little market town (now much decay'd) in Kent. Though the account of her life before her works pretends otherwise; some persons now alive do testify upon their knowledge that to be her original.'

The Earl of Winchelsea, her husband, had property in the Wye district so that it would have been quite possible for Anne Finch to have heard a verbatim report from 'persons now alive'. I think, however, that their memories were misleading them and her. The person I believe they had in mind was Aphra Beane of the village of Elmstead, a couple of miles from Wye, who had been by her first marriage, and by an odd coincidence, an Aphra Amis and mother of an Aphra Amis.[4]

It has been suggested[5] that there never was a Mr Behn and that Aphra Behn simply had Aphra Beane in mind when she decided to call herself Behn. This is the kind of fiction that has built up around her. There are indeed two more Mrs Aphra Bean(e)s among the Canterbury marriage licences[6] whom she could have had equally in mind. Bean in all its variant spellings is a fairly common name in Kent in the seventeenth century and Aphras are thick upon the ground, also with many variant spellings. These two were spelt Afry and Alfery. Aphra, which is to us so exotic a name, seems to have been very popular roughly in what was the lathe of St Augustine and particularly along the banks of the Stour. It was spread through the whole social range.[7]

The 'account of her life before her works' to which Anne Finch referred was *The History of the Life and Memoirs of Mrs Behn*, which appeared prefixed to a collection of her *Histories & Novels*, first in 1696, and then, expanded, in 1698 and anonymously attributed to 'One of the Fair Sex', though the first version is admitted to be by Charles Gildon, the editor, who indeed repeats the main biographical facts in his rewrite of Langbaine's *An Account of the Dramatic Poets*. The memoir runs: 'She was a gentlewoman by birth, of a good family in the city of Canterbury in Kent; her paternal name was Johnson.'

It's hard to see why, given this firm statement, biographers ever set off in pursuit of Aphra Amis. The reason must be that the memoir continues in a style and with incidents that seem to belong more to fiction or farce than to fact. This caused the whole account to become discredited and Anne Finch's comment to be taken so seriously. A certain amount of malice probably lies behind it. Perhaps the Countess of Winchelsea felt that if she couldn't outdo Aphra Behn in talent or reputation she could in birth. Dryden, however, seems to bear her out.

In a letter to Elizabeth Thomas, a young woman who had sent him some verses of her own for criticism, after a piece of advice on avoiding 'the licenses which Mrs Behn allowed herself of writing too loosely', he goes on: 'But this I need not say to you who are too well born .. to fall into that mire.'[8] This sounds very much as if he didn't think Aphra Behn was as well-born as the memoir claimed, a supposition which she herself bears out in a poem where she speaks of cursing 'my birth, my education'.[9] There's an element in this of regretting that she had been born a girl and hadn't therefore been given a classical education but had to rely on translations to make Greek and Latin works accessible. I think, though, that there's more to it than this. It was possible for a woman who was gently born to acquire the classics even if only by a kind of osmosis from her brothers. Girls from other classes found it hard enough to become truly literate.[10]

Late seventeenth-century snobbery would have inclined to improve on Aphra Behn's birth. In that political climate it would have done her reputation no good for her to have risen by her own efforts from mean parentage. The written lives of the regicides, which followed the restoration of Charles II and the execution or imprisonment of those of his father's judges who were still alive, described almost all of them as of low birth even where it was completely untrue and must have been known to be so. Mean birth meant mean behaviour, as Dryden's letter bears out. For Astrea, as the memorialist called Aphra Behn, to be worthy of remembrance she must have been gently born.

Only one family of Kentish gentry in the period was called Johnson. Its branches stretched from Thanet,[11] where it seems to have originated, to Canterbury and the neighbouring villages of Westbere, Fordwich and Sturry, where some of its members were Church of England clergy. Unfortunately, among all its daughters there's not a single Aphra that I have been able to trace. Suitable as this family's background would be at this period for the nurturing of a young poet, whatever gilded baroque angel has the ordering of such things passed them by.

Nor have I found an Aphra Johnson among all the extant published and unpublished parish registers and bishop's transcripts of Canterbury itself. There are of course many Aphras. Given the commonness of the name Johnson there are remarkably few of them and none in the magic combination. Anne Finch didn't call the name Johnson in question, only the status of Aphra Behn's father and the fact that he came from Canterbury, although it would have been perfectly possible for him to have moved there later and still fulfil her condition 'formerly of Wye'. Fortunately there is another contemporary witness whose evidence has been surprisingly neglected by biographers.

In his *Adversaria*,[12] a manuscript collection of eighteen volumes of notes now in the British Library, Thomas Culpepper wrote, some time before 1708 when he died in Westminster: 'Mrs Aphara Bhen was born at Canterbury or Sturry, her name was Johnson. She was foster sister to the Colonell her mother being the Colonell's nurse.' The 'Colonell' is Thomas Culpepper himself. The entry goes on to make it clear that he had visited her grave 'in the cloister at Westminster near the door that goes into the church'. Perhaps he was even at her funeral.

The term 'foster sister' suggests that Mrs Johnson was specifically Thomas Culpepper's wetnurse and fed him. He was born on Christmas Day 1637 in Hackington, a village just outside the walls of Canterbury and sometimes known by the name of its parish church of St Stephen's.[13] His sister, Roberta Anne, was born two years later and baptized on July 7th 1639. Their parents were Sir Thomas Culpepper, described in his marriage licence as of Dover Castle, and Dame Barbara, who had been born a Sydney and married first to Thomas Smyth, Viscount Strangford, by whom she had three children, Philip, Barbara and Dorothy.[14] Sir Thomas and Dame Barbara were married in 1637. He had been knighted just before and had bought the manor house and estate of Hackington.[15] To this house Mrs Johnson must have gone to feed the Culpepper children, unless, which seems less likely, they were taken to her.

The Culpepper parents died within a few weeks of each other in 1643, their wills being proved on the same day. It's not clear where the two families of orphaned children were brought up. Thomas Culpepper later became steward to his half-brother Philip at Westenhanger but during the Civil War the moated manor there was being used as a parliamentarian prison. Perhaps the children lived at Hackington. Certainly the Hackington manor house was still in Thomas Culpepper's possession in 1675 when he sold it. Both he and his half-brother were too young to be involved in the early years of the Civil War, but they grew up ardently royalist and joined in plotting for the restoration of Charles II as soon as they were old enough.

One and a quarter miles from the Culpepper home at Hackington and half a mile outside the walls of Canterbury is the village of Harbledown, to which Bartholomew Johnson, 'yeoman, about twenty-three whose parents are dead', brought his wife Elizabeth shortly after their marriage at St Paul's, Canterbury, on August 25th 1638.[16] On December 14th 1640 their daughter was baptized in St Michael's, Harbledown. Her name appears in the register as Eaffry; her father's as Batholemew.[17]

Dynhams of Bucks

Francis Denham = Dorothy Thurston
(*1611*)

Bartholomew Johnson = Elizabeth		?George	Samuel
b.*1615* ?d.*1663* (*1638*) b.*1614*		b.*1620*	
alive ?*1667*		d.*1700*	
		Denhams of Lincs	

Aphra (Eaffry)	?George	1 daughter	1 son
b.*1640*	d.*1656*	('my sister' –	('my brother' –
?d.*1689*		alive *1663*)	alive *1667*)

Figure 1   The family of Aphra Behn.

Elizabeth Johnson, who was one year older than her husband when they married, was the daughter of Francis Denham of Smeeth, who, at his own marriage to Dorothy Thurston of Faversham on May 3rd 1611, was described as a gentleman of Mersham.[18] The Denhams had lived at Smeeth at least since May 22nd 1620, when George, the son of Francis, was baptized, but the register has no baptism for Elizabeth, who must have been born about 1614. The register does have another recognizable variant of Aphra in Aufrey Mydlety who was baptized in 1623.

Bartholomew Johnson came from Bishopsbourne, a village

just off the Dover road and three and a half miles from Canterbury. The manor of Bourne Place had once belonged to
Cranmer as Archbishop of Canterbury. He had exchanged it
with an earlier Thomas Culpepper for some property in Canterbury, and Culpepper had immediately alienated it to Sir
Anthony Aucher, whose wife Affra Cornwallis of Norfolk bore
him four sons and a daughter. The black tablets showing the
family descent are still in place in the Aucher chapel in Bishopsbourne church. Many of them weren't inscribed till after 1800[19]
although they were already in place. They now include an
Affra as late as 1725.

To Bartholomew Johnson, then, the name was familiar as
attached to the local gentry. The minister[20] of Harbledown had
never been asked to write it in the register before and not surprisingly, given the number of possible variations, and the fact
that he misspelt Bartholomew as well, he produced the variant
Eaffry. If this is indeed Aphra Behn's baptism it began a series of
permutations on her name which included Aphara, Aphaw and
Fyhere and, after her marriage, Bhen, Bene and Behen.

The major objection to an identification with Thomas
Culpepper's foster sister is the gap of three years between his
birth and hers. This gap isn't impossible. The Johnsons may
have had another child, perhaps a miscarried child, before
their daughter, or Thomas Culpepper might have been sickly
and given the breast for longer than usual or it could have been
that, although Mrs Johnson was his nurse, she was wetnurse only
to his sister. There is also a very strong possibility that Dame
Barbara, Culpepper's mother, knew Mrs Johnson while she was
still Elizabeth Denham living with her father at Smeeth, which
is only a few miles from Westenhanger, Dame Barbara's home
during her first marriage.[21]

The likelihood that Eaffry Johnson is the infant Aphra Behn
is strong enough for it to be worth looking a little harder at the
background of Bartholomew and Elizabeth Johnson. On Aphra
Behn's mother's side at least, the description of the memoir can
be satisfied. The children of gentlemen began life as gentlemen.
Elizabeth Denham's mother also came from a very substantial
family, the Thurstons of Faversham, who were merchants,
mercers, haberdashers and so on and one of whom, William,
was a jurat, a species of alderman.[22]

Bartholomew, Aphra Behn's putative father, has left less information to posterity. There was a family of Johnsons in Bishopsbourne according to the registers but no child Bartholomew is recorded as being baptized there. Edmond Johnson, who by the time he died in 1628 was a householder and had been a churchwarden for many years, although presumably unable to write since he made his mark when he certified the registers, was described in his marriage licence as a husbandman in 1602. There were other Johnsons in the village. Alice Johnson, widow, who could have been Bartholomew's mother, died in 1626, while Anne Johnson married Thomas Michell Esq. in the same year. Perhaps Alice and Edmond were related.

A little more information can be gleaned from the friends who were bondsmen for Bartholomew's marriage licence: John Fuller and Cuthbert Hilton, both described as carpenters of Canterbury. Hilton became a freeman of the city by redemption in 1652, which argues a good financial position. Fuller married a girl from the Smeeth/Mersham area whose brother was a sergeant in the army on guard at Rochester Bridge in 1647.[23] Bartholomew Johnson was bondsman for Fuller's marriage in 1639 and when Edward Argoe of Faversham, glazier, married Mary Rich of Harbledown in the same year he testified to her father's or mother's consent. After that I can find nothing except one or two odd entries that may or may not apply to him. George, the son of Bartholomew Johnson, died in the parish of St Alphage in Canterbury in 1656 and was buried at St Margaret's.[24] This is a likely brother for Aphra Johnson, since Elizabeth Johnson had a brother George and names tended to run monotonously in families. In 1649 a Bartholomew Johnson, innholder, became a freeman of the city by redemption. The move from yeoman to innholder isn't impossible but it seems unlikely. A yeoman would usually rise through land to become a gentleman. Against this it must be said that Bartholomew Johnson had close friends among the trades and an innholder isn't the same as an innkeeper. Elizabeth too had strong trade connections.

I think the family moved from Harbledown in the 'forties. Certainly there's no further trace of them in the registers. If Eaffry Johnson is the child Aphra Behn there is a poetic coincidence in the fact that it was from Harbledown that the young Walter Pater took the footpath to Canterbury to school. In default of a better candidate Eaffry Johnson seems to fulfil most of the requirements, including Thomas Culpepper's statement that she was born in Sturry or Canterbury. Harbledown virtually is Canterbury. The Sturry registers record no Aphra Johnson. Culpepper's suggestion is probably based on the fact that he knew there were Johnsons in Sturry.[25]

Aphra Behn maintained her connection with the Culpepper family to the end of her life. Henry Crispe, Thomas Culpepper's young cousin,[26] became a close friend of hers in the 1680s and contributed many poems to her *Miscellany* of 1685. But there's another connection which was even more important for her. Thomas Culpepper's mother was the daughter of Robert Sydney, Earl of Leicester, and therefore sister both to Algernon Sydney, the republican, and to the poet Waller's Sacharissa, Lady Dorothy, who became Countess of Sunderland. It was to Sacharissa's son, Robert Spencer, that Aphra Behn dedicated the third part of her longest novel, *Love Letters Between a Nobleman and His Sister*. Her involvement with Waller, which culminated in a long and moving epitaph on his death in 1687, provided one of her earliest literary influences. His first volume of poems was published in 1645. They had already circulated in manuscript since he had begun his court to Dorothy Sydney at Penshurst in the 1630s. It was on them that Aphra Behn modelled her early poems, those 'prettiest soft engaging verses in the world' which the memoir of 1698 claims she wrote from infancy.

Waller kept up his contacts with the Kentish Wallers, even though he himself was from Beaconsfield in Buckinghamshire. Kent became involved in his 1643 plot to seize London for Charles I. At the same time Sir William Waller, his distant kinsman, was a Parliament man and general of the South Eastern Association. The world into which Aphra Behn had been born was one bitterly at war with itself, which was to provide, together with love, the major theme of her work.

II

Kent in the Interregnum

There are no records that I have been able to find for the first twenty years of her life[1] apart from the death of a possible brother. In 1666 she still had a brother and mother living, since her letters from Antwerp refer to them. In *Oroonoko* she also mentions a sister. Families before contraception tended to be large, even when you set against the high birthrate the almost equally high figures for infant mortality. Parish registers make terrifying reading. Every birth was attended with the strong possibility of death for mother and child. There may, then, have been other siblings who didn't survive. There's also more than a possibility that one or other of her parents had died and that the mother and father she refers to in *Oroonoko* are in modern terms stepmother and stepfather. I've been unable to find any record of a remarriage by either Elizabeth or Bartholomew Johnson but records during the interregnum were often poorly kept and may have been subsequently destroyed.

However, although there are no easily accessible records,[2] it's possible to reconstruct the kind of world Aphra Behn must have been brought up in and I believe it's important to try to do so for an understanding of her work and her later life. The writer, like all artists, remakes his childhood over and over again in his work and she was no exception. I found surprising confirmation of this in a book which isn't consciously about her at all, indeed I should think it unlikely that the author, a Fellow in urban history, had read her work when he wrote it, yet it gives an almost complete description of the influences that shaped her and that are discernible in her writing and personality. The book is Alan Everitt's *The Community of Kent and the Great Rebellion 1640–60.*

In the memoir, One of the Fair Sex speaks of Aphra Behn's father leaving his quiet retreat at Canterbury for his post in Surinam. As I've said before, there's a great deal of invention in the memoir but it's almost always based on some half-truth that can be seen just behind. The half-truth here, I believe, is the impression that Aphra Behn gave of her childhood as of a secure country upbringing although while she was growing up Britain was going through some of its most traumatic years. This rural security was part of the nature of Kent itself.

Even today Kent remains in many ways a secret county, in spite of the tourists who pour through Canterbury Cathedral in summer. It's a county principally of small villages, with a cluster of houses round pub and church, quite unlike, say, the more open urban countryside of Buckinghamshire with its many small market towns. By 1676 the village of Harbledown had 194 inhabitants, Bishopsbourne 130, Smeeth 257.[3] Even Canterbury had only about 4,500 adults, with an estimated total population of 7,500. On the other hand there was a surprisingly large number of gentry compared with other counties of comparable size.[4] This made for hundreds of small landowners, who are traditionally and notoriously insular and conservative. They spoke of Kent as their 'country' and they prided themselves on their birthright and their freedom to pursue their own local ways as their fathers had done. This gentry was largely native. Its fields came up to its backdoors and it tended those fields with loving and precise attention. It gave precise attention, too, to its marriages, which were contracts undertaken to add more, in money or land, to the family estate. Aphra Behn wasn't unique among Restoration playwrights in her exploitation of the subject of forced and unhappy marriages for money but she brings more compassion and depth to her variations on an accepted theme.

For a woman of fairly obscure birth who wished to make some impression on the world Kent was an impossible place to stay. The dominance of the local gentry, while it gave a patriarchal sense of security, would have made no accommodation for the phenomenon of a dowerless poet who in any case was little inclined to support herself by what she regarded as the legalized prostitution of arranged marriage. On the other hand it gave her a strong infantile predisposition towards Toryism and personal loyalty to the patriarchal figure of the King.

Everitt notes the high degree of literacy, indeed of actual scholarship, among Kentish gentry. They were particularly eloquent on local history and custom and on theology, where they were firm supporters of the Church of England. Hooker's *Ecclesiastical Policy* was partly written while he was rector of Bishopsbourne; Sir Roger Twysden wrote an *Historical Vindication of the Church of England* and Sir Edward Dering was chairman of the Committee for Religion, which included several other Kent M.P.s. Though wanting reform of the established church and the removal of Laudian accretions, Dering remained firmly for a form of primitive episcopacy rather than presbyterianism and eventually found himself in the Tower, with his speeches, which he had just published, condemned to be burned by the common hangman.

Politically the bulk of Kent seems at first to have been for moderation, for some reform without plunging into extremes in either church or state. Perhaps more than in other counties, too, neighbours managed at first to meet and remain on good terms even when on opposite sides.

> Henry Oxinden of Great Maydeacon, a parliamentary captain, freely corresponded with Sir Thomas Peyton and Sir Anthony Percivall, saw to their estates while they were in prison, and entertained Sir Thomas when released ..
> War was far from total, and it was certainly inconvenient – and there was a strong feeling even during the war that it was unchristian – to remain at enmity with your neighbours.[5]

'She was of a generous and open temper, something passionate, very serviceable to her friends in all that was in her power; and could sooner forgive an injury than do one,' says the memoir. I suggest that much of this attitude she had sucked in unconsciously as a child brought up in Kentish mores.

At the same time her heroes must have been the extremists: the cavaliers, of whom perhaps Richard Lovelace of Lovelace Place in Kent was the prototype, as Richard Hillary was the Second World War prototype of the fighter pilot or Rupert

Brooke of the Great War soldier. *To Althea from Prison*, with its combination of eroticism and loyalism, was written during his imprisonment for presenting the Kentish petition to Parliament in 1642. During his second imprisonment in 1648 he prepared for publication his volume of poems called *Lucasta; Epodes; Odes, Sonnets, Songs etc.* which appeared in 1649. He died in extreme poverty in 1658 'in a cellar in Long Acre',[6] having spent his estate for the royalist cause. Among those who, Aubrey says, gave him regular supplies of money was another poet, friend and admirer of Aphra Behn, Charles Cotton, who himself fell deeply into debt after the restoration. The poverty, swashbuckling charm, drinking and duelling of the cavaliers were written into her heroes, sometimes specifically as recreations of the roving cavaliers themselves, sometimes as attributes of contemporary beautiful gentlemen and desirable lovers. Her childhood idealization must account for the intense attractiveness of a character like Wilmore the Rover, of whom Dibdin says that when Queen Mary saw Mountford in the part she said it was dangerous to see him act, he made vice so alluring. The allure lay in the part itself as well as in the performer. Even the names of some of the local families suggest characters from plays: Paramore, Dering and Lovelace himself.

In her most baroque imagery there's still, I think, a trace of her upbringing. Remote as it may seem to us, the idealized convention of swains and nymphs keeping the white flocks takes on more of that closeness to Nature, in the seventeenth-century sense of naturalness, almost of realism, for which contemporaries praised her, if we see it in the context of the Kent hills with their flocks over which is shed the luminosity of the Golden Age of childhood. For many of the gentry it was to a pre-war rural parochial Golden Age that they longed to return and this strand runs through Aphra Behn's work, too, even though most of the time she was in the thick of the political struggle.

The course of her childhood saw the Kentish moderates forced to take sides; and mostly, after the execution of Charles I, they took, whether secretly or openly, the royal side. For a traditional, patriarchal county such an oedipal killing was a profound psychological shock, a shock which the child Aphra Johnson, who according to the memoir was as precocious as we would expect, shared even with the republican Algernon Sydney. Duty to kings and to fathers is very easily confounded. In the dedicatory epistle to Henry, Duke of Grafton, which prefaces *The Roundheads or The Good Old Cause*, she writes: 'You, sir, who are obliged by a double duty to love, honour and obey his Majesty both as a father and a King! O undissolvable knot! O sacred union! what duty, what love, what adoration can express or repay the debt we owe the first or the allegiance due to the last ...'[7] It's a pity we know no more about the man who must originally have inspired this emotion, Aphra Behn's own father.

Her attitude to her mother is more equivocal, to judge by the only small piece of evidence. In a letter from Antwerp, justifying the arrangements she had made for the collection of some money, she writes of her mother 'possibly I should be loath to let her have it for another reason'. Perhaps she was extravagant and her daughter feared she would spend it. The memoir says that both parents feared that because of her precocity she might die young, and she herself claims in *Oroonoko* that she was 'but sickly, and very apt to fall into fits of dangerous illness upon any extraordinary melancholy'. Such a child would sop up the atmosphere around it only too easily. It led to a lifetime's preoccupation with politics. The intensity of her preoccupation suggests that her father was himself a royalist. He died, she says, on a voyage to Surinam to take up an official appointment as 'Lieutenant-General of six and thirty islands, besides the Continent of Surinam'. This claim is very hard to reconcile with Bartholomew Johnson of Harbledown or indeed the husband of Thomas Culpepper's wetnurse. It becomes even harder when the official records of colonial state papers and all the extant private correspondence make no mention of any such person or, in those precise terms, any such job.

The interregnum was a period of great social mobility. Men who in normal circumstances would never have risen to sergeant became captains, majors, colonels. This was particularly true, of course, of the Parliament army, which, lacking many of those who were thought of as the natural leaders, the gentry, had to raise up its own officers. Such a rise was harder for a royalist. In the first place, the standing army, with an official hierarchy to rise through, wasn't accessible to them after 1646 and the royalist defeat (unless they were prepared to join the

Scots army), and secondly there were many more, both gentry and noblemen, to fill the officer ranks. To be a lieutenant-general, however, would seem to require some military training or experience.

An explanation which I've already suggested is that one of her parents, who in this case would have to be her mother, re-married. There is a further possibility: that she was adopted after the death of both her parents. However it came about, I'm convinced that some time in 1663 she set sail with her family for the West Indies and Surinam.

III

Surinam

To die on a voyage to the West Indies was common enough. Most men made their wills before they set out and many of those wills are calendared 'died at sea' or 'died abroad'. The journey to Surinam took several weeks and usually included a stop at Barbados, although in the 1670s, when the English were being evacuated from Surinam, the captains were ordered to go direct. I've been able to find no appropriate will for Aphra Behn's father but then there's none for herself either. Even someone as highly placed as George Villiers, Duke of Buckingham, refused to make a will. Then as now it was probably temperament as much as anything else which decided whether you did or didn't. If Bartholomew Johnson was her father and was still alive in 1663, he would have been about forty-eight, neither too old nor too young for some kind of colonial post.

The colony of Surinam was a relatively new development. There had been an attempt to plant a settlement in 1643 but in 1645 the Indians had massacred both the English and neighbouring French planters.[1] Then in 1650, Lieutenant-Colonel Anthony Rous, 'a gentleman of great gallantry and prudence and of long experience in the West Indies', settled 300 people from Barbados in Surinam, with the help of Francis, Lord Willoughby of Parham, who provided the ship to transport them and 'the loan of a parcel of Indian trade'. Willoughby also settled two plantations of his own, one of which has given its name to the capital Paramaribo.[2]

Rous left in 1654 and a Major William Byam was chosen governor, according to the author of the *Discription of Guyana*, who also calls him 'a judicious gentleman'. Both Byam and

Willoughby had been involved in, indeed the leaders of, the
rebellion of Barbados against Parliament, when an English fleet
under Sir George Ayscue had to be sent to restore Barbados to
its loyalty to the English government, since it had declared for
loyalty to the King and independence.[3] In the treaty which
followed the defeat of Willoughby and the Barbadians, he had
been allowed to retain his English estates and Surinam. He had
sent Byam as deputy governor to Surinam and had himself
gone back to England to engage in royalist plotting. On several
occasions he was ordered back to his government in Surinam
but he managed to avoid going and was still in England when
Charles II was restored.

Willoughby immediately set about getting royal patents for
his claim to the whole of the Caribee Islands and Surinam. He
was partially successful in both. Other claimants appeared for
the Caribees, representing the creditors of the deceased Earl of
Carlisle, his heir, the Earl of Kinnoul, who wanted to govern in
person, and the Earl of Marlborough. In Surinam Willoughby
was forced to compromise by taking Lawrence Hyde, second
son of the Earl of Clarendon, as partner in the royal grant.
Clarendon had already shown an interest in colonial matters
and had joined the Duke of York's pet Royal African Company
and was one of the Lords Proprietors of Carolina. In the *Continuation of the Life*, Clarendon claims that he had been Willoughby's 'chief friend in procuring that government for him
and in discountenancing and suppressing those who in England
or in the Islands had complained of him'. He took no money for
the service but had his son included in the Surinam patent.
Willoughby was commissioned governor of Barbados and the
Caribees on June 12th 1663 and on June 16th instructed to
'repair with all convenient speed to his government'. The grant
of Surinam 'by the name of Willoughby Land' had been made
earlier, on May 6th. It gives Willoughby and Lawrence Hyde
the usual powers, including that of appointing a 'captain
general'.[4]

At this point, then, he could have appointed a captain
general, not a lieutenant, for Surinam, not including the
Caribees, or the appointment could have been to some candidate of Lawrence Hyde's. The memoir says that Aphra Behn's
father was related to Lord Willoughby and that was why he

got the job, but she nowhere in *Oroonoko* makes any such assertion. She does speak of a kinsman, called by the Indians the
Grand Peeie or great priest because of the wonders he performs
with a magnifying glass, but that's all. Indeed her attitude to
Willoughby, whom she never mentions by name but refers to as
the governor, is rather cool throughout, perhaps because of his
association with Byam, whom she detested.

There's also extant an appeal by Willoughby for planters to
go to Surinam.[5] This is variously dated but could apply to
1663 as well as for the earlier period of his settlement under
Cromwell. Aphra Behn's father might have gone as a planter,
taking his family with him. The memoir suggests that she was
very young when she went, capable of inspiring love but not
gratifying it, which in seventeenth-century terms of early
marriage would have meant no later than thirteen or fourteen.

> Silvia the fair in the bloom of fifteen
> Felt an innocent warmth as she lay on the green

writes Dryden and again

> Take me, take me some of you
> While I yet am young and true;
> Ere I can my soul disguise;
> Heave my breasts and roll my eyes.
> Cou'd I find a blooming youth
> Full of love and full of truth
> Brisk, and of a janty meen,
> I shou'd long to be fifteen.

But in terms of Thomas Culpepper's foster sister, Aphra Behn
must by now have been in her early twenties and her own
narrative of this time, although remembered over twenty years
later, doesn't suggest that she was a child. Unless she went
twice to Surinam, the memoir must be romancing again,[6] for all
the internal references in *Oroonoko* date her stay in the country
to a period of a few months some time not long before August
1666, when Francis Willoughby was drowned in the hurricane
which she refers to.

Fortunately there's a series of private letters[7] which help to
confirm that she was there and to date her stay more precisely.
They were written to Sir Robert Harley, who had been ap-

pointed Chancellor of Barbados in 1662, which rather looks as if Willoughby had a private assurance from Charles II that he would get the governorship of Barbados, since he was allowed to appoint a chancellor.[8]

Willoughby belonged to the presbyterian royalist group and had indeed begun the war fighting on the Parliament side. Sir Robert, and his brother Sir Edward, both belonged to this group. Edward Harley was an attractive personality which his letters to his wife show up well. Robert was a very different character. They were both Willoughby's friends and this was why Sir Robert was given the appointment. He arrived in Barbados in February 1663 and two months later wrote home complaining that he had expected Willoughby to be there before him but that he had still not arrived. Willoughby eventually reached the island and held his first assembly, where among other acts he delivered the seal to Harley on August 25th 1663.

All soon began to go wrong. Harley's letters show a man of a rather haughty irascible turn who was also inclined to secretiveness. While waiting for the boat from Dover he sent home a cipher to his brother which he intended they should use in their correspondence. He soon began to find fault with Willoughby and with his treatment.[9] He therefore bought a plantation in Surinam with the intention of possibly going to live there. However, the quarrel between them erupted too quickly. Harley refused either to set the seal to a writ on February 5th 1664 or to deliver up the seal, and he was arrested and put in gaol on the 11th. On the 18th Willoughby wrote giving the King his version of what had happened and he also wrote to the Secretary of State, Sir Henry Bennett, that Harley had 'gone off in discomfort ... because he could not remain to do as he listed' but that Willoughby hadn't banished him. The letter was received in April. Harley's version to his brother in a letter of the same day is rather different. 'Upon my delivery of the seal he would have sent me to Surinam but upon much pressing ... will send me in a small vessel to New England, upon no terms will let me go for Old England.' Harley had had to eat a certain amount of humble pie. He was eventually allowed to return home. Meanwhile others had been writing to Sir Robert, in particular from his plantation in Surinam.

The first letter is from a William Yearworth who seems to have been some kind of employee of Harley's. He had been told by Harley to look for somewhere on the plantation to build himself a house and he explains his difficulties and final success. He asks for a young Negro to instruct in his own trade although sadly for history he doesn't say what that trade is. His letter continues and I give it, for interest, in the original spelling: 'Theere is A genney man Arived heere in this river of ye 24th of This Instant att Sande poynt. Shee hase 130 nigroes one Borde: ye Comanders name Joseph John Woode; shee has lost 54 negroes in ye viage. The Ladeyes that are heere live att St Johnes hill. Itt is reported heere that yowre Honoure have sould that Plantation toe my Lord Willoughby.' The letter is dated January 27th and is addressed to Sir Robert in Barbados.

In *Oroonoko* Aphra Behn says: 'As soon as I came into the country, the best house in it was presented me call'd St John's Hill.' In her party were her mother, her sister, 'my woman, a maid of good courage', her brother and herself: a sufficient female preponderance for William Yearworth to refer to them as 'the Ladeyes', since her brother was young and very much under her domination, as he still was three years later when she took him to Flanders with her.

The plantation was undoubtedly still Sir Robert Harley's, for a later letter in the series, written to him in London on March 3rd, has an offer to buy it from a George Needham, who later moved to Jamaica and became an important figure on that island. I think it was because 'the Ladeyes' had been lodged there that rumour said it had been sold to Willoughby. This suggests that they were thought to be in some way connected with Willoughby and bears out Aphra Behn's claim that her father was going to an official post. Since Willoughby's intention was to go himself to Barbados, he might very well have sent a lieutenant to Surinam, particularly since the contest over his claims looked like dragging on.

The family could have set out immediately after the royal grant was made on May 6th 1663 and arrived at most nine weeks later. Renatus Enys,[10] who arrived on August 27th, wrote home to Sir Henry Bennett that his prosperous voyage had taken nine weeks. He further says that the colony is in good order, being nobly upheld by those at the helm who though hitherto not commissioned by his Majesty suddenly expect the arrival of Lord Willoughby, and then to be 'bottomed' on royal authority, 'the want of which has given encouragement to incendiaries'.[11] Another traveller to Surinam, Capt. Henry Adis, wrote just over three months later, on December 10th, to Willoughby himself, speaking well of 'the Lieutenant General of the Continent of Guiana' but complaining of the settlers as more brutish by far than the very heathens themselves.[12] Some time between late August and early December, then, a lieutenant general of Surinam had been appointed and he was the man who was already governor, Willoughby's old friend from Barbados, William Byam.

Byam was in his early forties, son of a royalist, Dr Henry Byam, who was made a canon of Exeter Cathedral by Charles II, and married to Dorothy Knollys, whose father was a nephew of the Earl of Banbury. Aphra Behn should therefore have been predisposed to like him. In the event she turned him and his deputy into the villains of *Oroonoko*. She refers to Byam when she first mentions him as 'the Deputy Governor of whom I have had no great occasion to speak' and as 'the most fawning fair-tongu'd fellow in the world ... and, though he had nothing, and so need fear nothing, yet talked and looked bigger than any man. He was a fellow not fit to be mentioned with the worst of the slaves.' This is the kind of language she usually kept for the Whigs. That, writing over twenty years later, she should apply it to a royalist makes me think that her initial dislike was because Byam had stepped into her father's post by his death.

Perhaps at this point I should briefly tell the story of *Oroonoko*, the documentary novel she made out of this episode. It begins in Coramantien in West Africa. Oroonoko himself is a young black prince, grandson of the old chief. He has been trained as a warrior but has also contrived, through a French tutor and converse with European traders, to learn several languages. He falls in love with the beautiful Imoinda but the lovers find themselves in a Tristan and Isolde situation with the old King who, having enjoyed her as a concubine, eventually has Imoinda sold into slavery. Oroonoko, believing her dead, falls into a despair from which he is only roused when the country is invaded. Gradually his grief moderates a little and

eventually he even returns to court, only to be shanghaied by an
English captain who has invited him aboard his ship, and is in
his turn carried into slavery, along with his French tutor and
many of his followers. The ship arrives in Surinam, where he is
sold to Trefry, Lord Willoughby's overseer at Parham. Meanwhile Aphra Behn's family have themselves arrived in Surinam
a little before this and are lodged at the neighbouring plantation
of St John's Hill. By the kind of coincidence beloved of life and
fiction, Imoinda has also been bought by Trefry and the lovers
are reunited. Imoinda becomes pregnant and Oroonoko leads a
rebellion of the slaves, who march towards the sea to set up
a free colony of their own. Byam and the settlers go in pursuit.
After a battle Oroonoko surrenders in return for the promised
freedom of his family. He is betrayed by Byam and whipped
almost to death. Trefry befriends him and he recovers in order
to be revenged on Byam. In preparation for this he murders
Imoinda with her consent, so that she and her unborn child
shan't be left to his enemies. However, the act is too much for
him and he exhausts himself with grief and fasting so that when,
eight days later, a search party finds him he has only strength
enough to mutilate himself in attempting suicide. He is brought
back to Parham where his wounds are dressed but the surgeon
assures him he will die. While Trefry and Aphra Behn are both
absent one day Byam's deputy comes and takes him by force
back to the place where he was whipped, fastens him to the
stake and Oroonoko is gradually cut in pieces which are thrown
into a fire in front of him, while the crowd, which includes
Aphra Behn's mother and sister, stand watching, until he
dies.

I am concerned here with the book only in so far as it throws
biographical light on Aphra Behn. I will deal with it later as
literature along with the other work she was writing at the time,
though I should perhaps say now that I think it a masterpiece.

The four white men whom she mentions are all historical
people living in Surinam from 1662 onwards; two, Byam and
Banister, she portrays as villains; two, Trefry and George
Marten, she shows as sympathetic. On March 14th 1664, in a
letter to Sir Robert Harley, Byam adds as a postscript: 'Major
Bannister and his lady present their humble service to you.'
Aphra Behn describes him as 'a wild Irishman, one of the

Council, a fellow of absolute barbarity, and fit to execute any villainy, but rich'.

Colonel George Marten had been with Willoughby in Barbados in the 'fifties and had been sent home as an emissary to England to put the Barbadian case, no doubt because he was brother to the regicide Sir Henry Marten whom Aphra Behn describes as 'the great Oliverian'. He was 'a man of great gallantry, wit, and goodness, and whom I have celebrated in a character of my new comedy, by his own name, in memory of so brave a man. He was wise and eloquent, and, from the fineness of his parts, bore a great sway over the hearts of the whole colony.'

Trefry[13] she describes as having been 'carried into those parts' to manage Willoughby's affairs. He was a 'young Cornish gentleman ... a man of great wit and learning ... a very good mathematician and a linguist, could speak French and Spanish'. The Treffry family in fact appears in the Herald's *Visitation of Cornwall, 1619.*

These then were the people whom she admitted to have met in Surinam though others are mentioned in passing, not by name but as figures in the background. Renatus Enys estimated that there were four thousand people there at this time. Aphra Behn mentions that the militia consisted of about six hundred men. Yet even so small a community was split by factions. 'All hands were against the Parhamites (as they called those of Parham-Plantation) because they did not in the first place love the Lord-Governor', she says of those whom she describes as 'the men of any fashion ... they of the better sort'.

The state papers bear out this discord. Robert Sandford, for example, had petitioned Parliament against the high-handedness of Byam in 1662, and John Trefry, writing to Charles Pym on August 15th that year,[14] said that Mr Sandford had alleged that Byam, 'our noble governor,' had tried to poison him. Enys had mentioned the 'incendiaries' and when Willoughby eventually came to Surinam in 1665[15] he was attacked by one of the inhabitants.

Into this volatile situation came Aphra Behn and, if we believe her claim, Oroonoko. It has been alleged that she never went to Surinam at all but wrote the whole thing up from a little book published in 1665, *A Brief Description of Guyana* by

George Warren. What is possible is that she had the book with her when she wrote *Oroonoko*, which she did very quickly and, according to her editor, Charles Gildon, often in a room full of company and taking part in the conversation, as he had observed her.[16] But Southerne, who turned the novel into a very successful play, claimed that she told the story even better than she wrote it. No doubt over the years it had acquired embellishments of various kinds. None of this, though, invalidates her claim, repeated in the dedication to *The Young King*, that she had actually been there. Her knowledge of the historical people involved doesn't come from George Warren's little book, which mentions only Byam. It includes what looks like a practical joke on the governor's part, for he has persuaded Warren to include among the rarities he is describing a camel fly which Warren hadn't himself seen but which Byam said settled on a tree and turned into a plant.

Certainly Aphra Behn could have learnt about Byam, who circulated several short accounts of his own of contemporary events in manuscript. She could also have known of Banister from hearsay, for he was sent by the Dutch as a prisoner to Flushing and became the object of intense international negotiations for his release. Her estimate of his character is, I think, unfair, for when Surinam was ceded to the Dutch after the Treaty of Breda, Banister never ceased his efforts to get the miserable English settlers who were left behind ships to transport them to Jamaica.

If it's allowed that she could have picked up the names and functions of these two, the same can't be true of Trefry and Marten, who were relatively obscure except in their own circles.

The second proposition, that she did go there but invented the story of Oroonoko, is more difficult to prove either way. Certainly, unless there's some West African word or name which by accident sounds like Oroonoko, that wasn't his name, since it's of Indian origin. His slave name in the novel was Caesar and that this was a likely name for a slave is attested by the will of a Nevis planter, Henry Gillingham, in November 1662, which includes among his bequests 'my negro man called Caesar his freedom after ten years service'. For Oroonoko the name Caesar had a poetic justice in that he was a king, but it was a justice which the cultivated Trefry could well have seen in naming him. The state papers are spotted with slave rebellions and failed native kings. A short book called *Great News from the Barbadoes*, published in 1676, gives an account of one revolt, 'three years hence by the Coramantee or Gold Coast negros who had a design to choose a King, one Coffee, an ancient Gold Coast negro'. The barbarities inflicted on Oroonoko were nothing strange either, but then the English crowds were used to public executions, floggings, quarterings and so on. 'One ... being chained to the stake was persuaded to confess ... he was jogged by the next man Tony ... "Thou fool are there not enough of our countrymen killed already" ... Which the spectators observing cryed out to Tony, "Sirrah we shall see you fry bravely by and by".' Seventeen were convicted, 'viz. 6 burned alive, 11 beheaded their dead bodies dragged through the streets at spikes ... and were afterwards burnt with those that were burnt alive,' writes the author of *Great News*.

Such a happening then isn't an impossibility, though it may be that the erotic side, the love plot, was missing from the original. Something certainly took place, for Trefry was sacked. An uncalendared letter dated March 23rd 1664[17] from Trefry to Sir Robert Harley makes this clear, and says that Willoughby has been good to him, everything considered, and this he owes partly to Harley's intervention.

> The employ I had is now removed with as much submission on my side as my Lord could expect from a faithful servant. I owe great part of the thanks of my not utter deletion out of his Excellency's favour to your honour ... In the meantime I humbly recommend myself to your favour and beseech you that not anything may induce you to disrelish me but that you will permit that cheerful and free access to kiss your hand in Barbados as you did deign me in Surinam.

Trefry, then, had met Harley when Harley had visited Surinam some time before the end of 1663, when a letter from Clarendon says: 'I expected from you after your voyage to Surinam some description of that colony.' Presumably Harley had also met Aphra Behn's family if they had arrived by that time or perhaps the arrangement had been made for them to stay on his plantation. Trefry himself stayed on in Surinam, where he died in 1674 as one of those that Banister was trying so hard to get a ship for.[18]

George Marten died in the great sickness of 1666. Byam included him in a list of the dead he sent to Harley. He himself abandoned 'our unfortunate colony of Surinam, war and pestilence having almost consumed it', for Antigua, as he wrote to Charles Pym on November 8th 1668. He died there a couple of years later having planted a dynasty that expired only with a Waterloo general.

Aphra Behn knew when she wrote the book that Trefry had been dead some time, for he had intended to write the story of Oroonoko himself but 'died before he began it, and bemoan'd himself for not having undertook it in time'. She had kept in touch, then, with the colony, perhaps through the kinsman she mentioned.[19]

If she was unfair to Banister, was she equally unfair to Byam? I don't think so. She calls him a 'fawning fair-tongu'd fellow' and it's true that reading his letters does give this impression. It also seems from a letter of his to Harley on March 14th 1664 that Byam probably reciprocated her dislike. He writes:

> I need not enlarge but to advise you of the sympathetical passion of the Grand Shepherd Celadon who is fled after Astrea, being resolved to espouse all distress or felicities of fortune with her. But the more certain cause of his flight (waving the arrow and the services he had for the lodger) was a regiment of protests to the number of 1000 of pounds sterling drawn up against him. And he being a tender gentleman and unable to keep the field hath betaken himself to the other element as fleeting as himself, but whether for certain I cannot yet resolve you. Truly the brethren are much startled that the Governor of the Reformation should turn tail on the day of battle.

Byam expected Harley to understand the references in this letter, which was addressed to Barbados but followed Harley home to England. The literary references, which were to Honoré d'Urfé's *L'Astrée*, he undoubtedly understood since they were part of fashionable culture, but he was also expected to know the two people involved, whose relationship had obviously become common gossip. Astrea was Aphra Behn's pseudonym and so closely was she identified with it that her burial is even entered in the Westminster Abbey registers as that of 'Astrea Behn'. It was also the name she used when employed as a spy to Antwerp. The man she was sent to contact was known in the correspondence as Celadon.

IV

Scot

His real name was William Scot. The initials of the 'Grand Shepherd Celadon' by coincidence or design make a version of his initials if you take the Latin form of his name Guglielmus; GSc. Latin is particularly appropriate since he was a lawyer. His father was the regicide Thomas Scot, who had been executed for his share in Charles I's death. Even George Bate admitted that he was 'drawn with seeming cheerful gravity to Charing Cross' and died bravely.[1]

William was his eldest son. Another, Colonel Thomas, was in Ireland in 1663, under arrest for his part in Captain Blood's rebellion.[2] A third son, Major Richard, was a planter in Surinam where, in about 1662, he had married Bathshua, the daughter of the Reverend John Oxenbridge. Richard was another of those for whom Banister tried later to get a ship. He eventually got out with the other settlers who went to Jamaica and rapidly became first a member of the assembly and then of the judiciary.

The Scot family had been involved in the West Indies since at least 1650 when the Calendar of State Papers Colonial first begins to record the appearance of 'Mr Scott' on committees dealing with colonial matters. It isn't always clear from the context whether the reference is to Thomas Scot senior or to his son William. The matter seems to be settled by a letter of Thomas Povey: 'A general remove of governors in the several colonies was designed and particularly of the governor of Barbados which was aimed at invisibly by divers (whereof a son of Mr Scott's is one ...)'.[3] Povey, who appears often in Pepys, is variously described as merchant and civil servant.

At this time he was Secretary to the Committee for the Colonies. He had managed in the usual seventeenth-century way to place most of his relatives in lucrative jobs to do with the colonies. He and his friend, the merchant Sir Martin Noel, had a great deal of influence with Francis Willoughby. Thomas's brother, Richard Povey, was secretary to the assembly in Jamaica. Thomas Noel, Martin's brother, was on a plantation in Surinam.

There were probably other Scot relatives in the West Indies too. A now vanished stone in the burying place of the YS, Richard Scot's plantation in Jamaica, had the inscription: 'Here lies the remains of John Scott who had a hand and a heart in the execution of Charles Stewart.'[4] In 1668 in Jamaica a Timothy Scott married a Joanna Scott.[5] William Scot's second wife was a Joanna, so this could be either his wife or his daughter.

The web extends even further for the Scots were related by marriage to the Reymeses of Nevis and St Kitts. All these connections make it very likely that, after the execution of his father and the arrest of his brother, William Scot decided to try his luck in Surinam. He isn't to be found anywhere else at this time except possibly buying arms for the English exiles in Holland in 1663.[6]

Whether Aphra Behn first met him in Surinam or whether they were renewing an acquaintance I've been unable to discover. It's been suggested by Harrison Platt in his *Astrea and Celadon*[7] that she ran away to the colony as Scot's mistress. The tone of Byam's letter about Astrea and Celadon makes this unlikely. He suggests an affair that the colony had been watching develop with amusement. Further, if they had gone there together they would presumably have left together rather than first Aphra Behn with Scot following later. Byam's suggestion that Scot was using his grand passion as an excuse for leaving Surinam is very shrewd. What makes it even more likely that this Astrea is Aphra Behn is his describing her as 'the lodger', which is exactly what her family were in St John's Hill as she says in *Oroonoko*.

She and her family returned to England, according to her account. An undated copy of a letter from Byam to Sir Robert, from the Portland MSS. but now in the University of Nottingham, begins: 'I bless God I had a short and pleasant passage hither not full 7 days. I found ... a ship full freighted bound for London, on whom I sent off the fair shepherdess and Devouring Gorge but with what reluctancy and regret you may well conjecture.' Byam is back in Surinam from seeing Harley and Willoughby in Barbados. Harley was in no trouble when he left, which would date this about February. If the identification of Astrea with Aphra Behn is correct in the later letter, then this is a record of her departure towards the end of January or thereabouts. 'Devouring Gorge' I take to be her mother.[8] It's a good example of Byam's ingratiating bitchiness.

Scot himself went to join the English exiles in Rotterdam. Byam says that 'the Brethren' were much startled that the governor of the reformation should turn tail on the day of battle. Scot as eldest son of his father could have been expected to lead some kind of counter-revolution in the West Indies, to do in reverse what Willoughby had done in getting Barbados to declare for the King against the Parliament.

Willoughby had become a royalist but he still had many republican connections. His sister was married to Sir Bulstrode Whitelock, who was one of his executors.[9] Willoughby and Thomas Scot had been involved together in Irish affairs in 1647. They were also distantly related. V. L. Oliver believes that Thomas Scot married as his third wife Anne Baesh, daughter of Sir Edward Baesh, who had let his house in Stanstedbury to Francis Willoughby's brother William who succeeded him as governor of the West Indies when Francis was drowned in 1666. William was married to Anne Cary, whose brother John married Mary the widow of Sir Edward Baesh.[10] This meant that within the 'Dear Octopus' reach of seventeenth-century families Thomas Scot and the Willoughbys, particularly William, were kinsmen. To us it seems a long stretch but it made Thomas Scot William Willoughby's nephew. Such relationships could be used for profit but they could also be embarrassing. It was expected that kinsmen would support each other unless they made it quite clear that they wouldn't. From a contemporary point of view one of the most terrible effects of the Civil War was the tearing apart of these webs of relationships. Everitt has noticed that in Kent they were particularly strong and that royalist rebellions, for example, were usually caused by bands of kinsfolk in which the relationships would seem to us very tenuous indeed. Such extended family groupings helped to emphasize the importance of carefully chosen marriage alliances for it wasn't just the couple who married each other but the families, with all their intermarried appendages. Once again inheritance seems to lie behind it. Given the high rate of mortality, especially among infants, your property might pass further and further along the interlocking strands to some distant relative, or his to you. It was as well therefore to choose all possible heirs or their begetters as carefully as possible and to keep them as close to the family and its interests as you could. This meant political as well as religious, social, and of course financial interests in the broadest sense. In this way, too, your family merely reflected the royal family, which on its wider stage cemented international alliances with its marriages.

There was also the simple practical problem of how to meet people to marry unless you were brought together by kin or friendship. Marriages within the same two families were therefore very common, which reinforced the bonds. George Marten would, by his brother's necessary connection with Thomas Scot as a fellow parliamentarian and regicide, know the Scot sons and it could have been through him that Aphra Behn met William Scot. On the other hand there must have been some connection between her father and the Willoughbys for her family to be treated so well in Surinam and this may have led to their meeting. There are, however, other connections between the Scot family and Aphra Behn which I shall deal with later and which suggest that she could have known him before they both found themselves in Surinam. Perhaps their families were already acquainted but their erotic relationship was new.

'My stay was to be short in that country; because my father died at sea ... So that though we were obliged to continue on that voyage we did not intend to stay upon the place.'[11] The time span of that part of the novel which coincides with her being in Surinam is from a little before the arrival of Oroonoko to a little after Imoinda's pregnancy becomes apparent, which in a near-naked woman would be at about three to four months. By March 'Astrea' had left and Byam believed that 'Celadon' had followed her. Aphra Behn's stay then seems likely to have been at the most six months, from August 1663 to February 1664.

During that time she had in one way or another set the colony by the ears. She had given it cause for gossip in her relationship with the son of the notorious regicide and member of the republican faction whose brother Thomas had now turned King's evidence against his fellow plotters in Ireland. She had been involved in events which probably included a slave rebellion and Trefry's defiance of Byam which had cost him his job. *Oroonoko* says: 'Trefry then thought it time to use his authority, and told Byam his command did not extend to his Lord's plantation; and that Parham was as much exempt from the law as White-Hall ... So turning the Governor and his wise Council, out of doors (for they sat at Parham House) we set a guard upon our lodging-place, and would admit none but those we called friends to us and Caesar.' Byam would of course have complained to Willoughby on his trip to Barbados and the governor would no doubt have upheld his lieutenant, particularly once Aphra Behn and her family were gone. Trefry's letter is an account of humble pie. In a letter of August 15th Byam told Harley that Willoughby had ordered him to remove all Willoughby's negroes and stock from his plantation at Parham and from St John's, presumably since now he had sacked Trefry there was no longer anyone to oversee them. The plantation had gone to waste and only one of Harley's own men, William Gwilt, was still there with one woman to look after a few cattle for Harley. Gwilt had been there, from his letter home to his father, since July.

I don't know if this was the beginning of Aphra Behn's active political life or if she had been involved in similar events before. Certainly it made a lasting impression on her and she returned in her imagination to this short visit throughout her life. Perhaps her brother came back to the West Indies. As I said earlier, she knew of Trefry's death and presumably of Byam's, since she felt quite safe in making fiercely libellous statements about him.

When she was dead, by a final irony One of the Fair Sex felt forced to defend her against the charge of having been Oroonoko's mistress, presumably because she had shown such total sympathy for him. In George Warren's little book, which was published in 1665 and which she must have known, he writes of the slaves rebelling, attempting to escape, killing themselves and suffering torture bravely. Out of this Aphra Behn could have made the character of Oroonoko but equally George Warren could have based his remarks on events they had both just witnessed. There is still hope that Oroonoko himself may be more, or less, than a magnificent fiction.

V

Sir Thomas Gower

Mr Behn, her putative husband, has less substance than any character she invented. Beside Oroonoko and William Scot he has nothing but his name and even that's insecure, since she sometimes spelt it with and sometimes without a terminal 'e', while others made it into what seemed most familiar to them. This doesn't however mean that he was necessarily a fictional creation. The argument from negative evidence is as dangerous historically as it is prehistorically and it's apt to be refuted totally by a sudden lucky find.

The memoir says that he was 'a merchant of this city though of Dutch extraction'. On these few half bricks several flimsy structures have subsequently been erected, such as that she was sent to Antwerp because of her knowledge of the Dutch language.

The name Behn, however, isn't Dutch but what we would now call German. During the seventeenth century the change was taking place from one term to the other. There was Low Dutch and High Dutch. The *London Gazette* of September 6th 1680 carried an advertisement for a 'High Dutch' grammar for learning German and Clarendon remarked that it was particularly hard on German ships during wars with the Dutch for no one could tell them apart, language included.[1]

The word 'extraction' used in the memoir is itself ambiguous. Does it mean that although her husband's forebears were 'Dutch' he himself was English born? The phrase 'a merchant of this city' is equally ambiguous. The 'of' could mean that he was a Londoner born or simply that he traded in London.

The memoir also says that she married him when she returned

to England from Surinam (which would be about the middle of 1664). Her letters from Antwerp in 1666 make no mention of him although she is already 'A Behne'. Had he been still alive she would surely have sent him to collect some money she needed. Instead she sent a Mr Piers, was reprimanded for it and had to explain why she hadn't sent her mother or 'Sir Thomas'. It seems certain, then, that he was dead by August 1666 at the latest.

There are several collections of lists of aliens at this period and earlier published by the Huguenot Society. The first thing that you realize in looking through them is that the clerks who had to write them down had even more trouble with the spelling of foreign names than they had with British orthography. Their tendency was to anglicize whenever possible.

Among these lists is the perfect ancestor for Aphra Behn's husband, from the parish registers of St Olave's, Tooley St, Southwark: 'Haunce Bayne servant to Herman Conygrave 25 years born in Cullyn and hath been here a year and came to work Duch 1571.'[2] Translated back this becomes Hans Behn from Köln, German. Unfortunately there's no more mention of him that I've been able to find, although Herman Conygrave's family appear dutifully in the parish register, many of them under the burials of 1596 when an outbreak of plague visited Southwark. Conygrave himself, who also appears asking for denization (naturalization) a little earlier than Hans Behn, was a joiner from Lukeland or as we now call it Luxembourg. The neighbouring parish of St Saviour's, Southwark, is riddled with possible versions of Behn but none of them can be precisely identified apart from a much married Josias Ben, waterman.

Hans Behn seems by his denization application to be exactly the kind of young man to found a merchant dynasty. A child of his born about the time of his naturalization would be around thirty by the end of the century, probably married himself, and his child would by 1664 provide a suitably elderly husband for Aphra Johnson, thus fulfilling the stereotype of the aged merchant who marries the young gentlewoman in several of her plays.

I have a possibility for this role. I offer him in default of anything better, not because I have any evidence that he married an Aphra. On that point all the parish registers and collections of licences which I've been able to consult are negatively agreed, including, just in case she might have returned to a pre-Surinam home to be married from, those of Canterbury. He is Richard Ben of Popinsey Alley, St Bride's, who in the Hearth Tax returns of 1663–5 was taxed for seven hearths or chimneys and was therefore a man of some substance. He died of the plague in 1665. A Henry Ben of the same parish but a different address, in New Street, died shortly after and might have been his son. Richard Ben isn't an entirely maverick suggestion. He and Henry are the only two within the range of probable Behn spellings to die, as recorded in the Boyd index of London burials, in 1664–5,[3] which is the traditional date for her husband's death, and St Bride's is a very likely parish for her to have lived in.

She seems to have been living there at the end of her life, when a satire speaks of her as 'famed through Whitefriars'. It was the parish in which later stood Dorset Garden Theatre where many of her plays were performed and was a district where several writers lived, presumably to be close to the theatre, and to the publishers and booksellers. It was also near the Inner Temple where her lover John Hoyle, to anticipate a little, had chambers.

To revert to Haunce Bayne of Southwark for a moment, however, there is in the *Love Letters Between a Nobleman and His Sister* a passing reference to an old merchant of Cullyn, Vander Hanskin, with whom the villain-hero stays for a while.

If Richard Ben is too unlikely a candidate there's another possibility in John Behn who appears in the state papers on August 14th 1655. A ship from Hamburg, the *King David*, had put in to Barbados on May 2nd and had been seized as a prize. In a deposition those on board claimed that she had come to the island only for water. It was signed by Erick Wrede, commander, John Behn and Class (Klaus) Sure, cook. John Behn is given no position on the ship and it's therefore possible that he was one of the merchant venturers who had gone along on the voyage, since the accompanying item mentions both the merchants and the captain. The existence of this Behn on a ship from Hamburg makes it even more certain that any Behn was German, not Dutch. The *King David* or another vessel of the same name had been about in these waters for some time according to the state papers. Whether this is the same one that by 1663 is said to be of Rotterdam and transporting arms from Holland to the rebels in England and was later made a prize again I don't know. If so it would make this John Behn an even stronger candidate as Aphra's husband.

From Byam's letter to Harley which probably refers to their leaving Surinam I get the impression that she wasn't married at that time, unless she had already been married and widowed. I think it unlikely that he would have written that Celadon was prepared 'to espouse all distress or felicities of fortune with her' if she was leaving the colony as a married woman. I think too that Byam would have been more likely to refer to her as 'the widow', rather than 'the lodger', had she been one.

Interestingly the memoir nowhere says that Mr Behn died but Aphra certainly lived out the rest of her life as a widow. If, as is the tradition, he died in the great plague, what property he had would probably have been heavily encumbered with debts which, when once they were paid off, would have left his widow with comparatively little. By the time she went to Antwerp she was again living with her mother and probably her brother and there had come into their lives, if indeed he hadn't been there already, 'Sir Thomas' whom I can now identify as Sir Thomas Gower of Stittenham.

Stittenham, or Stitnam as it's often spelt, is in Yorkshire, a few miles from York itself near Sheriff Hutton and Maldon for which Sir Thomas was M.P. from 1661 to 1672, when he died. The family memorials are in the church of High Hutton. Sir Thomas was born in 1605. His mother was a Doyley from Merton in Oxfordshire. He had matriculated from Wadham in 1617 and was entered in Gray's Inn in 1621. In 1630 he was knighted at Whitehall by Charles I. His father, Sir Thomas senior, was made a baronet by James I, and Aphra Behn's Sir Thomas succeeded to the baronetcy in 1651.[4]

His education had followed a conventional upper-class pattern but for Sir Thomas it wasn't just a formality. Thoresby, the great Yorkshire antiquarian, recorded in his diary in 1680 that he had been to see Sir Thomas's library which was still intact, 'the best furnished with ancient fathers and commentators both Popish and Protestant upon the Scriptures of any that I have seen; the rest mostly on Medicine for which Sir Thomas was

justly famous'. If it also contained works by Aphra Behn
Thoresby wouldn't have thought them, as modern works, worth
mentioning. I believe she knew that library and that it was from
there she got her knowledge of the fathers which she refused to
display in her *Essay on Translated Prose* in case it should be
thought ostentatious in a woman. Sir Thomas undoubtedly
shared the seventeenth-century gentleman's passion for verse.
In a letter home written in 1669 he speaks of a letter in blank
verse promised for his daughter-in-law, 'but she is to expect
another from Sir Robert Howard unless his muse be out of
humour because my Lady Bathe won his money at hombre last
night'.[5]

Through his daughter-in-law, Lady Jane, the Gowers were
related to the Grenvilles, for she was the daughter of John, Earl
of Bath. This relationship and the Grenville connection with
the poet Edmund Waller leads to Aphra Behn's friendship with
George Grenville, Lord Lansdowne, a friendship which he
never repudiated even when she had been dead over forty
years.

Sir Thomas was a widower of sixty by the time he appears in
Aphra Behn's letters in 1666. He had married first Elizabeth
Howard, the sister of Charles later Earl of Carlisle, by whom he
appears to have had no children. I say 'appears' because the
Burke's *Peerage* entry under the Duke of Sutherland, whose
ancestor he was, is very unreliable. There are at least two sons
who don't appear there and it therefore isn't very clear whether
they were the children of his first wife or his second, Frances
Leveson. There's also a third wife, according to a Yorkshire
will and the state papers, Dame Mary Squier, who died in
1651.[6] She is not listed in Burke's either.

Frances Leveson, Sir Thomas's second wife, was the daughter
of Sir John Leveson of Lillshall, Co. Staffordshire, and Halling,
Kent. Her mother was another Frances, the daughter of Sir
Thomas Sondes of Throwley, Kent, by Margaret Brooke. This
link with Kent makes me think that Aphra Behn and her family
had known the Leveson-Gowers for some time. Sir Richard
Leveson, Sir John's brother, still had property in Kent in the
'forties and Sir Thomas's friend Sir Philip Musgrave had
estates there which were sequestrated during the interregnum.

By 1660 Sir Thomas was a confirmed royalist but in spite of

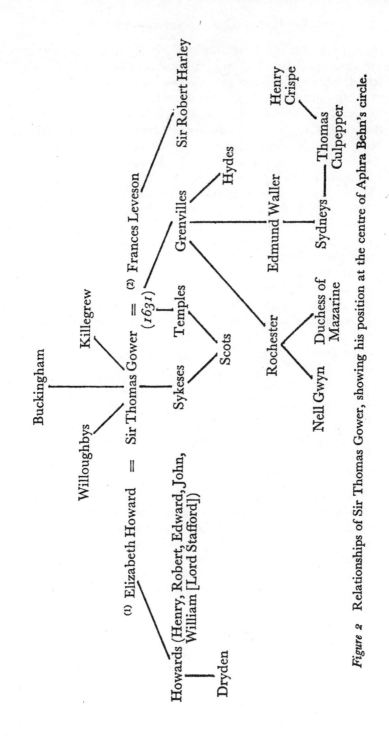

Figure 2 Relationships of Sir Thomas Gower, showing his position at the centre of Aphra Behn's circle.

the entry to this effect in Burke's *Peerage* this hadn't always been the case, not at least without some qualification. With his father, his brothers and his children he was fined and forced to compound for his sequestrated estates. In an attempt to get his fine reduced Fairfax himself put in a very interesting plea that Gower's 'moderation towards Parliament and their friends begat him a long imprisonment by the King'. Nevertheless he lent the King £2,500 which was paid to Lucius Cary, Lord Falkland, Edmund Waller's great friend. Unlike many, Sir Thomas was repaid after the restoration. His son John was killed fighting for the King at Scarborough and Edward, William and Doyley Gower all had to compound for delinquency in arms.[7] After this the Gowers seem to have kept their heads down and stuck to their estates, like so many other royalists waiting out the time till the King should be restored. They were helped by their relationship to Charles Howard, who was fighting for the Parliament until he switched sides in the late 'fifties. Writing to his uncle Sir Richard Leveson in 1657, Sir Thomas Gower reports that his two brothers have been carried prisoners to York

> and I have notice not to stir out of my own house ... The respect for my brother-in-law is the reason they extend not the full rigor to me. My brother William Gower and my son was but newly returned out of France and wishes himself there again having had no suspicion that keeping himself free from the company of those of whom they are jealous that he should be made a prisoner.[8]

In May 1653 Sir Thomas had had to beg his 'brother Howard's favour to get a pass ... to come to London'. His first wife had been dead twenty years, yet the family ties still remained and the young Gowers were brought up close to the Howards. In December 1660 one of Gower's sons went abroad with Sir Thomas's 'brother Howard', newly created Earl of Carlisle.

Aphra Behn also knew the Howards, 'coming, I may say, into the World with a veneration for your illustrious family, and being brought up with continual praises of the renowned actions of your glorious ancestors,' she wrote in her dedication of *The City Heiress* to Henry, Earl of Arundel, in 1682. She also knew the dramatist Edward Howard whose work she defended and who wrote her a panegyric. It was his brother Robert who had promised to write some verses for Lady Jane Gower.

Sir Thomas had another brother-in-law by his second wife who could also have stood him in good stead: the parliamentarian Sir Peter Temple, who had married Christian Leveson. Sir Thomas kept up with that side of the family too and was in partnership in property with them in the Temples' home county of Buckinghamshire. As well as being an M.P. Sir Peter sat on the county committee for Buckinghamshire in 1652 with Sir Richard Grenville and William Scot, and on the Committee for Scandalous Ministers with both William and his father in 1654. He was also on the Committee of Both Houses for Irish Affairs, with Colonel Thomas Scot, in 1648.

The connection between the Scots and Sir Thomas Gower was even stronger than would appear by this and may go back earlier. In 1620, a year before Sir Thomas Gower, Richard Scot of London, who was probably Thomas Scot senior's brother, after whom he named one of his sons, was admitted to Gray's Inn. Then in 1650, William Scot married into the Sykes family of Yorkshire. How, precisely, he met Elizabeth Sykes I don't know. His father knew Charles Howard in his days with the Parliament army and that might have taken him to Yorkshire. On the other hand he might have met her in London when she was visiting the London branch of the Sykes family.

Elizabeth has vanished from the Sykes family tree but there can be very little doubt that the marriage of Elizabeth Sykes and William Scot at Ledsam[9] refers to these two, for in common seventeenth-century style, their siblings, William's half-sister Elizabeth and Richard Sykes, were later married too. Elizabeth Scot seems to have died soon after her marriage, perhaps in childbirth, but Elizabeth Sykes survived into the eighteenth century outliving her husband.

Through the Sykes family the Scots and the Gowers were related by marriage, since both had married into the family of Lord Eure. The antiquarian Thoresby, who was married to Anna Sykes, the daughter of Richard and Elizabeth Scot, kept his father-in-law informed through a Dublin correspondent, the Rev. Joseph Boyse, of the later doings of Colonel Thomas Scot, who continued to live in Ireland and collected the rents from Richard Sykes's land there. So strong was the suspicion of the Scot family and all connected with them, that Richard Sykes and his old mother, Grace Sykes, were arrested in 1685 at Monmouth's landing. The old lady, who was in her eighties, died in prison, her only crimes being her relation to the regicide and her quakerism. Thoresby records her turning over some things that had been left her by 'her uncle Eure'.

The web of relationships then leads back again to the enigmatic figure of Thomas Scot himself. History has served him rather badly. His name is usually coupled with that of Sir Arthur Haselrigg as if he couldn't act independently, but Scot's deeply felt republicanism was his own.

William, his eldest son, was seven, according to his father, in 1634.[10] His mother was Alice, daughter and heir of William Allanson of London, who had married his father in 1626. Allanson is also a Yorkshire name. There were at least five children of this first marriage. Later Thomas married again. Grace, the daughter of a fellow regicide, Sir Thomas Maulever, came from another old Yorkshire family and was the mother of Elizabeth. Later still he married an Anne.

Aphra Behn never wrote directly about the Scots although she wrote about both periods when she was closest to them and those were the periods to which her imagination persistently returned for material. It was as if the act of repression itself made them more vivid and as if she was constantly skirting the things she dare not say. If she first met William in 1663 in Surinam, he was thirty-six and twice married; she was twenty-three. Given the close connection between Sir Thomas Gower and the Scots, however, it's possible, as I said earlier, that she had met him before.

There's also another piece of evidence for an earlier connection that fits into the jig-saw. On September 3rd 1651, the Committee for the Advance of Money recorded a claim for payment for a piece of detective work or simple spying, depending on which way you look at it. The entry reads: 'Thomas Scott [sic] or William that George Lord Cobham gave lands in county Kent which descend by entail to John Lord Cobham second son of Henry Brooke ... via the Duke of Lennox and Earl of Salisbury ... which are forfeit by the recusancy ...' The lands in question were originally forfeited by the attainder of

Henry Brooke for treason. Henry was brother of the Margaret Brooke whose daughter married Sir John Leveson. Sir John, or his father of the same name, was one of the trustees for the attaindered estate. Sir John Leveson senior had been one of Henry Brooke's father's executors. Henry Brooke was married to Frances Howard.[11] This curious piece of vulturizing, which the Scots must have been able to pull off through information given either by accident or design by Sir Peter Temple, brings together several strains in Aphra Behn's life: the Scots, the Howards, the Leveson-Gowers and Kent. It also introduces the Cecils, for a sister of Henry Brooke married a Cecil and to her contemporary James Cecil, Earl of Salisbury, Aphra Behn later dedicated *A Voyage to the Island of Love*.

Sir Thomas Gower, then, stands as a kind of keystone to her life. Through him she met the Grenvilles, Cecil, possibly Scot, probably George Villiers, second Duke of Buckingham, John Hoyle, her lover, and James, later to be King of England. Through him, too, she was sent as a spy to Antwerp. He was the man she said she would most trust in the world.

VI

The First Dutch War

In *Oroonoko* she says that on her return to England she presented
some specimens from Surinam to the royal antiquary and some
feathered Indian capes to the King's Theatre for the queen in
Sir Robert Howard's *The Indian Queen*. The first performance
was in January 1664 though Pepys still hadn't seen it by
February 27th, but he recorded that 'for show they say it
exceeds Henry the Eighth'. In a manuscript in Worcester
College, Cosmo Manuche writes of *The Indian Queen* that with
'speckled plumes brought such an audience'. There's a problem
of dating here. William Yearworth referred to 'the Ladeyes'
in a letter dated January 27th. By March 14th Astrea had gone
and Celadon after her. It could be that William Yearworth was
a little behind in his gossip because he was further up the river
and 'the Ladeyes' had in fact already left when he wrote.
There's no date for Cosmo Manuche's comment, which might
have settled the matter. Alternatively Aphra Behn's plumes
might have been used for the revival of *The Indian Queen* in 1668.
It's interesting that this first theatrical reference should be to
Sir Thomas Gower's friend Sir Robert Howard, Dryden's
brother-in-law.

Her position as a dowerless but beautiful woman, whose
beauty Thomas Culpepper testifies to in his note, left very little
room for manœuvre. The obvious course was a marriage to
someone who was substantial enough to buy good looks and
education, and who wasn't a member of the gentry trying to
improve his family estates by marriage. The obvious choice
would be a merchant or well-off tradesman of some kind. She
could not have been married long when the great plague began

to spread through the country.

Sir Thomas Gower had had a busy year in England while her family were on their abortive journey to Surinam and back, for the whole country had been put on the alert by the discovery of a plot to overthrow the King centred on Yorkshire and the North and connected with Colonel Blood's plot in Ireland. Opinions still differ about the importance of it as they did at the time. Sir Thomas as High Sheriff of Yorkshire tried at first to downgrade its seriousness, but as more and more reports came in of plottings, arms, ridings by night he was forced to act. The Duke of Buckingham was sent north with a troop of horse at the beginning of August 1663 and about a hundred of the conspirators were seized. Several of them turned informer, others fled to Holland. The plotting was allowed to continue but, with Sir Thomas now using a network of spies, he was able in October to make another eighty-eight arrests. Two nights later an abortive attempt at a rising was made in three places, the chief at Farnley Wood which has given the whole plot its name.

Most of the plotters were old republicans and old army men who had held office in the North before the restoration, indeed their names are often the same as those which appeared on the various Northern committees. Inevitably the name Sykes appeared among those tossed around as implicated, but this time the family seems to have been untouched. Not so lucky was the father of Ralph Rymer, antiquarian and poet, whose son gave evidence against him which helped to get him imprisoned while twenty or so others were hanged.[1]

One letter from a certain informer, John Ironmonger, may have stuck in Sir Thomas's unconscious mind:

> Designs are carried on chiefly through women, some the wives of prisoners, who have interests in their husbands' fortune, have access to them, and to others on pretence of soliciting for them and write in covert terms of trade or meet each other to convey intelligence etc. Secret meetings are often held at Channell's a milliner in Tower Street, also at Hackney, and at schools kept by matrons for young women.[2]

Sir Thomas on his visits to London stayed either at the pewterers next to the Swan Tavern in King Street, Westminster,

or at the Blue Lion, an apothecary's shop 'over against Salisbury House in the Strand . Aphra Behn's mother may have
had lodgings at or near this second address. If her daughter was
married to Mr Ben of Popinsey Alley they would have been
very close.

Late in 1664 came the first intimations of the plague, in
Yarmouth. At the same time England and Holland went to
war. This second event was what the English rebels at home and
in Holland had been waiting for. Sir Thomas was still collecting
information against them, though by now he had made himself
unpopular even with those faithful to the King who thought he
was being unnecessarily officious. He had many contacts with
informers who professed to keep him up to date with the plots
of the English abroad. In preparation for future needs a certain
Hieronymus Nipho was given a passport to return to Flanders,
'his own country', having 'served the King for many years'. His
job was to set up an efficient post service for intelligence from
Holland for Sir Henry Bennett. Sir Thomas and his friend Sir
Philip Musgrave continued their vigilance in the North.

At first both the pestilence and the Dutch maintained a
phoney war but with the spring of 1665 both began to hot up.
Clarendon writes that the plague made such early progress in
the spring that 'the ancient men, who well remembered in
what manner the last great plague (which had been near forty
years before) first broke out, and the progress it afterwards
made, foretold a terrible summer. And many of them removed
their families out of the city to country habitations.' Parliament
was prorogued in April, having voted money for the war, and
the fleet put to sea even though many of the ships were wanting
supplies 'even of beer and other provisions of victual', because it
was impossible to stop the sailors going ashore and bringing the
plague back on board with them.

The two fleets played cat and mouse until the beginning of
June. Meanwhile Lord Arlington, as Sir Henry Bennett had
now become, was receiving huge sums for the secret service and
Sir Thomas Gower, high in favour, petitioned for, and in
November received payment of, the £2,250 he had lent
Charles I. The great fear was that the dissidents at home would
combine with those in exile and with the Dutch, a fear that was
to haunt the Stuart Kings for the next twenty years until it

became a reality. Arlington tried to watch them all, putting spies into Holland and Flanders, infiltrating non-conformist groups at home, offering money and pardons for those who would come over. In the middle of it all the young Earl of Rochester abducted an heiress and was sent to the Tower.

The engagement of the two fleets finally took place at the beginning of June. The English were the victors but with much damage and heavy loss of life, including that of the young Earl of Falmouth over whom Clarendon alleges the King wept more than over anyone else. On the Dutch side Opdam, their naval commander, was killed.

William Scot was now in Rotterdam where the largest number of English and Scots had gathered. The English victory must have shaken him for he put out a feeler, through Sir William Davidson, offering to discover a plot for a rising in the west and north of England. 'The informer is much in favour with the rulers in Holland and is son to one of the King's judges who was quartered.' Davidson had promised him 'a large sum for his secret' but some of the information which Scot gave him was false. He said that the ringleaders of the plot were Major General Desborough, Colonel Ludlow and Colonel Farie, all names calculated to heighten the worth of the tale he had to sell as among the most respected of the old army leaders. But Ludlow in his *Memoirs* is adamant that he had no hand in any of this because he didn't trust the Dutch not to sell him to the English when it suited their turn, as they had done with others of the exiles, and he therefore, in spite of urgent requests from the exiles to join them, stayed quietly in Switzerland. Scot was lying and it was a powerful lie that gave rise to many rumours of Ludlow's being seen in unlikely places ready to lead a new revolt.

Scot repeated his tale to Sir George Downing, the English ambassador at the Hague, and incidentally Sir Thomas Gower's brother-in-law, and Sir George wrote it home to Clarendon. Scot alleged that the dissidents were at work round Poole in Dorset. Arlington had two agents in Holland: Nicholas Oudert who had been given a pass to go over in December 1664 and Thomas Corney, a merchant. Scot was taken into their counsel and promptly betrayed them to the Dutch. In July Downing wrote home to Clarendon that he had now found out that Scot was in league with De Witt and had betrayed Oudert and Corney.[3] An anonymous letter in the state papers of August 3rd reported that Corney thought that by means of William Scott [*sic*]

> he can discover all actions of the discontented party ... but he is filled with untruths by Scott, Colonel Bampfield and Lord Nieuport, late ambassador in England; they plotted together and took Corney prisoner and had his papers searched; Oudert corresponded with Corney, was also taken and his papers; the latter will die but Corney will be spared. Sandes Temple, Lieutenant of the Charity, was called in on pretence of giving bail, and taken close prisoner: he is a person much admired by the Dutch as a stout man and a perfect Englishman.

The writer goes on to say he will get Temple out of prison if he can and adds a note that he was liberated on bail of 1,000 rix dollars. 'Long John (De Witt) has given William Scott a place of 1,000 dollars a year in the Hague.'

Meanwhile John Ironmonger informed Sir Thomas Gower on June 20th that the dissidents were 'dead' on the news of the English victory but were building on the increase of the plague and hopes of a Dutch–French alliance against England. Charles had decided that it was too dangerous for the Duke of York as heir to the throne to go on leading the fleet in person. In the last battle he had been spattered with the blood of those shot down beside him. Command was given to the Earl of Sandwich and the Duke ordered back to court. But the plague was now raging so fiercely, two thousand dying a week, that the King was forced to move first to Hampton Court and then to Salisbury. General Monck, now Duke of Albemarle, and his friend Lord Craven bravely stayed on in London to help the Lord Mayor in keeping order. At the last minute it was decided, with the coaches standing at the doors, that the two courts should split, Charles to the West and James himself to York and the North so as to keep in touch with the fleet through Hull and the other ports on that coast and to use his presence to influence those parts 'where the most disaffected persons were most inhabitant'.[4]

Aphra Behn, I believe, went to Yorkshire too. I date her

deep personal attachment to James from this summer. It would be natural for her husband to stay on in London to attend to business while she went to stay with friends in the country. In the greater informality of the court at York and as part of Sir Thomas's 'family' in seventeenth-century terminology, it would have been easier for a woman of no aristocratic standing but of beauty and wit to be received and noticed. I think she gained the attention of James and of George Villiers, Duke of Buckingham, and that it's to this period she refers in the poem 'On Desire':

> Where wert thou, oh, malicious spright,
> When shining Honour did invite?
> When interest call'd then thou went shy ...
> When Princes at my feet did lye.

> When thou could'st mix ambition with thy joy ...

Dukes ranked as princes. Sir Thomas knew the Duke of Buckingham well, indeed they were distantly related through the Howards. Buckingham's duchess was Fairfax's daughter and Fairfax was an old acquaintance of Sir Thomas. Gower and Buckingham had raised and led a troop of horse together for the King immediately before the restoration and William Gower had been a sergeant of arms attending Buckingham at the start of the Civil War.[5]

Here too she could have met for the first time that bizarre phenomenon the female poet, for William and Margaret Cavendish came to greet James. Her 'behaviour was very pleasant but rather to be seen than told. She was dressed in a vest, and instead of courtesies, made legs and bows to the ground with her hand and head.'[6] 'Sure, the poor woman is a little distracted, she could never be so ridiculous else as to venture at writing books, and in verse too,' Dorothy Osborne had written of her in a letter to William Temple in 1653.

It was an indication of the opposition Aphra Behn would have to face if she wanted to be a poet; much of it was to come from women. Margaret Cavendish's only serious rival, Katherine Philips, 'the matchless Orinda', had died in 1664 after seeing her translation of Corneille's *Pompey* performed in Ireland. She was to be Aphra Behn's spiritual rival too. Both Margaret Cavendish and Katherine Philips were protected from the worst of the mockery and odium by the refuge of marriage. If tradition is right so too at this time must Aphra Behn have thought herself. Both her predecessors had sheltered behind romantic mythological pseudonyms. She already had hers. She had written part at least of her first play in Surinam. Perhaps the sight of Margaret, Duchess of Newcastle, determined her not to become a freak. I believe that at this time she had no idea that she would be 'forced to write for bread'.

The Duke of York returned to Oxford, where the King was now holding his court, in the middle of September 1665, having 'lived in great lustre in York all that summer, with the very great respect and continual attendance of all the persons of quality of that large county'.[7]

Mr Ben died, and was buried in St Bride's on September 13th. The plague wasn't kind to merchants. Their livelihood was in the city. They didn't come up from country estates simply to attend the court. The great merchant prince, Sir Martin Noel,[8] friend of Thomas Povey and Lord Willoughby, died too when the world might have thought that his enterprises might preserve him. Whether Richard Ben is Mr Behn or not, by 1666 Aphra Behn was a widow and, whatever had gone on in her marriage and whenever it had taken place, she was unwilling to repeat the experiment. At any time during the next twenty years she could have found someone to marry. In spite of her comparative poverty some tradesman or member of the lesser gentry would surely have made an offer. That she remained unmarried must have been her own decision, her own choice.

There was an alternative: she could be a 'miss', a mistress. She rejected that too while having immense respect for those who, like Nell Gwyn, could make it work. If James, Duke of York, or George, Duke of Buckingham, had offered at York, it must have been this that was offered. In 'On Desire' she attributes her own non-acceptance to a lack of emotional or physical involvement and discards any false notions of honour. She must have believed she could survive without such support. To prove it she went to Antwerp.

VII

The Spies

Like his father, William Scot was bred to the law but neither
he nor his brother Thomas, who was expelled from the Dublin
parliament in November 1665 with others who had been in the
Irish plot, had the stature of their father. Ironically Thomas
Scot senior had twice been in charge of intelligence during the
interregnum, first in 1649 and then again in 1660 after the
Rump Parliament had ousted Richard Cromwell. At the restoration he had fled to Flanders, using his first wife's name and
posing as a merchant. After 'eight days in a free country' he
surrendered himself and was sent home to England. His wife
petitioned to be allowed to visit him in the Tower and she was
probably instrumental in persuading him to tell all in the hope
of saving his life. Among those his confession implicated was
Waller, who, Scot claimed, had given him information about
the royalists while Waller and his relations, particularly
Hampden, were negotiating for him to be allowed to compound
and come home.

Intelligence was largely carried on through the post office,
the careful opening and resealing of letters being, apart from
the reports of actual agents, the chief source of information.
Thomas had employed his son William and Isaac Dorislaus to
manage the post office under him. Dorislaus's father had been
murdered in Holland by royalists, in revenge for the execution
of Charles I. Dorislaus transferred his allegiance to Thurloe
when he took over from Scot and then again managed to keep
his job at the restoration. Quite what William did I've been
unable to discover but in January 1657 his wife Joanna sued
to Cromwell for relief for herself and their child since William

had 'lost his office through his own fault'. In August Cromwell granted her £20 a year for life. In the previous December Thomas Scot had been forced to beg favours from Thurloe, as a result, he said, of William's behaviour: 'my improvident son in France and his only child here which his wife hath been pleased to send home to me'. In mitigation it was claimed that he had paid the clerks and had worked until September 1656.

William Scot seems to have followed his wife home and then gone again to France for he, or another of the same name, was given a pass for himself and a servant in July 1658. I believe he was communicating with the double agent Joseph Bampfield, who in July 1659 wrote to Thomas Scot enclosing a letter to his son. In his confession Thomas claimed that he had asked Colonel Bampfield 'to think of some means of making my peace with His Majesty'.

The popular charge, much exploited by royalist propaganda, against Thomas Scot was licentiousness, a vice he shared with his fellow regicide Henry Marten. The Clarendon State Papers contain a report in June 1659 of an attempt to whip up the populace against the government which failed until the speaker began on the theme of Scot, with a 'lewd son and 2 young women wives to them both'.

> Now look to your wives for I am informed
> That carnal Scot is again broke loose
> But the House that shelter'd his lust is
> Reformed ... [1]

Nothing could save Thomas Scot. The regicides were exempted from the Act of Oblivion and it was foolish of him to give himself up hoping perhaps that the Commons would save him. Bampfield, who had come home after Cromwell's death, was put in the Tower the day after Charles landed and kept there for eleven months before he was freed and began to try to worm his way into Charles's favour, but James took against him.[2] Realizing that he had no hopes at court, he went to Holland.

William Scot seems to have already left England before the restoration. In spite of his father's high position, a warrant for his arrest had been issued in March 1660 but there's no record of his being brought before the Council of State. Perhaps he had already decided that the interregnum was over.

At this point he was out of favour with both sides. He may have hoped to sue for pardon from the safety of the Continent. He had no intention of making his father's later mistake and coming home without one.

His crimes weren't capital but they were enough for at least a long imprisonment, which was usually as fatal as hanging. He had been one of the trustees for the sale of the royal property and this was unlikely to be easily forgotten. He must have seen the arrival of the disgruntled Bampfield in Holland as a chance to repair his fortune, for Bampfield set about forming an English regiment of exiled parliamentarians to fight for the States.

What, I think, Scot didn't know was that Bampfield was soon at his old game of double agent. In 1663, Bampfield was in correspondence with Bennett about earning a pardon. His failure to get it must have driven him to a more single-minded identification with the rebel cause. Scot meanwhile had been to Surinam and back, driven from there, if we're to believe Byam, by a thousand pounds of debts. In Holland he may have hoped to draw on the Sykes family, for a cousin John was trading at Dortrecht where there was a large colony of English merchants, and it was he who was married into the West Indian family of Reymes. Scot's merchant brother-in-law William Sykes was also in Holland.

William Scot must have been desperate for money. His step-mother had been allowed some of his father's estate by the King's mercy but bounty hunters were constantly claiming rewards for the discovery of bits of it.[3] Of his other relations his sister Alice Rowe had three children to support. His cousins had married into good city families but they were unlikely to be able to help him. His betrayal of Corney and Oudert was the surest way to make quick money and to get himself employment in the service of the States of Holland.

In October Sir Thomas Gower received information which he passed to Arlington that William Sykes, brother to Richard, 'who married the daughter of Thomas Scot, the traitor has been an agent in foreign parts for the fanatics ever since the restoration. He has been in disguise in England as a spy, and wants a license to come home ... He has been in counsel with Bampfield, Kelsey and other fugitives.' William Sykes was a merchant of Leeds and Hull. Foster in his *Yorkshire Pedigrees* says he was dead in 1665 but certainly Sir Thomas Gower believed he was alive in October of that year. Sir Thomas's advice was to capture him. It's interesting to see Bampfield's name and that of Kelsey who had been the parliamentary major general in charge of Kent. Unfortunately there are no further letters to show the progress of this move by Sykes.

Oudert and Corney had been kept prisoners all this time but were eventually released on January 22nd.[4] Corney was ordered to leave the country in twenty-four hours. Oudert was given longer and was recompensed by Charles for his sufferings. In February France declared war on England and English residents were given three months to leave France. England was therefore at war simultaneously with two of the most powerful nations of Europe and was driven back for an ally on the Spaniards. In March Sir Mark Ogniate came on an embassy from Bruges, as envoy from the Marquess of Castel Rodrigo whose relation he was. Ogniate was burgomaster of Bruges, had an English wife and was a great friend of Arlington. The Flemish were very much afraid that the French would gobble them up and feared the dangerous new alliance with the Dutch. They were therefore doubly anxious to remain on the best terms with England.

Fortunately for the English the plague was subsiding and the King was able to return to Whitehall in February. In April, in preparation for the summer campaign against the Dutch, a proclamation was issued recalling those who had 'not only remained beyond seas contrary to former proclamations but have treasonably served in the wars against their native country, to undergo their legal trial under pain of being attained and forfeited for high treason'. At the head of the list and sinisterly tagged as 'son of Thomas Scott lately executed for high treason' was William Scot. After him came Sir Robert Honeywood junior[5], Thomas Kelsey, John White, William Burton, Thomas Cole of Southampton, Colonel John Desborough (whose son Nathaniel was being used by Arlington as a double agent), Spurway, Redden, Dr Richardson (who had been involved in the Farnley Wood plot), John Grove and John Phelps. Bampfield's name is surprisingly missing, since he was the colonel of the English regiment in Holland.

The threat was clearly intended to put them all, but particularly Scot, under pressure. What should he do? If he gave himself up without a pardon he might go the way of his father, since the charge could now be treason. He must have quickly made some move, some offer of co-operation. Someone was needed to make contact with him. They had learnt their lesson, they thought. They wouldn't deal with him by letter. They had the perfect contact in Aphra Behn. They would trade on his reputation for 'lewdness' and on his former flirtation and of course on hers.

'They' included Arlington and Sir Thomas Gower, but it also included Thomas Killegrew, in some ways an unlikely figure to be involved in spying.[6] He was groom of the bedchamber and licensee of the King's Theatre. He was also Arlington's uncle, for they had both married Crofts. The Killegrews were related through their Cornish branches to Sir Thomas Gower's relations the Grenvilles. Killegrew knew the playwriting Howard brothers. But there is also some link that I haven't uncovered, for Aphra Behn writes to him in terms of, for the period, great intimacy as if he was a relation. However she had met Killegrew, between them all they fixed on her or she offered as go-between. In a letter to Arlington she says it was the former.

She accepted out of sentimentality, idealism, a desire like that of the cavaliers of her youth to serve her King, to bring a political sinner to see the error of his ways, to prove that she wasn't a child any more and probably to earn, if not money, prestige, some reward that would help to keep her. The arrangement to meet Scot must have been made before she left England, through some other go-between. From Arlington's underling, and Killegrew's fellow royal servant, the cupbearer James Halsall, she received a list of memorials much like those which were given to ambassadors, instructions and requests for information. From Arlington she received a letter to 'my good friend Ogniate'[7] who had now returned to Flanders.

After the success of the year before, the war now went badly for England. The country was impoverished by the plague which had ruined trade and by the sudden changes that inevitably followed the restoration. This led to the fatal economy measure of 1667, the decision not to set out one great fleet but to have smaller sections cruising on different parts of the coast.

At the beginning of June 1666 an inconclusive action was fought with both sides claiming the victory. Towards the end of the month they engaged again and this time the English drove the Dutch back. Once again there was heavy loss on both sides, but the English were left the weaker. It was a bad moment and Arlington needed all the information he could get. How heavy were the Dutch losses? Did their fleet plan to come out again? Had they any intention of invading? What were 'the fanatics' up to?

Instructions to spies sent from Holland to England included the spreading of propaganda that the Dutch would land headed by the Old English officers in the States' service, the collection of intelligence from ports about the sailing of convoys and merchant ships, and the establishment of correspondencies for passing information, including communication with 'Scott's brother-in-law', presumably William Sykes, 'and correspondent'. It's not clear whether this is one person or two. However, unless these instructions are a fake, they show how heavily Scot and members of the Sykes family were implicated. It's quite possible that the paper was passed on by Sir Thomas Gower's correspondent John Ironmonger.

On July 25th Sir Antony Desmarces wrote to Arlington from Margate where he was trying to get some horses shipped in the Flanders fleet for the Marquess of Castel Rodrigo. The customs were being difficult because Sir Mark Ogniate had left the pass for them at Gravesend. Desmarces had with him a boy called Robert Yard whom Joseph Williamson, Arlington's secretary, was sending abroad to improve his languages. They went back to Gravesend and shipped on board the *Castel Rodrigo* for Ostend. Among the passengers were Aphra Behn and her brother, and Lord Stafford and his son, the Honourable John Howard.

The usual method of travel to Ostend was by packet boat but the packet boats had been boarded and plundered on several occasions by the Dutch and French, 'the mails broke open, passengers ill-treated, women stripped and abused'[8] and it was safer to go in convoy. Ostend was badly hit by plague and boats were forbidden to enter to unload but went on to Paschendale. There Sir Antony and Robert Yard took boat for Bruges where they had arrived by August 7th. There's some discrepancy in the dating here because England was still using old style dating while the Continent had gone on to new style, causing a difference of a few days. Robert Yard eventually travelled on to the Hague.

Aphra Behn may have continued on with them to Bruges before going to Antwerp, from which her first letter is dated August 16th. She had struck up a friendship with Sir Antony on the journey which suggests more than just a couple of days' acquaintance on the crossing. My guess is that Sir Antony made the first move and that he had been instructed to do so. What she didn't realize was that he was an agent of long professional standing. He had been an official in the French Post Office working as a royalist spy before the restoration, opening the letters of the parliamentarian ambassador Lockhart, for which he was eventually knighted. Fearing detection he had fled to Brussels in 1660. He was a friend of Killegrew's and involved with him in the management of various lotteries but his chief occupation was on secret service missions. His courier was Hieronymus Nipho. Arlington knew Nipho well. On July 30th he had written to Sir William Temple, envoy at Brussels: 'P.S. Let your emissaries give you a particular account of the condition of the Dutch fleet gotten into New Zealand; and of the readiness they are in to come out again; with an exact account of their strength if it be possible. Monsieur Nypho will help to convey it speedily to us.'⁹

Later she was to say that her expedition was at the command of Charles II and that it was 'unsuited to my age and to my sex'. The truth was that she was bound to be out of her depth between two groups of professional spies both of whom were using her for their own ends. This made her seem a child, even in her own eyes looking back from fifteen years on. However, for a writer few experiences are entirely wasted and this one certainly wasn't. It brought her into close touch with the exotic high camp world of Hispano–Flemish counter-reformation which, although it never engaged her reason, excited her aesthetic sense much as the Catholic trappings later did for Ronald Firbank. The most complete expression of this is the short story, dedicated to the Catholic playwright and conspirator Henry Neville Payne, called *The Fair Jilt* but there is a great use of it too in *Love Letters Between a Nobleman and His Sister*.

VIII

Antwerp

When commentators stopped calling her work 'a reproach to
her womanhood and a disgrace even to the licentious age in
which she lived'[1] and suchlike things, they began instead to
call her a liar. There are two stories which she claims as true:
Oroonoko and *The Fair Jilt*. Of the two the second has always
been advanced as the more improbable, so improbable that it
has caused, by a classic example of a fallacy, *Oroonoko* to be
doubted as well. The argument runs: Aphra Behn said that
The Fair Jilt was a true story; she also said *Oroonoko* was a true
story. But the first is clearly untrue, therefore the second is too.
Even such a careful apologist as Cameron in his *New Light on
Aphra Behn* found the truth of *The Fair Jilt* hard to swallow,
though sensibly he was prepared to keep an open mind.

He points out that Aphra Behn never claimed to be an eye-
witness of *most* of what she was describing, only some, and to
have had part of the story as hearsay from some Franciscan
friars and from the protagonist. This turns out to be the simple
truth. In fact she could have read the first part of the story in
condensed form before she left home. Her writer's curiosity
would then have led her to find out the ending, which in any
case would have been the gossip of the town.

In the *London Gazette* for the week of May 28th–31st 1666 is
this news item from the Hague:

The Prince Tarquino being condemned at Antwerp to be
beheaded, for endeavouring the death of his sister-in-law:
being on the scaffold, the executioner tied a handkerchief
about his head and by great accident his blow lighted upon

the knot, giving him only a slight wound. Upon which, the
people being in a tumult, he was carried back to the Town-
house, and is in hopes both of his pardon and his recovery.

In the next issue the *London Gazette* reports from Middelburgh:
'From Antwerp 'tis said, that Prince Tarquino that so acciden-
tally escaped execution, has since obtained his pardon from
his Excellency the Marquis de Castel Rodrigo.'

The Fair Jilt has done Aphra Behn's reputation a great deal
of completely unjustified damage for it has altered the way in
which people have looked at her. That she was an obscene
writer and a disgrace to womanhood might be lived with on the
grounds that it was a licentious age but that she herself was a
liar is a very different matter. Once she was thought, beyond
doubt, to be a liar in this one thing, all her statements and
actions became susceptible to the worst interpretation and her
apologists were crying against the wind in trying to re-establish
her credibility.

Her version of the story differs in detail from the *Gazette*
report. She says nothing of the knot causing the blow to slip
but she explains the method of execution which made such a
happening more likely. Hers is probably the more accurate
account since she had more time to question people and then
wrote the story down in her 'journal-observations' which she
says she kept at this time. The *Gazette* report was probably based
on the first oral accounts of what people thought had happened.

It would be nice to think that somewhere that journal is
preserved. She suggests that it was still extant when she wrote
the story after the death of Charles II. Perhaps it also contained
her observations on Surinam which would account for the
fascinating detail in *Oroonoko*. Fortunately the series of letters
among the state papers gives some idea of the Antwerp episode
but they still leave a great deal to interpretation.

Before she left, the *Gazette* carried another news item, that
Major John Desborough, another of those on the list with
William Scot, had returned to England and given himself up.
Her hopes of persuading Scot to do the same must have been
very high. I'm not, however, convinced that that was what
Arlington and the authorities really wanted. Their greatest
need was for information and they intended to squeeze him for

that. But he wasn't a soldier or indeed a great leader as Desborough, Ludlow or Kelsey could have been and in this sense he was far less of a threat as the head of a potential rebellion.

Aphra Behn believed that the offer of both a pardon and a reward were genuine and she soon made contact with Scot. He arrived in Antwerp on the morning of August 15th so full of fears that he wouldn't stay in the house to talk and she was forced to hire a coach and go a day's journey with him. Obviously he thought the whole thing was a plot to capture him. At first he was 'extremely shy' but gradually as she reasoned with him he said he was willing to co-operate but that first she must go to Holland because it was too dangerous for him to come to Flanders which would make Bampfield suspect him. Bampfield of course had every reason to suspect the others since he had already tried the same thing himself and the defection of Desborough had no doubt made him even more suspicious.

Scot told her that he disliked his employment in the English regiment and intended to leave it. He also admitted his previous attempt to correspond with Arlington but didn't tell her that he had betrayed Corney and the others. He said that Bampfield had been told by 'the old man' that Aphra Behn was in Flanders and this had made him more suspicious. This must mean that Bampfield knew who she was and of Scot's previous involvement with her.

There seems to be a break in the writing of her first letter.[2] Between the account of their first meeting and the second part she has asked Sir Antony Desmarces's advice and he has spoken strongly against her going to Holland. It looks as if they were afraid that she might be captured and the authorities would be forced to trade concessions for her freedom. Sir Antony's advice has prevailed and she will go to Dort to meet Scot, presumably because he has the perfect excuse for being there, of visiting relations, since the Sykeses and the Reymeses were there.

Already she is plagued by that curse of all his majesty's servants, lack of money. 'Sir when I went from England I carried but fifty pounds with me upon bill and when I came there the exchange was so low I had but barely forty.' Her money is all gone and she is ashamed not to have more to show for it although she is able to warn them against 'the man in Ludgate' who is a spy for the Dutch and not to be trusted.

It's worth pausing a moment to notice a few things about this first piece of writing from her own pen. First the writing itself is neat and elegant although part at least of the letter was probably written in a hurry to catch the post. It's also fluent and literate. However she had acquired it, her education is evident. Already the prose has the easy flow that characterizes her literary work. What also emerges very strongly is how much both sides have concealed from her.

Her second letter to James Halsall was sent eleven days later. Sir Antony had now been joined by Hieronymus Nipho as her counsellor and all letters were to be sent through him. She was still in Antwerp because they had decided it was too dangerous for her to go to Dort where Scot had been expecting her for a week. Holland was in a state of excitement and all Dutch troops had been sent for from Germany. The reason for this was an exploit of the English which had taken place at the beginning of August, when the Duke of Albemarle had sent a thousand men to destroy the stores and ships on the islands of Vlie and Schelling. One hundred and sixty[3] merchant ships were burnt as well as the stores and houses on the islands, among them that belonging to the unfortunate Thomas Corney. The expedition had been guided by a renegade Dutchman. Sir Thomas Gower's kinsman Sir Philip Howard had 'assisted in the whole action very handsomely in his own person'.

She speaks in her letter of Scot as 'this rogue' and says she would come home if it weren't that she really believed she could accomplish her business 'it being no delight at all for me'. She will send her brother as soon as she has 'something worth his voyage'. Once again she asks for money and says she has had to pawn a ring. She will send someone to collect the money. Meanwhile Scot is coming the next day to a little house two miles outside Antwerp where he will give her 'every assurance of his life and service that can be desired'.

The only piece of intelligence as such in this letter is the comment about the recall of troops and the confusion and suspicion after the raid on the Vlie. She reports that two men and their sisters have been degraded from their offices. Ludlow in his *Memoirs* identifies them as Sieur Kievoit, the brother-in-law of Van Tromp, and one 'Vanderhulst' of the same place (Rotterdam). As Holland meddled in English internal affairs so did

England in those of the Dutch. Van Tromp was a naval commander, of the faction that supported the young Prince of Orange as ruler of a united Holland. Arlington had been supporting this faction through the Sieur Buat. He would have been interested, then, in this setback for the Orangist cause but Aphra Behn is diffident about offering it in case he has heard it already. Although her letters were addressed to Halsall she knew perfectly well that it was really Arlington she was writing to. One irony was that he was married to a Dutch wife.

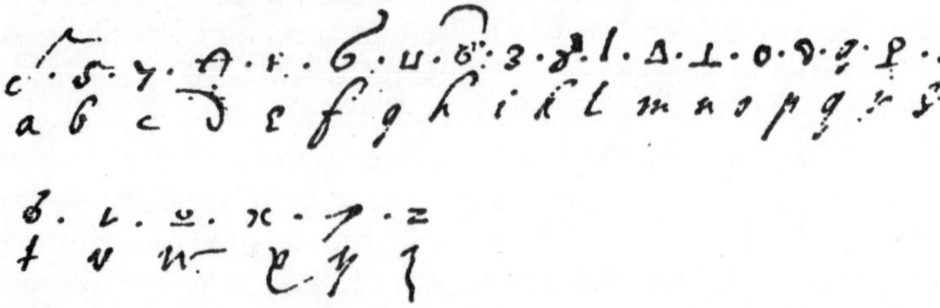

Figure 3   The code which Aphra Behn invented because she thought the one she had been given took up too much space. Some of the letters have obvious Greek derivations although she presumably knew no Greek.

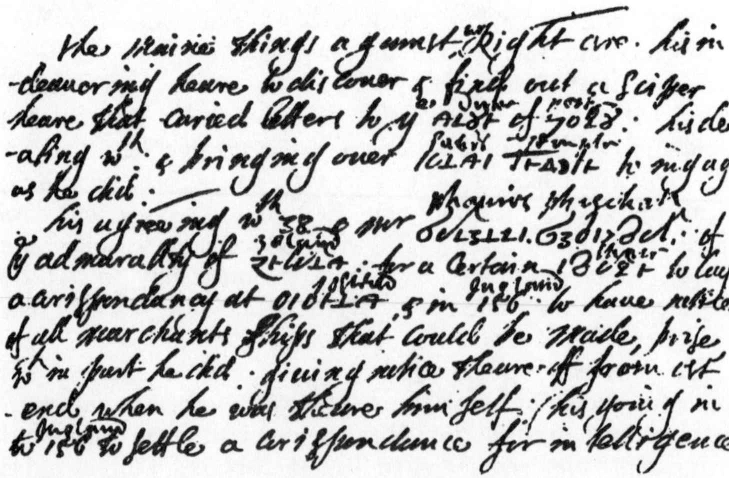

Figure 4   Part of a letter showing the two codes in use. An official of Halsall's has written in the decoded words above. The text is her transcript of Scot's original.

Sir Antony went home at the end of August. He had arrived
at Dover 'from Holland' and would 'report how affairs stand
there' by August 31st, presumably by English dating since it's
an English correspondent who reports it.[4] Aphra Behn's next
letter is dated the same day but would have been written
earlier because she was using new style dating. Originally it
contained an enclosure in Scot's own hand which, among other
things, informed them that Sands Temple had turned traitor
when he was arrested by the Dutch, if indeed he hadn't been
one already and the arrest was a blind. Scot was still trying to
leave his regiment and was working hard to charm Aphra
Behn. 'I am sure he wants no wit nor address nor anything to
manage this affaire'; 'I believe him in all things.'

On the same day, exasperated by Halsall's failure to answer
her letters and requests for money, she wrote directly to Thomas
Killegrew, at his lodgings in Whitehall, apologizing that her
letter wasn't merely to present her services but 'to give him
trouble'. She explains her lack of an answer from Halsall. Scot,
she says, hears the gossip of the slenderness of rewards to his
majesty's servants but he is resolved to do what he can to serve.
He has been to see her twice which has cost her ten pounds a
time because she had had to give him money to go back. All
their communication has, for safety, to be done by special
messenger. At the same time she and her brother are having to
spend ten guilders a day on their keep. Soon she will send him
home with what information she has.

To add to her troubles Thomas Corney had now turned up in
Antwerp, sent by Lord Stafford who had told him Scot was
there. It's an indication of how little was able to be kept secret
at this time that Lord Stafford not only knew of Scot's visit but
was prepared to tell Corney. Corney was almost out of his
mind, as well he might be, and was threatening to kill Scot who
was just outside the town. Corney boasted that he was employed
by the King 'so that I never heard such a rodomontade in all
my life'. At the end of her letter comes the strange statement
that she is the more willing to trouble Killegrew 'because it was
from you as well as any I received my business and from you I
shall expect a favour … '

Unless Arlington had complaints from others about Corney,
it was on her warnings about him that he acted. A letter to Sir

William Temple on October 12th runs: 'At my return I found yours of the 12th and 15th one part relating to Mr Corney: whom as I assured you in a former you are not at all censured for having employed. Therefore after the caution given you, concerning him, it is in your own hands to use him or not, as you see cause.' Corney continued to send reports to Arlington.

Wearily she wrote to Killegrew again five days later. She is nearly a hundred pounds in debt and the longer she has to stay where she is, expecting the money, the higher her charges will be. She begs him for a hundred pounds so she can pay her debts and go to The Hague, where she will be able to communicate better with Scot. She is expecting a copy of an incriminating letter from Sands Temple to Bampfield and gives Killegrew a little news from Holland. She has arranged for Mr Piers to collect her money and remit it to her. 'He is an honest man' and to be trusted.

It wasn't surprising that this letter, too, went unanswered, for on the night of September 1st (old style) the great fire broke out in London and burned for four days until two thirds of London within the walls was reduced to ruins. No one had time to worry about someone who was at least safe in Antwerp. Later that week she seems to have sent a copy in her hand of a letter from Scot dated September 7th from Rotterdam. It was full of caution. He had changed his address and was now living with one of the old army majors, Robert Luson.[5] He hopes she has sent her brother home for Scot's pardon.

On September 12th he sent another letter with more news of the fanatics, including Thomas Culpepper's uncle Algernon Sydney, who had joined them in exile and was in high favour with De Witt but not liked, Scot said, by Bampfield. His most important piece of news, though, is that an old Parliament captain, Thomas Woodman, had undertaken to sink ships and block up the Thames. One of the Fair Sex in the *Memoirs* says that Aphra Behn warned the authorities of the disaster of 1667 when the Dutch fleet sailed up the Thames and the Medway. This is the letter on which the claim is based. What we have is an abstract made in Halsall's office with certain bits which were thought of interest underlined. Among them is the plan to block the Thames.

She wrote again two days later but she was growing tired of

Scot. His letters were filled with 'the old story' most of which she didn't bother to transcribe. He urged the English to a speedy battle which he said they could win since the Dutch were in great disorder. But the English fleet was probably in no condition to take his advice even if they had thought it good, for the fire had disrupted everything. Aphra Behn had asked him to name a quaker who was high in the Dutch counsels and he did so: Benjamin Furley.

Perhaps Scot was aware of her weariness and afraid of losing his pardon for her next letter to Killegrew, of three days later, included a long one from Scot. In her own she complains that she has had three answers to those letters that accompanied her last to Mr Halsall but nothing from him. Her chief concern however is over the Mr Piers she had sent to him for her money. Apparently Killegrew had shown Sir Thomas Gower her letter which said that Piers was the only man in the world she could trust and Sir Thomas was angry. She is forced to justify herself. Sir Thomas is seldom in town. Her mother is 'not so fit being a woman and possibly I should be loath to let her have it for another reason and Sir Thomas I did not know but you might scruple at as much as any'. It's true she said Piers was the only man she could trust except, of course, Sir Thomas and so he might have told Killegrew 'but I find everyone has a prejudice to do me if he can'. As for Mr Piers, whom they call a 'base fellow', he is 'very honest in all his ways' and if he weren't she would be the one most in danger. Worst of all, however, 'they tell me his Majesty is displeased'. Her letter ends with a bitter cry: 'for Christ his sake sir let me receive no ill opinion from his Majesty who would give my poor life to serve him in never so little a degree'. This cry, I think, is the genuine reason for why she had gone in the first place. Now the enterprise was turning sour and it seemed she could do nothing right.

I've not been able to identify Mr Piers, the 'inconsiderat fellow' who was 'good enough to serve me in the nature of a servant'. Piers is another Kentish name and it could be that he was someone from her childhood now living in London. The clerk vestris of St Bride's at this time was a Philip Pierson and it could possibly be him but I have no definite proof and such an identification depends on her having misspelt or misremembered the name. Her spirited defence of him doesn't I think arise

merely from her having employed him. If that had been the
case she would have stopped at the argument that there was no
one else. When she warned in an earlier letter that she would be
sending him she spoke of his trustworthiness. High Tory as she
was, there were some forms of accepted snobbery that she
didn't subscribe to. In this case his honesty was to be preferred
to the implied unreliableness of her mother.

This is the only mention of Sir Thomas and she doesn't of
course give his surname but I have no doubt of the identification. He was on one of his visits to London from Stitnam. He
knows Killegrew but then he also knew Charles II. He has

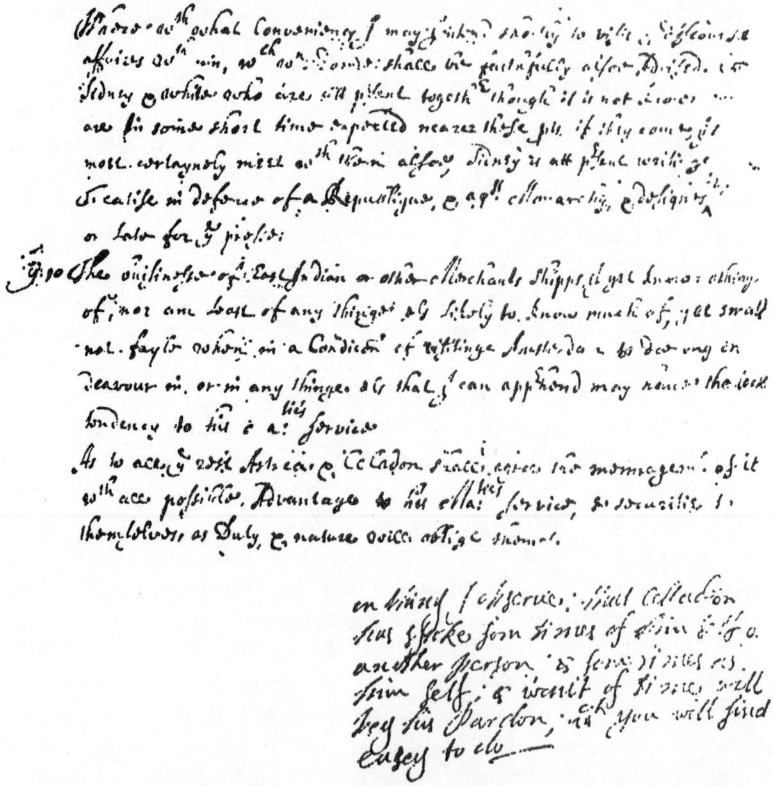

Figure 5   Scot's own handwriting with a scribbled footnote by
Aphra Behn. Part of his answers to the 'Memorials' she took
with her to Antwerp.

either written to her himself or got her mother to do so. The 'they' who have told her the King is displeased seem to be her mother and Sir Thomas. Perhaps Sir Thomas was her mother's lover or somehow a distant kinsman. Possibly they lived in the same house as I've said earlier. It's interesting that Thomas Culpepper's father and Sir Peter Temple had been neighbours in the Piazza at Covent Garden in 1642.

Still she worked on at transcribing Scot's letters. The one enclosed was four pages. His main news is of the English exiles but he also says that the Dutch fleet has gone westward and gives its strength. He reports the latest on the imprisoned Buat. This episode, which reads like something from *Carry on Spying*, is told at length by Clarendon in the *Continuation of the Life*. Buat was a Frenchman, married to a Dutch wife, and commander of the horse troop known as the Prince of Orange's Guard. Buat was both pro-Orange and pro-England. He found himself caught between two skilled manipulators, De Witt and Lord Arlington, and entered into a correspondence with the English to promote a peace between them and the Dutch. Arlington used this situation to forward the Orangist cause and sow dissension among the Dutch. Unfortunately Buat, who according to Clarendon was too fond of the bottle, confused two letters in cipher and handed the wrong one to De Witt, with the result that he was tried, imprisoned and eventually executed for treason. Scot in this letter says that he is reported to have made a confession implicating many people but he thinks it's only a rumour spread to cause others to panic and so betray themselves. Scot's own deviousness often shows through in his interpretation of events like this. He gives more information about the quaker Furley and a dissenting minister, Mr Hill. Scot accuses Hill of having betrayed him, Corney and Oudert to Bampfield and then goes on to give further details about a man called Wright.

His last paragraph is about a letter in 'a woman's hand' which has been discovered at The Hague. They have apparently examined Buat's wife about it but she knows nothing of it. Scot hopes it isn't Aphra Behn's because, since Bampfield knows Mrs Buat's writing, suspicion will fall on Scot. Aphra Behn adds a postscript that the letter is none of hers and gives another warning about Corney's loose tongue.

What was Scot up to here and was there such a letter? Was he trying to frighten her? If so he failed. She's only concerned to assure them that it isn't hers but with no trace of panic. There's the matter of language. Was the letter in English or Dutch? Mrs Buat was Dutch but presumably her husband's correspondence with Arlington was in English. Or was it in Dutch since his wife was Dutch? Does this mean that Aphra Behn could speak Dutch? She gives no sign of it in these letters yet it's always been supposed she was sent on this mission because she could speak the language. That ignores the fact that she went to Flanders, one of whose languages, French, she could speak. There she made contact with an Englishman. The whole theory that she spoke Dutch rested on the belief that her husband was of Dutch extraction and the man she had gone to contact was his (Dutch) friend, who as the memoir puts it 'had known her husband before the war'.

A letter at last reached her from Halsall with a promise of Scot's pardon. Accordingly Scot was now prepared to give more information. Arrangements were made in Aphra Behn's next letter on September 21st for his pardon to be given to a Matthew Pinder. Her letter reports Scot's transports and gratitude almost verbatim. He confesses the betrayal of Corney and Oudert but says he had no option but to be the first to tell the States of the conspiracy once Hill had spoken to Bampfield. Her own emotions are very mixed at this point. She feels some sense of achievement, for Scot, in his enclosure, with the scent of a pardon in his nostrils, has answered some of the questions in the memorials which she had taken with her. She's eager to know what they think of them. They must write to her by every post or at least once a week. At the same time she is 'worse than dead' with worries about her debts and fears of displeasing Killegrew. Finally she is worried that, in her haste because the post was going, she didn't make a very good copy of last Saturday's letters.

A draft of the original questions is calendared alongside Scot's answers and these are in his own hand. The three scripts make an interesting comparison of seventeenth-century hands. Scot's is very neat. He still uses the older form of the letter 'e' whereas Aphra Behn uses a modern 'e'. His is a style that appears consistently in legal and official documents. Halsall's official has a spiky, slapdash, illegible hand.

Scot begins by saying, in answer to a question about his conversion to the royal cause, that he doesn't need conversion having been long resolved to serve the King whose pardon he begs. After this preamble he gets down to facts, giving figures for the last Dutch losses. He warns that they had intended under the leadership of Samuel Raven to land near Harwich. Now they pretend not to be interested in a landing in England but he is quite sure from their dealing with such a fellow as Raven that they are 'really greedy of hankering for any such adventures'. Only Scot and possibly Phelps, who lodges in his house at Rotterdam, will know about it and he is confident he will be able to warn of any such intention.

In answer to another question he puts the whole management of agents and correspondence on to Bampfield and says that he is his majesty's most dextrous and malicious enemy. It was Bampfield who seduced Sands Temple into offering to mutiny and bring over his ship to the Dutch. Among other items he mentions a fact of interest to literary and political historians, that Algernon Sydney was already preparing his work, *Discourses of Government*, for the press although it wasn't actually published until 1698.

The most important information Scot has to offer them is his conviction that the Dutch intended to invade and land if they could. Following on his earlier suggestion that it would also involve blocking the Thames and sinking ships, it should have alerted Arlington. The authorities, however, decided to ignore it and, since it was his strongest card, ignore him. These answers were what Arlington had played for and he had them now. There was no point in wasting a good pardon.

On September 25th she transcribed another short note from Scot and dispatched it with a covering letter of her own to Halsall. The next, which is dated October 5th, is another abstract by the same person in Halsall's office. There are no underlinings. Scot is unable to join the other dissidents, who have gone to Utrecht, because he has no money. They are now under the command of Dolman and waiting for the return of Colonel Sydney.

Once Arlington had decided there was no more to be got from Scot, he took steps to get himself another agent, the strongest proof that he had done with Scot and, by implication, Aphra Behn. This agent was called Van Ruyben: 'a poor unfortunate man ... who about two years since, was my correspondent, and not a very ill one ... he is fled to Antwerp and may be heard of at Mr Shaw's' as he described him in a letter to Sir William Temple on October 15th. 'It will be worth your asking him what way he can put you into of getting such accounts, as he usually sent me; assuring him they shall be paid for, as he punctually was, till I dismissed his correspondence, having met with a better.' On the swings and roundabouts of espionage it was now Van Ruyben's turn to be the 'better' while others were dismissed, this time without pay.

By November 3rd it must have been clear that no pardon and no more money was likely to come and Aphra Behn wrote to Lord Arlington himself. The letter has been superscribed 'wants money' in a new hand. 'I did believe when I came out of England that it was in order to ... a service to your lordship ... I am very confident that no person in the world could have drawn him to a resolution of that kind, besides myself.' She was now in 'extreme want', having pawned everything she had, and was likely to be imprisoned for debt. She begs for the 'least note to Mr Shaw' which would give her credit for anything. 'For God's sake my Lord do something to help me out of my affliction for I am not able to live and suffer so.' She signs herself 'Astrea'. It's not clear whether the Mr Shaw she refers to is the Treasury official or a Shaw who worked for Alderman Backwell the goldsmith. He was in Antwerp managing the English bribe to the Bishop of Munster and therefore had money. Arlington mentions him several times in his correspondence with Sir William Temple.

How she spent Christmas I don't know. Her last long letter, again to Arlington himself, was written on Boxing Day. Scot has been imprisoned for debt. She has sent home copies of his letters from prison but to none of them has she had any answer. She no longer dares to answer his letters herself because she has 'fooled him so long with vain expectation'. Now she doesn't even know where he is. This sentence is underlined in the copy.

She has been sent for from home but 'they' knew quite well she 'had no money to come home with'. She begs Arlington only to lend her a hundred pounds on her being able to satisfy him when she gets home, which she truly wants to do in spite of 'those excuses which others make for my stay (as if I had a mind to do)'. She doesn't believe, though, that her 'little services are at an end'. She expects Scot to be set free in a few days if he isn't already and she encloses a quotation from one of his 'too long' letters.

Once she is home she hopes[6] she will be able to return any money lent her and Arlington will see what a just and good account she will give 'of what I am now so ill thought on for. I neither petitioned for nor desired the place I now have nor voyage I have taken ... ' She begs him in a postscript not to let her 'eate out my head'. Finally she gives a quotation from a letter from Scot in prison which she has already reported by the last post to Mr Halsall. That letter, like many others in the sequence, is missing. In particular there's a long gap in November and December when she had continued to write by every post but many of her letters had miscarried. Scot's letter begs her not to go home without his seeing her again, when he will tell her matters of great importance, 'such things as you cannot imagine'. Nothing, he also says, will make him fail in his 'duty to them'. This is in answer to a letter in which she had told him there was no hope of anything from Arlington. Whether she had been told this or deduced it from the English silence it's hard to say.

The tone of this last fragment we have from Scot is very interesting. He is playing, as he has done throughout, the character of Celadon, the suffering faithful lover. In the novel Astrea's is the more dominant role. She commands, he obeys. When she rejects him he submits with patience. But by the end Aphra Behn was no longer the dominant one. By the authorities' silence and refusal to co-operate they had taken her role away and left her reduced to herself, begging for help. Even so she isn't entirely subdued. She would be 'wild' with her treatment. However, that most dangerous of transpositions has taken place and she is now identifying with Scot, the agent she is supposed to bring in. It's a situation familiar to readers of the more intricate modern spy novels.

She begged Arlington not to let her miss the next convoy or she would have to stay another two months. The memoir says she came home with Sir Bernard Gascoigne and the state papers date a pass for him into England on March 11th which is just over two months after this last letter. It looks as though the money wasn't sent and subsequent events bear this out. She was forced to borrow £150 from an Edward Butler. It's always been assumed that the money was sent from him in London but there was an Edward Butler in Flanders, a correspondent of the Duke of Ormonde. I will return to him later.

The story of all that appears in the letters and state papers is retold in the *Memoirs* heavily disguised. Scot is a Dutchman, Vander Albert, of Utrecht not Rotterdam. It was his love for her that caused him to give her secret information including 'one piece of intelligence, which might have sav'd the nation a great deal of money and disgrace, had credit been given to it'. This is of course the plan given in some detail 'to sail up the river of Thames'. Astrea immediately sent off her dispatches but they weren't credited and indeed were shown around and mocked. A friend sent her word of this and she was very angry. This part looks like a version of Killegrew showing her letter to Sir Thomas Gower. The *Memoirs* then go off into a series of letters telling first the story of Lucilla, Don Miguel and Don Lopez and then returning to Aphra Behn's own supposed adventures in Antwerp. She is alleged to have agreed to marry Vander Albert but on his return to Holland, to make ready for his marriage trip to England after her, he died of a fever.

By the time of her last appeal to Arlington, Scot had become 'my friend' and 'the poore man'. She was undoubtedly pulling out all the stops to get some money, which she said she intended to share with him. She obviously felt deeply the betrayal of him which had been forced on her. She would be honourable no matter what the others did or rather didn't do. Several times she speaks of the disgrace of her debts and begs to be allowed to come home with honour, having paid them. Her cavalier heroes, however, had thought it no shame to be in debt, to abscond to another place when debt collectors became too pressing or, at last, to be imprisoned. It was a nuisance but a kind of natural hazard of loyalty. Her condition was neither unique nor remarkable except that she felt it so. This argues for a fairly comfortable and sheltered upbringing which hadn't accustomed her to such situations.

She makes no mention of her brother in her later letters.

I think it likely that he had been sent home with the long answer in Scot's own hand. Unfortunately I can't identify him among those mentioned in the state papers as coming and going between England and the Continent at this time.

The authorities had decided that Scot wasn't worth bothering with. They were, I believe, very wrong. He now had nothing to lose and turned coat again. He didn't warn them when Dolman planned to land at Harwich or about the Thames–Medway expedition. Indeed their rejection of his usefulness and his previous warning may have helped to breed a false sense of security in England that the Dutch would never come.

These were negative acts of revenge but Scot had his revenge also in a more positive way. He lost Surinam to the British crown.

IX

To Prison

He got the idea from the 'Memorials for Mrs Affara', those questions which she took with her for him to answer. There are two separate questions that deal with a possible landing. One is simply 'whether they have any design of attempting anything by land and at what place'. The other, however, speaks of the 'landing of men in *any of the King's dominions*', my italics. The colonies and plantations were also the King's dominions. Since the English authorities neglected Scot's advice about possible landings in Britain, he advised the Dutch, in particular Zealand in whose jurisdiction he lived at Rotterdam, to attack Surinam.

My evidence for this is a letter from Byam to Sir Robert Harley of November 6th 1668, which gives a full account of the taking of the colony by the Dutch and says quite unequivocally: 'In February following [1667][1] arrived a Dutch fleet from Zealand, by the advice of Scott, to take the colony, which found us in a most weak condition, near half our men dead and half that were living, miserably weak, ill armed, and our fort not half built, but one bastion perfected.'

The depleted state of the colony was the result of the sickness which carried off George Marten. Byam goes on: 'I had about ninety men, such as they were, with me most of which immediately clave to the Dutch.' These would be the parliamentary faction, the 'brethren' whom Byam had spoken so slightingly of before.[2] Richard Scot might have been one of them. William Scot would have known the weakness of the colony from his relations and friends there but also from his own observations. The English retook the colony under Sir

John Harman the following October but the politicians were already busy trading for the Treaty of Breda and Surinam reverted to the Dutch.

Was the advice to attack the colony Scot's trade for the opening of the prison gates and was this the important news he begged her to wait for, the 'such things as you cannot imagine'? Did he in fact tell her? In *Oroonoko* she says of Surinam: 'certainly had his late Majesty, of sacred memory, but seen and known what a vast and charming world he had been master of in that continent, he would never have parted so easily with it to the Dutch'. I suspect that behind the righteous indignation she expressed about the Dutch in the Thames lies also some for the Dutch in Surinam.

She had continually urged Scot's importance on Halsall and Arlington but they had disregarded her advice and refused to send her money because of her 'small services'. They had decided Scot was of no account yet even as they decided, that is if they hadn't thought so even before they sent her out there, he was plotting the taking of the colony. The journey to Surinam without a stop at Barbados must have taken about eight weeks. The plot must have been finalized in early December. The account in the state papers says Admiral Crynsens set sail on the 20th (new style).

When the attack came, Aphra Behn was still in Flanders waiting for the next convoy. News of the taking of Surinam wouldn't have reached Europe till the end of March. In June followed the attack on the Medway, Landguard Fort and the Thames. The 'land soldiers' were commanded by Dolman.[3] Heads rolled as a result of these disasters and Clarendon was forced into exile. Yet as early as December 1663 he had asked Harley 'in what security' that colony is 'against any attempts of an enemy'. Miraculously Arlington survived.

The Dutch attack on Surinam was no doubt forwarded by the news, which reached London at the end of November 1666, that Lord Francis Willoughby had been lost in a hurricane, with many others, while on an expedition to the Leeward Islands. Aphra Behn mentions this in *Oroonoko*. The news must have reached her in Flanders before she left.

The summons home was an official one and angered her with its imputation of failure. It didn't come from Arlington in person but since she speaks of those who sent it in the plural it must include Halsall and either Killegrew or Sir Thomas or both. 'They' knew she hadn't the money; she was forced to borrow.

Edward Butler is a depressingly common name to hunt down. It was particularly common about the person of James Butler, the Duke of Ormonde, and the bearers of it were probably members of minor branches of his own family. There are among the Ormonde papers several letters from an Edward Butler who was a steward or bailiff, but also two from another Edward Butler who was a soldier in Flanders, dated from Brussels in 1660 and 1668.[4] These two letters are in different hands. Either there were two Edward Butlers, perhaps father and son, in Brussels within a few years of each other or there was one who considerably altered his handwriting in those few years.

It makes far more sense if she borrowed the money in Flanders. It would also explain how she managed not to pay it back until the following year. There are three undated petitions in her name among the state papers for 1668. The first one[5] is in her own hand, in her best writing. It hints at a former petition: 'your petitioner is again forced to make her humble applications to your Majesty which nothing but an execution against her this next term could have made her do.' She has had 'more than two years suffering' all which time she has received 'no small hopes from some about your Majesty.' She asks for an order for payment to 'Mr May or Mr Chiffinch who say they will willingly obey it'. She refers to it as 'Mr Butler's business'.

The second says that Mr Edward Butler 'being come to Town' has given her a week to pay. She had managed so far because Mr Butler was out of London. The second Edward Butler letter is dated from Brussels in October 1668 asking for the Duke of Ormonde's recommendation to the place of Major in the Irish regiment. This isn't incompatible with a trip to London where the Duke was, according to the address, to solicit the favour in person.

The handwriting of this second petition is clerkly or legal, much like William Scot's. Mr Butler, it says, is resolved to use all imaginable severity. 'If your Majesty will not that she shall languish in prison' your Majesty 'will order this money to be paid him which Mr Halsall and Mr Killegrew know is so justly due'. Her name on this is spelt Aphara.

No money came. The week passed. In desperation on the last day before the execution of the order, she wrote to Killegrew begging him to send some money that night. The writing is jagged and blotched as if with tears. 'I have cried myself dead and could find in my heart to break through all and get to the King and never rise till he were pleased to pay this, but I am sick and weak and unfit for it or a prison. I shall go tomorrow but I will send my mother to the King with a petition.' She had been trying the day before to get a few days more but 'they say, they see I am dallied with all and so they see I shall be for ever'. She ends with what is almost a command: 'Sir ... you must send me something to keep me in prison for I will not starve.'

This too failed. The next petition says 'Mr Butler being out of all patience hath taken his revenge in arresting your petitioner.' Presumably this is the one carried to the King by her mother. Most cruel of all is the little episode revealed in the first few lines, that Killegrew had sent her to Arlington 'whom he said had order from your Majesty to pay it' but Arlington had denied that he had either orders or money. The King, who was susceptible to such pleas especially when they came from beautiful women, had no doubt told Killegrew he would give the order and then forgotten to do so.

Pepys had recorded on February 14th: 'Secretary Morrice did this day in the House, when they talked of intelligence, say that he was allowed but £700 a year for intelligence whereas in Cromwell's time he did allow £70,000 a year for it.' Almost in the next dip of ink he records that Lady Castlemaine had won £15,000 one night at play and lost £25,000. Later on the 21st he records 'it is pretty odd that the very first sum mentioned ... is £5,000 to my Lord Arlington for intelligence, which was mighty unseasonable so soon after they had so much cried out against his want of intelligence.'

There were other agents as well as Aphra Behn petitioning. Nicholas Estoll asked for money for discovering the 'horrible plot of some in Holland and others here in 1665'; Johann Boeckell presented his accounts and Mr Nipho's 'for journeys to gather information of the state of shipping, naval stores etc and for entertaining spies where he could not go himself. £506 16s. and £240 paid to him by Nipho on account.' 'All who have been in Holland know how dear living is there.' The same was true of Flanders. His petition is the more interesting in that it suggests Aphra Behn might have been able to borrow money from Nipho but perhaps Boeckell had had it all.

The wretched Thomas Corney had petitioned, too, in March 1668 for the place of storekeeper at Chatham with a long list of his sufferings. Killegrew had done his best in getting a promise from the King. Now he must have stirred himself again, unless someone else paid the debt for her. She didn't starve in prison nor did she succumb to that terror, gaol fever, which did more executions than the public hangman.

The Fleet had been burned down in the great fire. An entry in the *London Gazette* for January 19th 1671 gives us a possible place for her imprisonment. The Fleet had just been rebuilt 'where antiently it stood' with 150 rooms new furnished and well fitted with all manner of necessities for prisoners: 'The prisoners upon Saturday last were all removed from Croome House at Lambeth unto this new prison.'

Once she was out, however, the problem of how to survive presented itself again. She could marry. She could be kept. Or she could try to keep herself. Incredibly, it must have seemed to many people, she chose the last.

There was just one more possibility which she considered or which was suggested to her: a convent. In the story which she dedicated to Hortense Mancini, the Duchess of Mazarine, in 1668, which is called appropriately *The History of the Nun*, she says that she was once designed for a convent. This statement, extraordinary because of her firm protestantism, has gone unremarked by biographers. If she isn't speaking merely in the anonymous persona of the writing 'I', however, it needs some consideration. 'I once was design'd an humble votary in the House of Devotion, but fancying myself not endu'd with an obstinacy of mind, great enough to secure me from the efforts and vanities of the world, I rather chose to deny myself that content ... '

When could it have taken place? There are three moments, I think, when it would have been possible; the first when she returned from Surinam and before her marriage, the second when she was in Flanders and the third on her release from prison. As I've said, Flemish Catholicism[6] made a strong impact on her, as did the presence of Lord Stafford, the Catholic member of the Howard family. The portrait of her which was reputed to be by Lely, and was exhibited as such in the National Portrait Exhibition of 1866, was then in the possession of another Catholic branch of the Howard family, that of Corby Castle.

I think that, if this isn't just a statement put in for the benefit of a cardinal's niece but has some basis in fact, she came closest to conversion at this time. There's also, of course, the possibility that one of her parents was a Catholic. Her mother seems the likelier candidate if pressure was put on Aphra Behn to enter a convent after her father's death. Convent life certainly fascinated her but it's more a fascination with the externals, anticipating the gothick of the eighteenth century, than a religious fascination.

There's some evidence for Catholic connections among her friends. I've already mentioned Henry Neville Payne, to whom she confessed 'particular obligations' in the dedication of *The Fair Jilt*. But I think she also had an acquaintance with Walter, Lord Aston of Staffordshire, who was a great friend of Lord Stafford and whose family later intermarried with the Howards of Corby.

My evidence for this is in a collection of letters of the Aston family, published in *The Tixall Letters* from the name of their family seat. Aphra Behn could have met Lord Aston through Sir Thomas Gower's Leveson relations, since their home, once they had withdrawn from Kent, was in Staffordshire.

Walter Aston, who spent a lot of his time in London even though he was barred from public office because of his Catholicism, was a great playgoer. In 1669 he was entertaining his cousin Elizabeth Cottington, who was in some family disgrace and was on her way to France. It's hard to work out quite what she had done but it had caused her estrangement from a powerful member of the family, Winifred Thimelby, Abbess of St Ursula's, the Convent of English Nuns, Augustines, at Louvain in Flanders.[7]

Elizabeth Cottington wrote to Herbert Aston on January

17th: 'you must know cousin Aston is this day gone to a new play which was never acted but by the Lady Castelmaine'. There's only one recorded instance of Lady Castlemaine acting and that was in Katherine Philips's *Horace* on Tuesday February 4th 1668. The performance caused a great stir and Elizabeth Cottington would easily remember it. One account says that Castlemaine was adorned with £200,000 worth of jewellery 'the Crowne Jewells being taken from the Tower for her'.[8] This dates the letter as I've said,[9] because Pepys saw the third night of the public production of *Horace* at the King's Theatre on January 19th. Her letter goes on: 'We are in expectation still of Mr Dryden's play. There is a bold woman hath offered one: my cousin Aston can give you a better account of her than I can. Some verses I have seen which are not ill; that is commentation [*sic*] enough she will think so too, I believe, when it comes upon the stage I shall tremble for the poor woman exposed among the critics.'

It was Orinda's *Horace* which cousin Aston was seeing while she wrote her letter, that caused her, by association of ideas, to give this tantalizing fragment which may be the earliest mention of Aphra Behn in a literary context. It sounds as if the play had been accepted. If so it must be *The Forc'd Marriage* which had its first known performance on September 20th the following year.

X

First Plays

The idea of becoming a playwright must have come partly from the success of Katherine Philips's translation of Corneille's *Pompey* which was first produced in Dublin in 1663. *Horace* was left incomplete by Katherine Philips's sudden death from smallpox in June 1664. Sir John Denham finished Act V. *Pompey* also had a probable production later in 1663 in London. Langbaine in his *English Dramatick Poets* says he had seen it acted 'with great applause at the Duke's Theatre'.

There were two main companies licensed by the King: the King's Company, which was Killegrew's and acted at the Theatre Royal in Bridges St, Drury Lane, in 1668, and Sir William Davenant's, known as the Duke's Company, which acted at the Playhouse in Lincoln's Inn Fields. Sir William, who was the last of the pre-Civil-War generation, and wasn't averse to being known as a natural son of Shakespeare, died in the spring of 1668 and the management of the company passed to the actors Thomas Betterton and Henry Harris on Lady Davenant's behalf. A third group, known as the Nursery, for young actors, played at Gibbon's Tennis Court in Vere Street, which was, as its name suggests, a converted indoor court where the King's Company had played before the building of the Bridges St theatre.

Each company had its own actors and dramatists. Dryden wrote for the King's Company and had been made laureate on April 13th after Sir William Davenant's death.

Shadwell wrote for the Duke's Company. At this date the Duke of York hadn't declared his conversion to Catholicism and it was therefore not so inappropriate that the chief Whig dramatist should be the principal writer for his company.

The obvious company for Aphra Behn to identify herself with was the King's because of her connection with Killegrew. More, Sir Robert Howard was a shareholder in the theatre. That she didn't requires some explanation. I think she offered first to them. Elizabeth Cottington's letter suggests this. She suggests that the Astons were in some way connected with the King's theatre by the intimate mention of Dryden. How else would she know that a 'bold woman had offered one'? But if this is Aphra Behn, and it's hard to suggest anyone else, there's a very long gap between the offer and the first performance in September 1670. A possible explanation is that Killegrew accepted and then changed his mind so that the play then had to be read by the other company, all of which, as any writer knows, takes a great deal of time. Her troubles with Edward Butler and her spell in prison must also have held things up.

Why, if he did, did Killegrew change his mind? There are several possible reasons. There had been two fairly successful plays by a woman performed by his company, *Pompey* and *Horace*. But they had come as rarities; the second with the glamour of the court production behind it. The 'matchless Orinda' was already a sanctified legend. The plays in any case were translations. The experiment of a woman dramatist writing 'for bread', as Aphra Behn describes her situation, might have been thought improper. Neither is it clear whether she was restored to royal favour after her return from Antwerp. It was the Duke of York who became her patron, not his brother.

Another suggestion is that she was in some sense a political plant in the other company. Shadwell had the patronage of Charles Sackville, the Earl of Dorset, at this time Lord Buckhurst, but the court may have felt that a Tory playwright in both companies would be no bad thing. The playwrights attached to the King's Company might also have felt there were enough of them. Dryden had entered into an agreement in 1668 to provide the company with three plays a year and this could have caused Aphra Behn's play to be finally rejected.

The Duke's Company had also made trial of a woman dramatist, Margaret Cavendish, though the play *The Humorous Lovers* as printed is attributed to her husband, William, Duke of Newcastle. Certainly those who saw it, including Pepys, believed it was hers.[1] He was there on March 28th 1667 and called it 'the most silly thing that ever came upon a stage. I was sick to see it, but yet would not but have seen it, that I might the better understand her.' The duchess at the end of the play 'made her respects to the players from her box, and did give them thanks.' On May 6th the King and all the court were there with the duke and duchess. It had a relative success, for three performances wasn't a bad run. The third night was the author's benefit, and the Newcastles' play probably had more than three performances. However, the duchess didn't repeat the experiment unless the other plays put out under her husband's name were in fact her own.[2] If Pepys's reactions were typical, the heavy chauvinism may have been too much even for someone so used to braving out her eccentricity.

The eminence that Dryden gave to the rival company probably had a part in the decision by the Duke's Company to put on another play by a woman, even a talking horse if it had novelty, although they themselves had the enormous pull of Betterton's acting. Someone, if Farquhar's account[3] of how a new playwright got accepted isn't too satirical to be true, must have recommended her and the play. Elizabeth Cottington had seen 'some verses' which had presumably been circulating in manuscript. Any one of a sizeable list of gentlemen could have been her sponsor, including Sir Thomas Gower, the Duke of Buckingham, Killegrew himself, Sir Robert Howard or his brother Edward also a playwright, Lord Aston and so on.

Aphra Behn's reputation as a poet was already well known. Otway had sought her out and, stagestruck himself, had begged a part in her first play. Unfortunately there's no way of knowing, among those of her published poems which can't be dated by internal evidence, which are her earliest and therefore the likeliest for Elizabeth Cottington to have seen.

The play was the first production of the new season and it ran for six nights. Otway played the old King on the first night and suffered paralysing stage fright. 'The full house put him to such a sweat and tremendous agony, being dash't, spoilt him for an actor.'[4] Downes calls it a 'good play' that 'made its exit ... to give room for a greater. The Tempest.' The part of the old King was given to a professional actor after the first night.

It's easy to imagine Aphra Behn's emotions on the first night. The house was full because of the kind of curiosity that would go to see a talking horse. For her biographer a great loss is that Pepys, frightened for his sight, had stopped his diary with its incredible contribution to dramatic history, at the end of 1669. He must however have seen *The Forc'd Marriage* and it probably made him 'sick'. It was still being performed in the following January and was published that year with the epigraph '*Va mon enfant! prends ta fortune*'.

She was proud of this first child by the time it came to be published but the prologue shows the misgivings of its first night. It's addressed to the men in the audience and spoken first by one of the actors. As the best form of defence is said to be attack, the prologue is about this new phenomenon, the woman dramatist. Women, no longer relying only on beauty which 'goes now at too cheap rates', will join wit to beauty so that even when they're old they'll still retrieve 'the wandring heart'.

> Today one of their party ventures out,
> Not with design to conquer, but to scout.
> Discourage but this first attempt, and then
> They'll hardly dare to sally out again.

Then comes a curious passage which suggests that Aphra Behn's reputation as a spy was well known; either that or she herself was unable not to pick at that particular scab:

> The poetess too, they say, has spies abroad,
> Which have dispers'd themselves in every road,
> I' th' upper box, pit, galleries; every face
> You find disguis'd in a black velvet case.
> My life on't; is her spy on purpose sent,
> To hold you in a wanton compliment;
> That so you may not censure what she's writ,
> Which done they face you down 'twas full of wit.

Masks were usually worn by the prostitutes who plied the theatres, though ladies who wished to be incognito also took to them on occasion.

After a few more lines the actor is joined by an actress to refute his charges. There's not a vizard, a common term for a

prostitute from those very masks, among them. Prostitutes are
only after money, she says, with an image from naval warfare.

> Ours scorns the petty spoils, and do prefer
> The glory not the interest of the war.
> But yet our forces shall obliging prove,
> Imposing naught but constancy in love:
> That's all our aim, and when we have it too,
> We'll sacrifice it all to pleasure you.

These last two lines make two rapid disarming shifts, first in
praise of constancy, which would be received with satire by the
fashionably inconstant, and then an elegant double shuffle
which turns the laugh against them followed by a mock-modest
curtsey in 'to pleasure you'.

The prologue must at once have nailed up her colours. This
was no Katherine Philips who could write: 'sometimes I think
that employment (writing) so far above my reach, and unfit for
my sex, that I am going to resolve against it forever ... '5 Nor
could it be said of her work as Sir Edward Dering did in his
epilogue to *Pompey*:

> ... No bolder thought can tax
> Those rimes of blemish to the blushing sex
> As chaste the lines, as harmless is the sense,
> As the first smiles of infant innocence.

By her prologue Aphra Behn claimed the right to deal with sex
as outspokenly as the male playwrights did. It must have
brought down the house with its daring. Such a success was it
that her second play, *The Amorous Prince*, was produced only six
months later in February 1671.

The two plays are similar in style. They are both in the vein
of romantic tragi-comedy so popular until Buckingham laughed
it out of court with the revised version of *The Rehearsal* in 1674.
They reflect the literary debate which Dryden had put into his
An Essay of Dramatic Poesie, published first in 1668, which
crudely put is: to rhyme or not to rhyme. Aphra Behn seems
to have been unable to resolve this problem in her first two
plays and compromises by doing both. Her natural talent was
for blank verse and already this is beginning to assert itself.
Two short examples from *The Jealous Bridegroom* will give some

idea of her developing fluency. The first anticipates her use of blank verse in the later comedies for the cut and thrust of dialogue.

> Yes, he might have lain by,
> Like rusty armour, else,
> Had she not brought him into play again;
> The Devil take her for't.

The second has an echo of Polonius speaking to Ophelia and is an example of how she could in a moment move into a speech of remarkable emotional power and beauty.

> Away, away, you are a foolish girl,
> And look with too much pride upon your beauty;
> Which like a gaudy flower that springs too soon,
> Withers ere fully blown.
> Your very tears already have betray'd
> Its weak inconstant nature;
> Alcippus, should he look upon thee now,
> Would swear thou wert not that fine thing he lov'd.

I chose the second one deliberately for its Shakespearean echoes to illustrate this strongest of all influences on her dramatic writing. These two plays are full of lines behind which it's possible to pinpoint a Shakespeare original. It was a passion she shared with her friend Henry Neville Payne whose own plays show the same fathering genius.[6]

The vogue for plays in rhyming couplets was given impetus by the work of French dramatists, particularly Corneille and Racine. Katherine Philips had translated *Pompey* and *Horace* into them and the early plays of Dryden and those of the Earl of Orrery were in this form. It was the language of tragedy.

In practice few plays fall into the category of unrelieved tragedy or comedy. Most are tragi-comedies which lie at different points along a scale that reaches from farce to tragedy. Aphra Behn's first two plays are technically comedies in that they end happily but, in so far as their form of expression is mainly serious, rather than witty or comic, and their situations have the potential for tragedy, they must be called tragi-comedies.

She was perfectly well able to manage rhyming couplets and

at great lengths. It was the form she used magnificently in the last year of her life for her translation from Cowley which ran to over 1,500 lines. But her ear must have told her that the rhyming couplet isn't the unit of expression for English drama, perhaps because our blank verse tradition is too old and through the influence of Shakespeare too powerful. Nevertheless, rhymed dialogue, the theory ran, with the influential backing of Dryden, gave dignity to drama.

Ironically, I believe, it was the ease with which she wrote it that made the rhyming couplet unsuitable for her use in a dramatic context. Dryden, as he says in his dedication of the 1684 edition of *An Essay of Dramatick Poesie* to Charles Sackville, found it 'troublesome and slow' and that was why he later abandoned it, but it came so readily to her that the verse lacks dramatic intensity and easily deteriorates into the merely facile. To abandon it, however, meant to reject the side of the gods, to set herself up against the prestige of Dryden. At least three times in her life she felt she had to do this, twice in literary matters and once in religious. It gave her no pleasure because she disliked faction, although she was constantly involved in it, and she valued Dryden's genius above that of any of her contemporaries.

It would have seemed effrontery for her to have immediately abandoned in her very first production the accepted mode for the kind of play she was writing, against not only its living protagonists but also against the reputation of the dead Orinda, particularly since in every other way the play continues the daring promises of the prologue. Its theme is exactly what the title says. Erminia who is in love with and has exchanged vows with the prince Alcander is forced by her father to marry Alcippus. Alcander spends their wedding night torturing himself with images of them in bed together. In fact Erminia has contrived to sleep alone. The whole of Act II plays around the representation of the sex act with an outspokenness not in the least obscured by the romantic colouring of the language. It was for this that she was to be esteemed by her admirers and criticized by the puritanical.

The revolutionary impetus which had brought about the political and religious changes of the interregnum had now shifted to the moral sphere and the initiative had passed from roundheads to cavaliers. In place of the saints, God's elect, was a new race of baroque secular saints, love's elect. This revolution was the fiercer because the presbyterian establishment, as it had become, had been authoritarian and repressive in the area of personal morality, rejecting its own extreme wing, the sect of the ranters, along with the dissolute cavaliers.[7] Perversely it was the High Tories who were now the radicals but their radicalism was moral and sexual. Like the political revolution before it, theirs too was to be progressively eclipsed throughout the next century and more.

Freedom in religion applied now to the new religion, love. This didn't mean that there weren't many conflicting sects within it or indeed that it didn't have its own rules. It was, like its predecessor, an anti-authoritarian revolution. As such its first target was bound to be the arranged marriage and, its obverse, the forbidden marriage, which interfered in matters of sexual conscience. Freedom of individual conscience led inevitably to freedom of sexual choice. The very protestant ethic which decreed that the ultimate judge was a man's own inner conviction meant that, in the ethic of sexuality, love, not parental authority, was the ultimate arbiter.

In this religion the King and court formed, as it were, the high priests while the poets wrote its scriptures. Traditional history deals with commerce, warfare and power structures and tends to ignore the history of sexual mores or relegate it to a paragraph, yet nothing so affects the individual as the sexual climate in which he finds himself. Religions have always recognized this and subsumed sexual morality into their systems.

The Forc'd Marriage deals not only with those who love against their parents' will but those who choose love objects outside their social class. Erminia loves a prince. The princess loves a commoner. This situation, which can seem the stuff of romance or pantomime, was in fact an image of a very real situation: the marriage of the Duke of York to Anne Hyde. Clarendon's *Continuation of the Life* gives a lengthy account of his reactions to the discovery of a liaison between the heir to the throne and his daughter, which were no less violent than those of Erminia's father. Indeed Clarendon says that he strongly urged his daughter's imprisonment and execution for her presumption.

The epilogue to *The Forc'd Marriage* which is by 'a woman', is a piece of disarming throwaway. The prologue to *The Amorous Prince* is a very different matter. Aphra Behn's success had increased her confidence and she uses the prologue to defend her form of tragi-comedy, rejecting both the school of Ben Jonson and the other extreme of farce which relied on funny clothes, jigs and 'smutty jest'.

The prudes must have been disturbed by the opening scene between two unmarried lovers just come from bed, she in her night clothes and he dressing. What was even more disturbing was the growing conviction that this woman intended to go on writing for the public theatre. The play keeps up the increased confidence manifest in the prologue. Her talent for the writing of true comedy, which the prologue shows is a considered intellectual choice not simply a lucky hit, really begins to assert itself in her second play. *The Forc'd Marriage* had had one comedy character, Falatius, a coward. In *The Amorous Prince* the comedy is diffused throughout, both in the dialogue and among the characters. Technically it's an enormous advance on its predecessor and leads on naturally to the next stage in her development.

I've said that it was this second play that showed she wasn't just an amateur. She had joined a very select company. Of the fifteen living dramatists who had had two or more plays produced since the theatres reopened in 1660, two were earls, one a duke, one was to be a titular baron, four were knights.[8] Of the remaining seven one was Thomas Killegrew, another the actor-manager Thomas Betterton and three were members of the Howard family (including Dryden). The other two were Shadwell and Flecknoe. Shadwell came of a 'good family' and had been educated at Oxford. Flecknoe's origins are less known but since he was rumoured to be a Jesuit he too had probably had what we now call further education. Andrew Marvell had visited him in Rome and he had travelled to many other countries and presumably had some knowledge of languages.

The preponderance of Howards makes it even likelier that it was through Sir Thomas Gower that Aphra Behn had her first introduction to this society. He was in London in February 1669, attending the Treasury with his brother-in-law, Sir George Downing, about Yorkshire affairs. It was then that he wrote home about the verse letter for his daughter-in-law and Sir Robert Howard's own verses. It's even possible that the verse letter was from Aphra Behn. There had been a rush of new plays and writers when the theatre first reopened but by the end of the decade it had slowed to two or three new writers a year. Some, like Frances Boothby, seem to have been so discouraged at their first trial that they never attempted the stage again. The most prolific were Sir William Davenant himself, Dryden, Roger Boyle, Earl of Orrery, and the Howards, with Shadwell coming up strongly at the end of the period. Her fellow newcomer in 1670 was Thomas Betterton who hardly qualifies for the term.

In 1671 the most important additions were William Wycherley, Elkanah Settle and John Crowne. They did nothing materially to alter the pattern of educational and social background from which the dramatists came. Most were of the gentry or nobility, and almost all had university or Inns of Court education. Compared with such a company Aphra Behn's pretensions must have seemed even more extravagant.

XI

Early Poems

The first Dutch war had ended in 1667. In the same year the French invaded Flanders. Aphra Behn followed the campaign and its successor, the siege of Candia by the Turks, in the news bulletins for she used these events later as background material for *The History of the Nun*. One of her earliest extant poems was dated to this period by *The Muses Mercury* after she was dead, with the title 'On Capt —— going to the Wars in Flanders'. This could have been one of the verses seen by Elizabeth Cottington. It was first published in 1672 in *Covent Garden Drolery or a Collection of all the Choice Songs, Poems, Prologues and Epilogues, (Sung and Spoken at Courts and Theaters) never in print before. Written by the refined'st Witts of the Age. And Collected by A B.*

There was a great vogue for Scottish songs and tunes. Purcell was to write some and Aphra Behn used the convention more than once with great skill and charm. This early poem with its imitation Lallans and its folksong-like quality has no underlying stratum but later she used the same convention to lament over Monmouth's ingratitude and rebellion. The early poem uses the pastoral but dresses it in plaid.

> When Jemmy, first began to love,
> He was the finest swain:
> That ever yet a flock had drove,
> Or danc'd upon the plain.
> 'Twas yau that I, way's me poor heart,
> My freedom threw away,
> And finding sweets in every smart
> I could not say him nay.

The interchange between folksong and court song was very common at this period. Both were hawked as broadsheets and all levels of society enjoyed singing them. The greatest collection was Durfey's *Pills to Purge Melancholy*. Such songs were particularly popular in plays and Aphra Behn had a great talent for them. She was probably a little in love with gallant Captain ———, enough to give him this charming leaving present. But she associated this period with another happening as well, an association that came out when she was looking for someone to dedicate *The History of the Nun* to in 1688.

The *London Gazette* reported from Paris on June 23rd 1668 that the Comte de Chenilly on his return homewards had 'met upon the way at Ligny in Barre a coach well attended and therein a person attired like a gentleman of quality which he perceived to weep, hast'ning towards Lorrain and is since thought to be the Duchesse Mazarine disguised and intending for Italy'. Following up the story on August 1st the *Gazette* reported that 'the Duc de Nevers Mancini has obtained leave of his Majesty to pass some time in Italy tis believed with an intention to overtake the Duchess Mazarine his sister'. This was the beginning of the wanderings of the 'vagabond duchess' who had left her husband and who was to come to rest at last in Charles II's bed.

The Spaniards and the French declared a year's truce in February 1669 in order to fight the Turk. The Duc de Beaufort was put in command of the Christian forces by the Pope. He was not to return to France but died a year later at Candia.

Meanwhile in England Abraham Cowley had died in 1667 and Thomas Sprat, the Duke of Buckingham's chaplain, had produced an edition of his works and account of his life. In a literary sense it was as if God was dead and in the political sphere the death in 1670 of Monck, Duke of Albemarle, who had brought in the restoration must have had much the same *fin de siècle* feeling. The older generation were being removed by time and the younger were cut loose to make their own impression on events.

She produced no plays in 1672. What was she doing? I think she was the editor of *Covent Garden Drolery* and this must have brought her in a few pounds. Figures are very hard to estimate but she might have had £100 each from the performances of her two plays and then something from their publications. She felt she must, or she was forced to, take a year off in 1672. It was the year that Sir Thomas Gower died.

Her precise relationship to him may perhaps never be unravelled. When he was dead it continued in relationships to members of his family which can be traced in dedications and associations. His patronage of her, which was almost paternal, passed for the time being to the Duke of Buckingham and then to Gower's relative by marriage Henry Howard, 'Maecena of my muse, my patron lord'. But I think Sir Thomas had been her prop and his removal must have affected her deeply. Perhaps she fell ill as she was liable to do, as she says in *Oroonoko*, in situations of emotional stress.

Certainly about this time and before 1674 she went to the spa at Tunbridge Wells. The visit can be dated by a poem 'To My Lady Morland at Tunbridge'. Carola, daughter of Sir Roger Harsnett, married Sir Samuel Morland, the inventor, on October 26th 1670. She died in October 1674. The poem must therefore lie between those dates. The season at the wells was in the summer so that would make a possible date of any of the summers from 1671–4. The last seems unlikely since the poem shows no sign of Carola Morland's illness or pregnancy. However, the Duke of York was there in 1670 and again in 1674 which might have provided an added incentive for Aphra Behn to go there.

Mount Sion was then the fashionable part with its own ballroom, bowling green and houses for the accommodation of visitors, some of them built on sledges for easy removal. Grammont described the life there in his *Memoirs*.

Tunbridge (Wells) is the same distance from London that Fontainebleau is from Paris, and is, at the season, the general rendez-vous of all the gay and handsome of both sexes. The company though always numerous, is always select: since those who repair thither for diversion ever exceed the number of those who go thither for health, everything there breathes mirth and pleasure: constraint is banished, familiarity is established upon the first acquaintance, and joy and pleasure are the sole sovereigns of the place ... here one may live as one pleases: here is, likewise, deep play, and no want of amorous intrigues. As soon as the evening comes, every one quits his little palace to assemble, on the bowling green, where, in the open air, those who choose dance upon a turf more soft and smooth than the finest carpet in the world.[1]

Lady Morland was twenty-two when she died. Aphra Behn must have been in her early thirties. Lady Morland had stolen the attention of her lover whose identity is disguised under the soubriquet Amyntas. Aphra Behn hearing reports of Lady Morland's beauty had gone to church to see what her rival looked like and, always susceptible to beauty whether in men or women, had been immediately captivated. The very priest at the altar forgets where he is in the service and the congregation are all as affected. Aphra Behn admits defeat.

> I call'd Amyntas Faithless Swain before,
> But now I find 'tis just he should adore.
> Not to love you, a wonder sure would be
> Greater than all his perjuries to me.
> And whilst I blame him, I excuse him too;
> Who would not venture Heav'n to purchase you?

There's a sting in the end of the poem. She suggests that such a well-used lover isn't worthy of such a prize which deserves a 'virgin-heart' that

> ... ne'er found
> It could receive, till from your eyes, the wound.

The church must have been Speldhurst for there was no church at the wells before the chapel dedicated to Charles the Martyr, for which a plot of ground was given by Lady Purbeck in 1676. It took eight years to collect enough money to build on it.

The poem accords well with Grammont's description of life at the spa. What's hard to know is how seriously to take the emotion expressed in it. In the dedication of the first part of *Love Letters Between a Nobleman and His Sister* she says: 'who can be happy without love? for me I never numbered those dull days amongst those of my life, in which I had not my soul fill'd with that soft passion.' Not all such relationships, how-

ever, ended in bed. Pepys and Mrs Knep, the actress, are a
case in point. Kissings and pettings there could be, a great
deal of courting went on, but in the days before contraception
anything more led almost inevitably to pregnancy. Aphra
Behn's intellect and temperament would both, I believe, have
caused her to shy away from such a situation. Even the word
lover, it's clear from its contexts, didn't mean what it does now,
when it's used to describe a relationship where 'making love'
has occurred in the modern sense. To 'make love' in the
seventeenth century meant, as it does in the title of her poem
'To Clarinda who made love to me imagined more than a
woman', to court. The love game was played rather like
Monopoly with a great deal of fake coin and a constant going
back to square one. Its motto was often that old saw that it's
better to travel hopefully than to arrive. Amyntas had professed love but had now transferred his devotion to Carola
Morland who was in any case fairly recently married. Sometimes, as in the case of Congreve's devotion to Mrs Bracegirdle, the courtship went on unrewarded till death removed
mistress or lover.

Two other poems date from about this time. In March 1671,
shortly after the production of *The Amorous Prince*, Edward
Howard's *The New Utopia* was produced by the Duke's Company. It was damned and failed. Undaunted, Howard nevertheless published it the same year with a preface and commendatory verses by Aphra Behn, Edward Ravenscroft and
others. In return he wrote a poem to her. Howard had
threatened not to write any more which is always a two-edged
weapon for a writer to try to use.

Aphra Behn's poem suggests that she already understands
the feelings of the writer who has been heavily criticized. Put
briefly her message was: don't give up.

> Should you that justice do
> You must for ever bid adieu,
> To Poetry divine,
> And ev'ry Muse o' th' Nine
> For malice them with ignorance would join
> And so undo the world and you:
> So ravish from us that delight,

Of seeing the wonders which you write:
And all your glories unadmired must lie,
As vestal beauties are intomb'd before they die.

It was a temptation she must have faced herself as the criticism of both her work and her right to do it deepened.

I hope that the other poem which I date to this period brought her some money. It's called 'A Farewell to Celladon On his Going into Ireland' and refers, I believe, to the appointment of Arthur Capel, Earl of Essex, as Lord Lieutenant of Ireland in 1672. Often, though not always, the initial letter of the romance name under which the person is disguised is the same as their real initial. Carola Morland was Cloris in the Tunbridge Wells poem. Thomas Sprat is Thyrsis.

One thing which might argue against its being to Arthur Capel is the fact that by the time she decided to include the poem in a published collection Capel was dead, having committed suicide while in the Tower on a charge of treason. From certain evidence it seems likely that Charles would have pardoned him since in any case his involvement in the plot hadn't included knowledge of or consent to the murder of the King. The Tower itself, in which Capel's father had been imprisoned and executed, seems to have overshadowed his mind. Many writers wouldn't have included such a poem in a collection, though written ten years before, but Aphra Behn never abandoned those in disfavour unless she thought that they were wrong. She wrote against Monmouth while he was still only a potential rebel. She dedicated a work to Henry Neville Payne, who had been in prison, and wrote with unequivocal admiration for Lord Stafford after his execution.

There are a couple of other candidates for Celladon in this poem but they would date it earlier and make it indeed the earliest poem extant, apart possibly from one or two songs like the one discussed earlier, 'When Jemmy, first ... ', which were included in *Covent Garden Drolery*. The candidates are Lord John Berkeley and Sir John Robartes, both of whom were sent to Ireland as governors. Sir John was there from 1669 to 1670; Lord John Berkeley from 1670 to 1672. Neither of them seems to me to fit the description of Celladon. Both were well on in years with long military and diplomatic careers behind them.

Arthur Capel was forty-one. He had been Lord Lieutenant
of Hertfordshire and Wiltshire, both of which might lie behind
the rural imagery. His only diplomatic appointment had been
envoy to Denmark in 1670. As a young man he had fought for
the King and therefore fits the poem's comments about early
loyalty. He was known for his honesty. Celladon is undevious,
frank, charming.

> Farewell the Great, the Brave and Good
> By all admir'd and understood.

He has spent his youth in the country on country pleasures,
which in the pastoral conversion of *L'Astrée* means love. Now:

> Bus'ness debauches all his hours of love;
> Bus'ness whose hurry, noise and news
> Even Nature's self subdues;
> Changes her best and first simplicity,
> Her soft, her easie quietude
> Into mean arts of cunning policy,
> The grave and drudging coxcomb to delude.

Is there a reflection here on the treatment she had had from
Arlington?

> ... bus'ness which alone was made
> To teach the restless statesman how to trade
> In dark cabals for mischief and design ...
> Leave then that wretched troublesome estate
> To him to whom forgetful Heaven,
> Has no one other vertue given,
> But dropt down the unfortunate,
> To toil, be dull, and to be great.

That last line has a leaden droppingness reminiscent of Pope
on dullness.

Capel kept the vice-regency of Ireland until it was given
back to Ormonde in 1677. The aging though still magnificent
Duke was clearly not the sitter for this portrait. The next man
in the job was Henry Hyde, Clarendon's eldest son, but that
wasn't until 1685 and the collection in which the poem appears
was published in 1684. Capel was admitted by his contemporaries to be the most honest and hard-working of them all.

It's an important poem because it's the first of a whole series of state poems which she was to write up to the last months of her life and which was to include her finest poetic achievement, the great pindaric for the coronation of James II.

XII

The Dutch Lover

Such a poem as 'A Farewell to Celladon ... ' was written to be paid for and was recognized as such. She must have got some money too for *Covent Garden Drolery*. The editorship of this has been disputed but I give it to Aphra Behn, partly on the grounds of several previously unpublished poems of hers which appear in it. An enormous number of the pieces in it are by Dryden, which I take as evidence of the close and friendly relationship between them at this time. Her admiration for his work was very real. She knew he was a greater writer than herself and in the preface to her next play, *The Dutch Lover*, she says so and calls him 'our most unimitable Laureat'.

The choice of 'unimitable' is significant, I think. However else she had spent 1672, a great deal of it had been spent in thought and probably in discussion about literary matters, questions of both dramatic principle and technique. I don't intend to spend much time in refuting every criticism that has been levelled against her work and character but one particular comment seems to me to have been sufficiently far-reaching in its denigratory effects to need disposing of. This is the view, which permeates Victoria Sackville-West's short biography, that she was slapdash, a thoughtless hack with occasional flashes of talent. Sackville-West pictures her in a rather grubby *robe-de-chambre* dashing off her careless dialogue with Grub Street knocking on the door. Nothing, I maintain, could be farther from the truth. She wrote quickly, as most of her contemporaries, Dryden in particular, were forced to do.[1] She wrote often in a room full of people as did Jane Austen. These were the conditions of the times before writers aspired to 'a room of one's own'. Such a room was likely to be a garret. The writer who wasn't on the run from the bailiffs was a social animal. She wrote for bread, but she thought about her craft, its purpose and practice. I think she felt in 1673 that she had perhaps been too influenced by Dryden's dramatic views and had in some sense been imitating his technique, which wasn't best suited to her own talent.

Several of her friends would have inclined her to this kind of stocktaking at this particular time. The poem in defence of Edward Howard hints at the same kind of discussion as in her own prologue to *The Amorous Prince*, which is continued in the preface to *The Dutch Lover*, on the nature of true comedy, distinct from farce and from the Jonsonian rules of unity and heavy dependence on classical learning. In short, the model for comedy was 'the immortal Shakespeare'. Howard's own preface to *The New Utopia* also discusses dramatic technique.

At the same time Henry Neville Payne's first two plays had been performed by the Duke's Company in 1671 and 1672. They, too, lean heavily on Shakespeare. Willard Thorp, Payne's only modern biographer, has recognized thirteen Shakespearean reverberations in the first, *The Fatal Jealousy*.[2] Aphra Behn's long friendship with Payne must date from this time. He had been in Ireland in the train of Lord John Berkeley where he had helped to stir up a great deal of mischief which Arthur Capel had to cope with on his arrival. 'If you desire a little character of the man,' Capel wrote from Dublin in January 1673 to Sir Joseph Williamson, 'he was first a prompter of plays, afterwards Sir Ellis Leighton's broker to make his bargains, and the principal person who put this city into that disorder that I found it at my first coming, and continues still by his intelligence to do what mischiefs he can to the government here.'[3] If Capel was the Celladon of Aphra Behn's poem, she may well not have known of Payne's machinations in Ireland. However, Capel says he had been 'a prompter of plays' so presumably he had been about the theatres for some time before going to Ireland as secretary to Sir Ellis Leighton in 1670.

The greatest influence, however, must have been Buckingham and his satire on the romantic tragedies, *The Rehearsal*. Aphra Behn's works were included among its many references,

according to the key published with his collected works in
1715. So strong was the tradition of her association with
Buckingham that the collected works included not only her
epitaph on him but also her portrait, and claimed that her
translation of a poem by Sappho was written to Buckingham
in 1680. For some reason biographers have ignored this
association, possibly because there's no evidence for it in
contemporary letters or diaries.

To have been left out of *The Rehearsal* would have been a
slight. It would have meant quite simply that she wasn't important enough to satirize. The satire wasn't too harsh because,
I believe, both Buckingham and Rochester thought well of her.
She seems from references in her poems to have been on
friendly terms with Thomas Sprat, whom she called Thyrsis,
Buckingham's chaplain and collaborator in *The Rehearsal*. If she
was living in the parish of St Bride's, Sprat was her neighbour.
So too was Shadwell.

The Duke's Company had opened a magnificent new theatre
in Dorset Garden in the November of 1671. In the following
January the King's Company's Theatre Royal was destroyed by
fire and they took over the old theatre in Lincoln's Inn Fields
which the others had just moved out of. The Dorset Garden
Theatre was provided with a hit almost at once in Edward
Ravenscroft's first play, *The Citizen Turned Gentleman*,[4] which
opened in July 1672 and was a great favourite with the court,
particularly Prince Rupert to whom it was dedicated on
publication.

Ravenscroft was an important figure in Aphra Behn's life,
made all the more so by a rumour that he helped her write her
plays. In fact she had had two plays performed before his
theatrical career began, though he had joined her in the poems
prefixed in defence to Edward Howard's *The New Utopia*. Her
lover John Hoyle was later cast in the role of Svengali by those
who couldn't believe she had written them, much as Bacon and
Walsingham were suggested as the true authors of Shakespeare's
plays.

In the preface to *The Dutch Lover* she had been honest,
and perhaps foolish, enough to admit that she had consulted
'most of those who have a reputation for judgement of this
kind; who were at least so civil (if not kind) to it as did en-

courage me to venture it upon the stage, and in the press: nor did I take their single word for it, but us'd their reasons as a confirmation of my own.' Malice found it very easy to substitute creation for consultation.

The argument was a circular one: if a woman wrote it, it can't be very good and if it's any good a woman can't have written it. 'Indeed that day 'twas acted first, there comes me into the pit, a long, lither, phlegmatick, white, ill-favour'd, wretched fop ... This thing I tell ye, opening that which serves it for a mouth, out issued such a noise as this to those that sate about it, that they were to expect a woeful play, God damn him, for it was a woman's.'

But Aphra Behn had reached that moment in her art when confidence comes, a moment so well caught by Yeats in

> Because I have come into my own
> And words obey my call.

She goes on:

> For waving the examination why women having equal education with men, were not as capable of knowledge, of whatever sort as well as they: I'll only say as I have touch'd before, that plays have no great room for that which is men's great advantage over women, that is learning ... I dare to say I know of none that write at such a formidable rate but that a woman may well hope to reach their greatest heights.

No woman had ever addressed the public in such terms before, except maybe a queen, and indeed few men. No woman writer had ever made such claims for her right to work or, implicitly, for the merit of the work itself. She was claiming that she was as good as everyone else except Dryden. In terms of the literary hierarchy, she was claiming to be as good as Shadwell and this made him her enemy and would have done even had their politics not been so opposed. Not only that but she rejects in the preface the theory, which Shadwell and his supporters advanced, that plays are meant to instruct and 'to amend men's morals and their wit'. 'Comedy', she says, 'was never meant, either for a converting or a conforming ordinance.' Art is not life and isn't meant to be. Plays are 'intended for the exercising of men's passions not their understanding'. Modern terminology would express this as 'the appeal of drama is to a more fundamental psychological level than simply to the intellect.'

Buckingham had pilloried the conventions of romantic tragedy. In her reappraisal, she largely abandoned couplets in *The Dutch Lover* and for the first time in her plays she introduced prose. She was to push this experiment further until she found the right mix for each play. Not that the mix in *The Dutch Lover* isn't right. It is. The play could be put on tomorrow, with only those adjustments that are usually made during rehearsal, and be an enormous success if we could find the right theatrical idiom. Unfortunately Restoration drama presents as many problems to us in performance as *opera seria* and therefore those plays which, like Handel's operas, should be a permanent part of our national repertoire are as unperformed as they are.

The Dutch Lover was a failure on the stage. Aphra Behn claims in the preface that the actor who played the Dutchman, Edward Angel, ad libbed so much that she didn't recognize most of his lines 'which though I knew before I gave him yet the part, because I knew him so acceptable to most o' th' higher Periwigs about the town ... ' Angel had since died[5] so she's unwilling to speak ill of the dead. A comment like this is invaluable for the light it throws on theatrical practice. From this and her giving the part of the King in *The Forc'd Marriage* to Otway, it's clear that the author did the casting and this is important in considering the cast lists of her later plays.

She criticizes the costumes too, justifiably since the comedy of situation in the play depends on mistaken identity, the hero dressing as the Dutchman Haunce Van Ezel. But there was probably a political reason for the play's failure. It came at the end of the second Dutch war, which had gone badly for England so that Charles, who had engaged in it largely because of his treaties, both secret and acknowledged, with the French, was forced to conclude a peace in February even as the play was being staged. Even Angel's comic business was unable to make a Dutchman very acceptable at that moment. She was, however, in good company for Dryden's *Love in a Nunnery* had been damned the November before. What makes me suspect even more that there was a political element in these two failures of plays by supporters of the court party is the enormous success of Shadwell's *Epsom Wells*. Plays didn't rise or fall simply by their own merits but also as 'court' or 'country' party gained the political ascendency, and depending partly on the allegiances of the playwright and his friends who packed the first night.

It sounds from the preface as if *The Dutch Lover* didn't last till the vital third night whose receipts went to the dramatist. She had a further cause for complaint in that she had been promised an epilogue which didn't materialize. Instead, the delinquent got someone else to write one 'as you see ... The prologue is by misfortune lost.'

I believe the delinquent was Ravenscroft and that the reason he didn't fulfil his promise was that he was taking the cure for one of the venereal diseases. In 'A Letter to a Brother of the Pen in Tribulation' she has a footnote to the lines:

> Pox on't that you must needs be fooling now,
> Just when the wits had greatest need of you.

which runs 'I wanted a prologue to a play.' The footnote was written a decade later and the epilogue has become a prologue. Ravenscroft had produced no play since *The Citizen Turned Gentleman* in July 1672. In Lent of 1673 he produced *The Careless Lovers*, he says in a week, at the request of the company. The 'Lenten Plays' were usually for the benefit of the younger members of the company.

> Is this thy writing plays? who thought thy wit
> An interlude of whoring would permit.

The footnote to this couplet runs: 'He pretended to retire to write.' The cure was usually taken at the baths in Leather Lane. The treatment was lengthy and unpleasant, consisting largely of sweating in a tub and taking mercury. Henry Savile wrote to Rochester from the house he was staying in in 1678, 'I confess I wonder at myself and that whole stock of mercury that has gone down my throat in seven months.' However he had been joined by their mutual friends, Mr Fanshawe and Mrs Roberts, and they were contriving to be merry together and to make the best of their enforced confinement.

Venereal disease was a hazard of sexual activity. Some people used a condom of linen or sheep gut as an attempt at protection but, not surprisingly, these weren't popular. By this time

syphilis and gonorrhœa had reached almost epidemic proportions in Western Europe. Ideas on hygiene were very primitive
and its practice even more so. Pepys records the infrequency of
his wife's bathing. Cures must simply have allayed the symp-
toms and driven the diseases into the dormant state where they
could be passed on without the carrier or recipient realizing.
In such a situation some attitude had to be assumed, either of
condemnation or acceptance or a mixture of both.

> Now could I curse this female, but I know
> She needs it not, that thus could handle you.
> Besides, that vengeance does to thee belong ...
> Curse then, dear swain, that all the youth may hear,
> And from thy dire mishap be taught to fear.
> Curse till thou hast undone the race, and all
> That did contribute to thy Spring and Fall.

The poem has already made it clear that it's written in
anticipation of Spring and contrasts the welcome of nature,
meadows and groves in flower, to young lovers with Damon's
situation 'in close rooms pent' and 'codling every morning in a
cask'. Those who have accused Aphra Behn of libertinism
haven't read her with much attention. She doesn't condemn
her brother of the pen. She does condemn prostitution, though
not the particular prostitute who is already cursed enough in
her disease.

Ravenscroft has often been suggested as one of Aphra Behn's
lovers but this poem makes it pretty certain that he wasn't.
He's very much a brother, a friend. His promise of a prologue
was made good by an epilogue, one for *The Town Fop*. When
they were both dead Tom Brown revived the gossip in his
Letters from the Dead to the Living: The Virgin's answer to Mrs Behn:
'if you give yourself but the trouble of examining an old poet's
conscience who went lately off the stage, and now takes up his
lodging in your territories, and I don't question but there you'll
find Mrs Behn writ as often in black characters, and stand as
thick in some places, as the names of the generation of Adam in
the first of Genesis.' Ravenscroft's last play was produced in
1697 and he is said to have died a couple of years after and not
long before Tom Brown's fake letter which can be dated by a
reference to Jeremy Collier.

I think Ravenscroft is also the Damon of another poem 'To Damon: to enquire of him if he could tell me by the style who writ me a copy of verses that came to me in an unknown hand'; and the Damon once again of 'A Pastoral Pindarick: on the marriage of the Right Honourable the Earle of Dorset & Middlesex to the Lady Mary Compton'. In this Aminta is Aphra Behn and old Colin, I believe, is Abraham Cowley.

Ravenscroft may have known Aphra Behn before they both became dramatists for there's a curious entry in the state papers for 1663 which suggests that he knew Charles Howard, Sir Thomas Gower's brother-in-law. He and a Katherine Metham were stopped on their way to France by the Mayor of Rye who believed Ravenscroft was running off with an heiress. The Earl of Carlisle had to intervene to get them freed and in the process said that the girl was his kinswoman. In both the other two Damon poems the tone towards him is the same: that of a brotherly friend with whom she discusses both literature and her emotional life.

> Oh Damon if thou ever wert
> That certain friend thou hast profest ...
> Oh thou that knowst each shepherd's strains
> That pipes and sings upon the plains ...

The failure of *The Dutch Lover*, though it brought forth such an aggressive and amusing piece of self-defence from her, must have once again caused Aphra Behn to rethink her position. She produced no work, or at least none was performed, in the next two years. She was never again to afford herself such a luxury.

XIII

Abdelazer

I think she spent part of the time abroad, on the equivalent
of the young man's grand tour. I can see no other period in
the rest of her life when she could have done this though I
believe she did go to France from time to time. I base my
suggestion of a longish trip abroad on three small bits of
evidence. The first is her knowledge of languages other than
French. French she obviously spoke very well indeed. Where
she had originally learned it I don't know. A comment in
Oroonoko suggests she knew French before she went to Surinam.
French would have been a great help to her in Flanders. Sir
John Reresby in his memoirs speaks of the Duke of York's great
liking for the French language and those who spoke it. If she
met James, as I've suggested, in Yorkshire in 1665, this would
have been a great point in her favour and would have en-
hanced her attraction.

She also had a smattering of Italian and Spanish, both of
them, it seems to me, to the kind of level a sharp ear picks up as
a tourist, though her Spanish was a bit stronger than her
Italian. A story which was published posthumously, *The Dumb
Virgin or the Force of Imagination*, is set in Venice with the author
as a witness of some of the events. It's one of those novellas
where she speaks in her own person and makes a reference to
using the name of a certain person in one of her plays as she
does with the name of George Marten in *Oroonoko*. In this case
the name is Dangerfield and as far as has been found she never
did use it in a play. There was, however, a very good reason
why she shouldn't, for it was the name of the notorious plotter
who was involved with Henry Neville Payne and Elizabeth

Cellier in what was known as the meal-tub plot. Curiously enough Dangerfield's pseudonym was Willoughby.

The fact that she didn't publish the story and didn't use the name as she intended to do doesn't mean that she was never in Venice. There is, though, another small piece of evidence for travel in the dedication of *The Young King* to Philaster in 1679. I shall have something to say later about the identity of Philaster. For the moment I'm only concerned with the sentence which referring to her muse runs: 'Three thousand leagues of spacious ocean she has measured, visited many and distant shores and found a welcome everywhere ... ' The phrase 'many and distant shores' suggests to me more than a return from Surinam to England followed by a single visit to Antwerp.

One further small comment which I'd also like to tie in here comes from One of the Fair Sex. After including several letters from Aphra Behn to Lycidas, the *Memoirs* go on: 'Here I must draw to an end; for tho' considerable trusts were reposed in her, yet they were of that import, that I must not presume here to insert them.' This may be the biographer romancing again or there may be some foundation as yet undiscovered for this tantalizing fragment. Perhaps those 'considerable trusts' included carrying messages abroad.

As far as Aphra Behn was concerned, the most important political event of these years must have been the Duke of York's avowal of his Catholicism which posed an enormous problem of conscience for devoted royalists who were members of the established church.

James's conversion is generally supposed to have taken place during the family reunion at Dover in 1670 when their sister the Duchess of Orléans came over to seal the secret treaty between Charles and Louis. The Test Act which was passed in 1673 brought his conversion into the open when he was forced by the Act either to conform or to surrender his offices. His marriage to the Catholic Mary Beatrice of Modena in the same year did nothing to restore the nation's confidence. Feeling ran high against all Catholics and especially against those about the Queen. Philip Howard, the so-called cardinal of Norfolk who had founded two English convents in Flanders, was forced to leave England and was compensated by the Pope with a cardinal's hat. His entry into Rome in 1675 was very magnificent and among his train was the Honourable John Howard, Lord Stafford's son, whom Aphra Behn had already met on her way to Flanders. In the dedication of *The City Heiress* to Henry Howard she says that she had seen when abroad the populace acclaiming members of his family when they walked through the streets. She could have meant Stafford in Flanders. Sir William Temple wrote home to Lord Lisle at that time that it was 'a credit to be an Englishman; and not only here but in Amsterdam itself; I am told my Lord Stafford who went lately thither about a process, has more hats and legs than the burgomaster of the town'.[1] However, it could be that she was in Rome in 1675 and saw the Howards' triumphal and magnificent public entry.

Her patron to be, Henry Howard of Arundel, publicly conformed and took the sacrament though James never quite gave up hopes of converting him back. Buckingham meanwhile attacked Arlington and was himself dismissed while Arlington managed to survive to become Lord Chamberlain.

Her own reputation was given recognition in 1675 in the publication by Edward Phillips, Milton's nephew, of a little book *Theatrum Poetarum*. His entry is inaccurate and incoherent but it's the first piece of objective comment there is extant about her work and status, and I therefore give it in full. The book was licensed in September 1674 when, presumably, the text was already written. 'Astrea Behn a dramatic writer so much the more considerable as being a woman, to the present English stage, to which she hath contributed two comedies, the Dutch Lady, and the Amorous Princess, the Forc'd Marriage, a tragy-comedy, and the Fatal Jealousy, a tragedy.'

This last is actually by Henry Neville Payne. It's interesting that Phillips has, wherever possible, made the titles feminine to agree with the sex of their author. The other women writers he mentions are Katherine Philips, Anne Broadstreet[2] and the Duchess of Newcastle.

Tragedy was in favour by the time she returned to the theatrical scene, and the summer of 1676 saw the production of her own *Abdelazer or The Moor's Revenge*. By this time Elizabeth Barry had joined the Duke's Company. She appears on the lists from 1673 onwards but her first recorded part was in Otway's *Alcibiades*, for from would-be actor Otway had progressed quickly to playwright and it was his talent that was partly responsible for the vogue for tragedy. Elizabeth Barry played Leonora, the second female lead in *Abdelazer*, while the part of the termagant queen was taken by Mary Lee. Tradition identifies Elizabeth Barry as Amoret in Aphra Behn's poems and judging by the number of times she cast Elizabeth Barry in her plays, Aphra Behn, like most of her contemporaries, thought highly of her work.

If the identification is correct, she's the 'My dear Amoret, Mris B' of a poem called 'Our Cabal' which I date to either just before or just after the gap in Aphra Behn's playwriting from 1673 to 1676. It's closely linked in mood with the Celladon poem ' ... On his Going into Ireland'. By inference through its title, it contrasts the cabal of lovers in their pastoral disguise with the cabal of busy statesmen. The affairs of state of 'Our Cabal' are affairs of the heart. The little band of lovers is setting off to the country for a *fête galante*, a land voyage to their own Cythera. What she describes is exactly the sort of gathering that Watteau was to paint so exquisitely. There are the bagpipes and the dancing of the fake shepherds and shepherdesses:

> The sun is up, the day does waste:
> Dost thou not hear the musick loud,
> Mix'd with the murmur of the crowd?
> How can thy active feet be still,
> And hear the bagpipes cheerfull thrill?

The Muses Mercury for January 1708 identifies two of the people as 'Mr Edward Butler and Mrs Masters' and promises to speak of the others 'hereafter'. Unfortunately this promise was never fulfilled but the identification of Edward Butler is interesting in itself.

I date the poem to this period because in it Aphra Behn hasn't yet fallen in love with John Hoyle, although he appears in it as Mr J. H. Lysidas, and already he's involved in a homosexual situation with the young Philander, Mr Ed. Bed.[3]

> He cannot guess what passion is.
> But all the love he ever knew,
> On Lysidas he does bestow:
> Who pays his tenderness again,

> Too amorous for a swain to a swain ...
> His eyes towards Lysidas still turn,
> As sympathising flowers to the sun;
> Whilst Lysidas whose eyes dispense
> No less a grateful influence,
> Improves his beauty which still fresher grows:
> Who would not under two such suns as those?

This wasn't the first time she had shown herself aware of homosexuality. Lorenzo in *The Amorous Prince* has a passage with Cloris who he thinks is a 'smooth-fac'd boy' and offers to set up as his favourite. Her own relationship with Elizabeth Barry is intense enough, to border on the erotic. Another poem, 'On Mr J H to Amoret', where Hoyle appears under the guise of Amyntas, begins:

> My Amoret, since you must know
> The grief you say my eyes do show:
> Survey my heart, where you shall find,
> More love than for your self confin'd.
> And though you chide, you'l pity too,
> A passion which even rivals you.

'Our Cabal' presents Mr Je B. as Amyntas 'the author of my sighs and flame'. I believe he was Jeffery Boys of Kent. He was then at Gray's Inn and his pocket diary for 1671 records that on July 1st, 'Astrea's boy brought me her play of *Ye Amerous Prince*,' and that on May 29, he 'g Astrea 5s for a Guiny if she live halfe a year'. J.B. may be James Boys and N.R.V., the Nick Vernatty who appears in Boys's diary, and in Pepys's as a cunning knave. Aphra Behn loves Je B while Amoret loves N.R.V., 'the lovely Philocles', the epitome of faithlessness.

> And if inconstancy can seem
> Agreeable, 'tis so in him,
> And when he meets reproach for it,
> He does excuse it with his wit.

This is the game of love as played in *L'Astrée*: the heavy flirtation, the rejections, the jealousies and accusations, the changes of partner; the sex game played as it was among groups of adolescents, before the general availability of contraceptives, at university, youth club, harvest camp and so on. One of its strongest factors is the repression of complete sexual expression and this gives it its hothouse atmosphere. The pastoral idiom provides a dress for sexuality to play in which protects the wearers with its images of innocence from the ultimate reality of physical sex as the end of courtship for as long as possible. It didn't of course always work. The loveliest of the shepherds was Strephon, John Wilmot, Earl of Rochester, by whom Amoret had a daughter in 1677.

Aphra Behn's own meeting with him may have been at this time but I think it was earlier and probably came about through Buckingham. In a poem written after his death to Anne Wharton she implies such an early meeting. Imagining his spirit has appeared to her she says (my italics):

> With the same wonted grace my muse it prais'd,
> With the same goodness did my faults correct,
> And careful of *the fame himself first rais'd*,
> Obligingly it school'd my loose neglect.

With Edward Phillips's comments in 1674 about her in mind these lines suggest that she met Rochester about the time Elizabeth Barry joined the company or perhaps even before, for he had been a theatregoer as early as 1667 when Pepys saw him at *Heraclius* with his new wife. It also suggests that it was his verdict which got her work accepted. This wasn't impossible. Wycherley's *The Plain Dealer* was saved in 1676 when 'the Town appeared doubtful what judgement to form of it' by the applause of Buckingham, Rochester, Dorset, Mulgrave, Savile, Buckly, Sir John Denham and Waller, who made up 'the wits'.[4] Of those eight names at least five were known to her as patrons or friends.

Cibber thought *Abdelazer* poorly written. Aphra Behn never again wrote a full-blown tragedy, which suggests that, like marriage, it was an experiment she was disinclined to repeat. It contains however one of her finest and most anthologized songs which indeed opens the play: 'Love in fantastic triumph set.' Unfortunately when *Abdelazer* was produced again in the 1690s with music by Purcell he doesn't seem to have set this but simply to have provided new incidental music to replace that by Francis Forcer.

Was it only the fashion for tragedy that caused her to write it and what was behind her choice of subject? It's an adaptation of a play published in 1657 called *Lust's Dominion* and provided an excellent vehicle for the company's two finest tragic actors, Thomas Betterton as Abdelazer and Mary Lee as Isabella, Queen of Spain. I think it's fair to say that the main technical difference between the tragedies of Otway and Dryden on one hand and *Abdelazer* on the other is that in the first case the emphasis is on the poetry, in the second it's on the action, both physical and emotional. In spite of its unclassical setting *Abdelazer* is closer to Racine and Corneille than to Shakespeare. Otway's plays however are much more in the English tradition where the drama often seems simply a vehicle for the verse.

The lustful termagant queen must have made a magnificent part for Mary Lee who specialized in tragic roles and was eventually ousted from them by Elizabeth Barry who here appropriately played her daughter. Is there, I wonder, an element of Mrs Johnson in Isabella? If Byam's 'Devouring Gorge' was Aphra Behn's mother there might indeed be. Unfortunately Elizabeth Johnson is such a common name I've been unable to make even a guess at whether she was still alive at this time.

Two letters suggest that Aphra Behn spent the summer following the production of *Abdelazer* in the country, in Oxfordshire, presumably writing *The Town Fop or Sir Timothy Tawdry* which was produced in the September of 1676. The letters are to the actress Emily Price who had joined the company in 1675. The letters have to be treated with some caution because they were both published in 1718 by Tom Brown in his *Familiar Letters of Love and Gallantry*, after Aphra Behn's death. His dislike of her may have caused him to tinker with the texts. They don't ring to my ear completely true but yet not so false as to cause me to reject them as complete fakes. One is a partly verse letter which gives us the location.

My Dear,

In your last, you admir'd how I could pass my time so long in the country: I am sorry your taste is so deprav'd, as not to relish a country-life. Now I think there's no satisfaction to be found amidst an urban throng (as Mr Bayes calls it).

The reference to *The Rehearsal* in the last sentence dates it to after 1671. The letter then goes into a verse description of country pleasures which is very close to the libretto for Handel's *Acis and Galatea*. The lines which locate the poem in Oxfordshire follow.

> Here Gentle Isis, with a bridegroom's haste,
> Glides to o'ertake the Thame, as fair, as chaste;
> Then mixt, embracing, they together flie;
> They live together, and together die;

It sounds as if she might be in the city of Oxford itself though the implication in the rest of the poem is that she is somewhere outside, probably in a country mansion. Rochester's own home wasn't far away at Adderbury.

The second letter pins down the time.

My Dear,

In your last, you inform'd me, that the world treated me as a plagiary, and, I must confess, not with injustice: But that Mr Otway shou'd say, my sex wou'd not prevent my being pulled to pieces by the critics, is something odd, since whatever Mr Otway now declares he may very well remember when last I saw him, I receiv'd more than ordinary encomiums on my *Abdelazer*. But everyone knows Mr Otway's good nature, which will not permit him to shock any one of our sex to their faces. But let that pass: For being impeach'd of murdering my Moor, I am thankful, since, when I shall let the world know, whenever I take the pains next to appear in print, of the mighty theft I have been guilty of; but however for your own satisfaction, I have sent you the garden from whence I gather'd, and I hope you will not think me vain, if I say, I have weeded and improv'd it. I hope to prevail on the printer to reprint *Lust's Dominion* etc that my theft may be the more public. But I detain you. I believe I shan't have the happiness of seeing my dear Amillia 'till the middle of September: But be assur'd I shall always remain as I am,

Yours, A Behn.

Tom Brown has used these two letters to repeat a charge of plagiarism and to suggest an overfondness for Emily Price in the postscript to the first letter which is a love song presumably addressed to her. She was to play Lucretia in Aphra Behn's *Sir Patient Fancy* in 1678.

At this time Aphra Behn seems to have lacked the confidence to produce a play which wasn't based on an earlier one. I call it lack of confidence because I believe that's what it was and that it derived from the criticism she had to undergo for writing plays at all. Part of her seemed still to half believe she couldn't do it. By reworking earlier material in this way she of course ran into the charge of plagiarism, and this went so far that she was forced to add a postscript to a play the following year rebutting the charge.[5]

A culture which encouraged the rewriting of Shakespeare should hardly have jibbed at new versions of older, cruder material. Shakespeare himself after all didn't scorn to use other people's work of all sorts as his source. Not even the famous 'the barge she sat in' speech is without an earlier source. But in her it was somehow worse. It was no doubt thought to prove something about women's minds. The epilogue to *Abdelazer* written 'by a friend' shows the unease still at work. It was spoken by 'little Mrs Ariell'.

> But now not pity but my sex's curse,
> Whose beauty does, like monarchs, give you laws,
> Should now command, being join'd with wit, applause.
> Yet since our beauty's power's not absolute,
> She'll not the privilege of your sex dispute,
> But does by me submit –

Rehearsal usually took a month, so for a September production of *The Town Fop* she must have been back in town by August, since rehearsal usually began with the author reading the play to the cast. The play was licensed for printing almost immediately, which suggests it was a success, and it was still running on November 1st when Nell Gwyn went to it. Once again it's a rewrite but one with a particular significance for Aphra Behn since it was based on something originally called *The Yorkshire Tragedy*. It may be no coincidence that about this time she fell seriously and physically in love for the first time in her life, and with a Yorkshireman.

XIV

John Hoyle

He was admitted a pensioner of Emmanuel College, Oxford, on May 14th 1658. I've not been able to find his baptismal record, which isn't among those of several of his brothers and sisters in the registers of St Martin cum Gregory, York. He must however have been about sixteen or eighteen at the time of his admission to Emmanuel, which would make him roughly the same age as Aphra Behn.

His father, Thomas Hoyle, had been both alderman and M.P. for York and almost certainly knew Sir Thomas Gower. He had begun as a parliamentarian, co-operating in 1640, and he appears quite often in the state papers in connection with the governing of the city. But the execution of Charles I seems to have worked on his mind to such an extent that he hanged himself exactly a year later on January 30th 1650. His suicide made a great stir and was recorded in Smith's *Obituary*.[1] It also got into verse and was published eventually in the collection called *The Rump* in 1662, which consisted of royalist verses that had passed round in manuscript during the interregnum. By the time of its publication John Hoyle had been admitted to Gray's Inn, on February 27th 1660. The poem is worth giving in full because of the traumatic effect it must have had on John Hoyle. It's called 'On the Happy Memory of Alderman Hoyle that hang'd himself'.

> All hail fair fruit! may every crabtree bear
> Such blossoms, and so lovely every year.
> Call ye me this the slip? Marry 'tis well,
> Zacheus slip'd to Heaven, the thief to Hell:

But if the Saints thus gives the slip, 'tis need
To look about us to preserve the breed.
Th'are of the Running game, and thus to post
In nooses blanks the reckning with their Host.
Here's more than trussum cordum I suppose
That knit this knot: guilt seldom singly goes!
A wounded soul close coupled with the sense
Of sin, pays home its proper recompense,
But hark you sir, if haste can grant the time?
See you the danger yet what 'tis to climb
In King's prerogatives? things beyond just,
When law seems brib'd to doom them, must be truss'd.
But O I smell your plot strong through your hose,
'Twas but to cheat the hangman of your clothes.
Else your more active hands had fairly stay'd
The leisure of a psalm: Judas has pray'd.
But later crimes cannot admit the pause,
They run upon effects more than the cause.
Yet let me ask the question, why alone?
One member of a corporation?
'Tis clear amongst divines, bodies and souls
As jointly active, so their judgement rolls
Concordant in the sentence; why not so
In earthly sufferings? States attended go.
But I perceive the knock: old women say
And bee't approved, each dog should have his day.
Hence sweep the almanac: Lilly make room,
And room enough for the new saints to come,
All in red letters: as their faults have been
Scarlet, so limn their anniverse of sin.
And to their children's credits and their wives
Be it still said, they leap fair for their lives.

It's not surprising that John Hoyle was 'an atheist, a sodomite professed, a corrupter of youth and a blasphemer of Christ', as Bulstrode Whitelock described him in his commonplace book under the date of Hoyle's murder.

After her husband's suicide John Hoyle's mother, whose name was Sussana, invested money in the Irish Adventurers' Scheme and was lucky enough to win some property in the

lotteries. In this connection she appears in the Irish state papers
as Dame Sussana. I've not been able to find that Thomas
Hoyle was knighted and indeed all the evidence of the entries,
which give him as 'Alderman' or 'his worship' or simply,
'esquire deceased', suggest that he wasn't. It looks therefore as
if Sussana Hoyle had some rank in her own right.

John Hoyle began to acquire notoriety quite early in his
career. In 1665 he was bound over to appear at the Middlesex
Session to answer a charge by the vicar of the parish church of
Hackney, Thomas Steddle, that he had misbehaved himself in
church during sermon-time by speaking 'disgraceful words' of
the preacher 'and disturbing several gentlewomen by uncivil
language and threatening the said Thomas Steddle for re-
proving him for so doing'.[2]

A much more serious crime in the same year may also have
been his, bearing in mind that he died violently. On August
10th a John Hoyle Esq. assaulted Francis Torado junior, a
watchmaker, at St Andrew's, Holborn, and murdered him by
giving him 'with a rapier in the left part of his belly a mortal
wound' of which he died on the 16th. Hoyle was subsequently
tried and found not guilty.[3]

The plots of Aphra Behn's plays contain a great deal of
fighting and duelling. To a twentieth-century audience this
seems part of the theatrical idiom, a machinery for action rather
than the realism which it is. Dozens of instances could be
collected from letters and papers of the time, giving accounts
of such fights.[4] Gentlemen were quick to take offence or to out
with their swords to rescue themselves from any predicament.
Her plays are basically realistic too in their accounts of love
affairs which the mid- and late 'seventies were particularly rich
in. Looking back from the political turmoil of the 'eighties this
must have seemed the golden age of the country shepherds
when England was still Arcadia. Among the shepherds was
John Hoyle who appears under several different names in
Aphra Behn's poems: Amyntas, Lysander, Lysidas.

He was already part of their group, their cabal, and accustomed to flirt with both sexes. She has two versions of how she
fell in love with him. One is the pastoral poem I've already
mentioned, addressed to Elizabeth Barry.

Amyntas on a Holy-day
As fine as any Lord of May,
Amongst the nymphs and jolly swains,
That feed their flocks upon the plains:
Met in a grove beneath whose shade,
A match of dancing they had made.

With all these charms he did address
Himself to every shepherdess:
Until the bagpipes which did play,
Began the business of the day;
And in the taking forth to dance,
The lovely swain became my chance.

To whom much passion he did vow ...

The poem which follows this in *Poems on Several Occasions* is
'Our Cabal', and in that 'Mr J. H.' is Lysidas:

... that haughty swain,
With many beauties in a train,
All sighing for the swain, whilst he
Barely returns civility.
Yet once for each much love he voic'd,
And strange fantastic passion show'd.

This poem tells us that like Charles II he was a 'black' man.

His eyes are black, and do transcend
All fancy e'er can comprehend,
And yet no softness in 'em move
They kill with fierceness not with love.

Another poem, 'To Lysander at the Musick Meeting', says
that she fell in love with him at a concert. John Bannister
instituted a series of public concerts in December 1672 at his
house in White Friars, known as the Musick School, 'over
against the George Tavern'. Two years later he moved to
Chandos Street, Covent Garden, and 'there intends to entertain, as formerly, on Tuesday next, and likewise every evening
for the future, Sundays only excepted'. The concerts began at
four o'clock, the play at three.

Aphra Behn was always susceptible to the combination of

love and music. She has a poem on the same theme, 'A Pindaric to Mr P who sings finely'. In the case of 'Mr P', whom I tentatively identify as Daniel Purcell, Henry Purcell's brother, since he is Damon in the poem,[5] she resisted the erotic impulse; with Lysander she succumbed.

> Beauty and music must the soul disarm;
> Since harmony, like fire to wax, does fit
> The softned heart impressions to admit:
> As the brisk sounds of war the courage move,
> Music prepares and warms the soul to love.

She was now in her late thirties and for the first time she felt real physical desire. This was no longer a love game but a painful obsession.

> What art thou, oh! thou new-found pain?
> From what infection dost thou spring ...
> Thou haunt'st my inconvenient hours;
> The business of the day, nor silence of the night,
> That shou'd to cares and sleep invite,
> Can bid defiance to thy conquering powers.

Desire has usurped her concern with her work and her literary reputation. Never before has she felt its power, even when it would have been to her advantage.

> When thou coud'st mix ambition with thy joy,
> Then peevish phantom thou wert nice and coy,
>   Not beauty cou'd invite thee then
>   Nor all the arts of lavish men;

Read carefully these lines and the following ones suggest several offers for her to become a kept mistress of some 'lavish' man, all of which she refused

> Oh! wou'd you but confess the truth,
> It is not real virtue makes you nice:
> But when you do resist the pressing youth,
> 'Tis want of clear desire, to thaw the virgin ice.

Now to Lysander she has yielded her heart, and bed.

The course of the affair is plotted fairly clearly by her poems and there's also a sequence of letters which were published posthumously, first separately as *Love Letters to a Gentleman* and

then as a kind of appendix to the *Memoirs* by One of the Fair
Sex. The letters aren't dated. They are addressed to Lycidas
and signed Astrea. To me they have the ring of authenticity
especially since they often repeat, or reflect, happenings in the
poems.

One of the Fair Sex claims that she has put them in their
correct order and, without the dates, this has to be accepted
since there's unfortunately no internal evidence to tie them to
an external event. The first letter is written in a period when
she has forbidden him to see her but wishes he had disobeyed.
Instead he is going to a dance and she is jealous and appre-
hensive.

In the second letter they have met the night before but in
public so that she was unable to speak to him and he went away
taking the letter he had brought with him. "Tis a wonder a
woman so violent in all her passions as I, did not (forgetting all
prudence, all considerations) fly out into absolute commands,
or at least entreaties, that you would give me a moment's time
longer ... I am undone, and will be free; I will tell you, you
did not use me well: I am ruined, and I will rail at you –' He
is to come tonight and in a better humour than he was last
night.

The uneasiness of the whole relationship comes out in the
third letter. He had refused to sit next to her. 'Was that my
friend, was that the esteem you profess? Who grows cold first?
Who is changed? and who the aggressor? 'Tis I was first in
friendship, and shall be last in constancy. You by inclination,
and not for want of friends, have I placed highest in my
esteem ...' The next letter continues this theme. He wants her
to love him but he doesn't want to love her. She calls him
'scrupulous'. She fears his 'severe prudence and discretion' will
condemn her. This fourth letter gives an interesting small insight
into her character which One of the Fair Sex describes as 'of a
generous and open temper, something passionate'. She had
described herself as 'passionate' before and now she says that
she 'so naturally' hates 'those little arts of my sex, that I often
run on freedoms that may well enough bear a censure from
people as scrupulous as Lycidas'. When she last saw him she
resolved not to see any man til she saw him again and she has
kept to this.

This carries on in the next letter. She has been writing and has seen no one 'save my own people'. It's very late. He has been to see her earlier in the evening 'and 'twas I hope and believe very innocent and undisturbing on both sides. My Lycidas says, he can be soft and dear when he please to put off his haughty pride, which is only assumed to see how far I dare love him unrequited.' It's depressingly clear to a reader of this that having got her love, and seemingly got her to bed, he is now tired of her and merely playing with her, and that there was never any emotional commitment on his side. It can be objected that she knew what she was letting herself in for since she had already described him as 'haughty' in 'Our Cabal' and described his Don Juan behaviour of losing interest as soon as he aroused it. The end of this letter is particularly affectionate but Hoyle didn't want affection. He wanted to play the love game, perhaps to hide his homosexual activities, for sodomy was a capital crime.[6]

The most interesting of the letters from the point of view of insight into her life is number six, once again written late at night.

> I stay'd after thee tonight, till I had read a whole act of my new play; and then he led me over all the way, saying, Gad you were the man: and beginning some rallying love discourse after supper, which he fancy'd was not so well received as it ought, he said you were not handsome, and called Philly to own it; but he did not but was of my side, and said you were handsome: so he went on a while and all ended that concern'd you. And this, upon my word, is all ... Pray make haste to see me tomorrow; and if I am not at home when you come, send for me over the way, where I have engaged to dine, there being an entertainment on purpose tomorrow for me.

I can only suggest various identifications here but I think they're worth offering. The new play she was reading was, I believe, *The Rover*, Part One of which was produced some time in March 1677. The 'he' who led her over it was implying that Hoyle was the original for Wilmore, the Rover. 'He' is obviously connected with the theatre and may be any one of a list which must include Thomas Betterton, Charles Davenant and

the wits Rochester, Sackville, Sedley and so on. 'Philly' I take
to be the 'Philaster' to whom she dedicated *The Young King* and
I'll say more of him later. The scene of both the reading and the
entertainment 'over the way' is, I believe, the house next to the
Duke's Theatre in Dorset Street where Lady Davenant, her
son, Betterton and Henry Harris lived with several of the
principal actresses.[7] The picture it gives of Aphra Behn at this
period is of someone both successful and popular.

The rest of the letter is concerned with some articles he has
drawn up for their relationship, a very lawyer-like thing to do.
By the next she has realized that he is not only 'haughty' but
unfaithful too.

> What shall I do to make you know I do not use to con-
> descend to so much submission, nor to tell my heart so
> freely? Though you think it use, methinks I find my heart
> swell with disdain at this minute for my being ready to
> make asseverations to the contrary, and to assure you I do
> not, nor never did love, or talk at the rate I do to you,
> since I was born ... However I conjure thee, if possible, to
> come tomorrow about seven or eight at night that I may
> tell you in what a deplorable condition you left me last
> night ... you went for joys, and left me to torments! You
> went to love alone and left me love and rage, fevers and
> calentures, even madness itself ...

The last letter is written after they have agreed not to meet
and not to write but he has broken the agreement and asked
her to write to him. She does so, while prophesying that it's a
mistake. She has learned her lesson and will never agree to hide
her love. He has only put up with her love out of vanity at being
loved by her.

> How could anything, but the man that hates me, entertain
> me so unkindly? Witness your excellent opinion of me, of
> loving others; witness your passing by the end of the
> street where I live, and squandering away your time at
> any coffee-house, rather than allow me what you know in
> your soul is the greatest blessing of my life, your dear
> *dull* melancholy company; I call it dull, because you can
> never be gay or merry where Astrea is.

It's hard to say how long this painful phase of their friendship continued. These must be only some of her letters to him. The rest of the story can be pieced out in such poems as 'On the first discovery of falseness in Amintas', 'To Lysander, on some verses he writ, and asking more for his heart than it was worth', 'To Lysander who made some verses on a discourse of love's fire', 'On Mr J H in a fit of sickness'. This last comes early in their relationship. He is Amyntas and he is ill.

> In pity to Astrea live,
> Astrea, whom from all the sighing throng,
>   You did your oft-won garlands give:
> For which she paid you back in grateful song:
> Astrea, who did still the glory boast,
> To be ador'd by thee, and to adore thee most.

Once again, as with William Scot, her love affair was the gossip of the town, gossip which was still current in 1707 when *The Muses Mercury* published versions of several of the poems with Hoyle's name firmly attached to them. It was also alluded to in a poem published in 1682 in Radcliffe's *The Ramble: News from Hell*.[8] This repeated the old charge that someone else wrote Aphra Behn's plays. This time Hoyle is intended as their putative author.

> The censuring age have thought it fit
> To damn a woman, 'cause 'tis said
> The plays she vends she never made.
> But that a Gray's Inn lawyer does 'em
> Who unto her was friend in bosom,
> So not presenting scarf and hood
> New plays and songs are full as good.

Scarf and hood are given by the groom to the bride. Hoyle moved from Gray's Inn to the Inner Temple on January 26th 1679. Radcliffe's poem, then, must have been written either before that date or not long after when John Hoyle was still thought of as 'a Gray's Inn lawyer'. However, the poem uses the past tense in describing him as her 'friend in bosom'. A verse letter of hers written at the beginning of 1683 shows that she still knew him, but he has become simply 'honest Hoyle', which no longer suggests passion but friendship,[9] though I believe her emotions remained involved with him for much longer. In 1677 however I believe he sat in part for the hero of her greatest box office success, *The Rover*, which brought her the patronage of James II.

XV

The Plagiary

The play which she made out of *The Yorkshire Tragedy* came to her through another version called *The Miseries of Enforced Marriage* by George Wilkins, published in 1605. Enforced marriage was a theme that appealed to the period and particularly to her to judge by the number of times she treated it. In this case it's the young man who is forced by his guardian to marry against his will and his promises to marry the girl he is in love with. Langbaine in his *An Account of the Dramatic Poets* claimed that *Sir Timothy Tawdry* was 'stolen from' *The Miseries of Enforced Marriage* both in plot and in language. Nothing however could be less true. The two plays belong to totally different worlds in both plot and dialogue though beginning from the same basic situation and having some of the same characters.

A few comparisons from the plots will do to illustrate this. In Wilkins's play the girl the young man is forced to break his promise to dies and he has two children by his wife to whom he is reconciled in the last scene. In Aphra Behn's play the girl runs away from home disguised as a young man and makes pretended love to her lover's wife Diana. The young man refuses to consummate the marriage and the couple are divorced to marry the partners of their choice. *Sir Timothy Tawdry* isn't just a rewrite, it's a retreatment of an old theme and it's most successful the farther it goes from its original.

In *The Miseries of Enforced Marriage* the wife is a cipher. Diana in *Sir Timothy Tawdry* is a character in her own right. Aphra Behn has opened out the plot to make a classical structure of two interleaving couples. The development of the women is all her own. If it owes much to earlier material it's to *Twelfth Night*.

The echoes of Wilkins's dialogue occur at those few points where the plots are closest, that is in an occasional speech at the beginning. From then on the major part is her own except where the plots touch again, where for example the young man attempts to debauch himself in revenge for his enforced marriage. Sir Timothy Tawdry of the title, the town fop, is a new character, in place of Sir Francis Ilford in Wilkins's play, who is a brutal opportunist, whereas Sir Timothy is a fool who keeps a mistress, that splendid invention Mrs Betty Flauntit.

The world of Aphra Behn's play is that of classical baroque, full of light and elegance even when set in a brothel. Wilkins's world is the gloomy half-timbering of its period, violent and unpolished. It would be a mistake to think of it either as more realistic or reaching a deeper psychological level. The difference between the plays is of two dramatic conventions which are equally valid.

Nevertheless there are moments when the older material seems to poke through the baroque fabric and give it a Hogarthian twist in, for instance, the brothel scenes, though the sentiments are very much in line with those she expresses elsewhere.

> *Bellmor:* Gods what an odious thing mere coupling is!
> A thing which every sensual animal
> Can do – as well as we – but prithee tell me,
> Is there naught else between the nobler creatures?
> *Flauntit:* Not that I know of, sir – Lord he's very silly or
> very innocent, I hope he has his maidenhead; if so
> and rich too, Oh what a booty were this for me!

By introducing the brothel and Betty Flauntit's attempts to get Bellmor for his money, Aphra Behn has made a parallel between prostitution and forced marriage for money that isn't in the original.

> *Bellmor:* Will you not show me some of your arts of love?
> For I am very apt to learn of beauty – Gods –
> What is't I negotiate for? – a woman!
> Making a bargain to possess a woman!
> Oh, never, never!

It's a cliché that the introduction of women to play female roles had a profound effect on the writing of them. It's not of course true. Shakespeare's women make it a gross simplification: Millamant is no more true or convincing than Rosalind. It might even be more true to say that Shakespeare's women led to the introduction of actresses. Celinda, who is the Viola character to Diana's Olivia in *Sir Timothy Tawdry*, is typical of many Restoration drag roles. The 'new woman' of the late seventeenth century fascinated by her very ambiguity like a bright young thing of the 'twenties. Faced with a wandering lover she doesn't die passively, she changes sex and sets out after him. One layer in the sexual confection that is Rosalind and Viola is lost. Boy isn't playing girl playing boy. Yet the urge to ambiguity with its particular kind of sexual excitement remained even when girls were playing girls and when there was no longer the justification for it that it was easier for the actors. Art was fed by life in the person of Hortense Mancini wandering about Europe in men's clothes. In 1676 she settled in England to remain till her death. Art fed life, I suspect, when she went out in St James's Park in the mornings to practise swordsmanship with Jane Middleton or one of the other ladies of the court.

The costume of the period gave realism to the transexual roles, and women had themselves painted in male dress. A period as sexually conscious as this was free to enjoy the implicit homosexuality of drag, which came into play when either male or female characters found the drag character physically attractive. Aphra Behn shows herself aware of part of this in the poem 'To the fair Clarinda, who made love to me, imagined more than a woman'.

> Against thy charms we struggle but in vain,
> With thy deluding form thou giv'st us pain,
> While the bright nymph betrays us to the swain.
>
> In pity to our sex sure thou wer't sent
> That we might love, and yet be innocent:
> For sure no crime with thee we can commit;
> Or if we should – thy form excuses it.

This is a long way from the intense but platonic relationships of Katherine Philips's circle. As far as I can trace it was the last time a woman was to write publicly and with witty eroticism about such a subject in English for two hundred years.

Sir Timothy Tawdry is the last of what can be called her theatrical juvenilia. There are three plays about this time which are variously attributed to her but were never given to her by earlier writers like Downes and Langbaine who were her contemporaries. These were published anonymously and were all prose rewrites of earlier works. They are *The Woman Turned Bully* produced in March 1675, *The Debauchee or The Credulous Cuckold* printed in February 1677 and therefore presumably performed about that time, and *The Counterfeit Bridegroom or The Defeated Widow* printed in October of that year.

They were all performed by the Duke's Company and the other most frequently suggested author for them is Thomas Betterton himself. Critics who attribute them to Aphra Behn generally do so because of their quality as stageable pieces. There is, of course, no reason why she couldn't have joined Betterton in writing them as part of her goodwill to the company. Ravenscroft wrote an epilogue for one of them as he did for *Sir Timothy Tawdry*. The only cast list we have is for *The Counterfeit Bridegroom* and it doesn't look much like an Aphra Behn cast.

It's true that by the time it appeared Elizabeth Barry was probably far too advanced in pregnancy to take the stage. Her daughter was born on December 16th. Henry Savile, his friend, wrote to Rochester the next day:

> The greatest news I can send you from hence is what the King told me last night, that your lordship has a daughter born by the body of Mrs Barry of which I give your lordship joy. I doubt she does not lie in much state for a friend and protectress of hers in the Mall was much lamenting her poverty very lately, not without some gentle aspersions on your lordship's want either of generosity or bowels towards a lady who had not refused you the full enjoyment of all her charms.[1]

The 'protectress' was Nell Gwyn. Both Rochester and Buckingham were close friends of hers and Rochester some-

times managed her business affairs, as when he wrote to Arthur
Capel in Ireland in 1677 about some rights she had there.[2] The
letter is interesting for Rochester's professed esteem for Capel,
which helps to bolster my identification of him as Aphra
Behn's Celladon in the poem discussed earlier. There's a tradition which makes Otway tutor to Nell Gwyn's sons. His unrequited passion for Elizabeth Barry, who appeared in many
of his plays, is documented by a series of published letters which
were believed to have been written to her. The circle of Aphra
Behn's close friends then was wide and brilliant. As far as I can
judge she remained faithful to them for the rest of their lives.
Perhaps they made up for some lack of closer family. One little
comment in a letter to Hoyle makes it sound as if 'my people'
didn't include her mother and brother by the time the letters
were written. 'I have nobody to fear, and therefore may have
somebody to love.'

If *The Debauchee* is hers it comes very close indeed in time to
The Rover, since only a month separates the licensing to print
of one and the first known performance, which may not be the
première, of the other. *The Rover* too was produced anonymously; indeed the prologue positively uses the masculine
pronoun for the author. It lends some colour to the suggestion
that the other three anonymous plays of this time are hers but
if that had been so I think she would have acknowledged them
when they got into print as she did *The Rover*. They were after
all her children as she had called her first play, though she
might have felt at this time that their mother (or father) was too
notorious to give them a good start in life. Both *The Rover* and
The Debauchee appear in the same bookseller's advertisement in
the *London Gazette* of August 6th–9th, but whereas *The Rover* is
said to be 'Written by A.B.', *The Debauchee* has no origin
attached to it. The Stationers' Register follows the same
pattern except that 'A.B.' is expanded to 'Mrs A Behn'. The
date of registration is July 7th, 'as it was acted at His Royal
Highness the Duke of York's Theatre'.

From the beginning of its run the court, and particularly
James, Duke of York, approved *The Rover*. It was constantly
called for at court and it was even put on after Aphra Behn's
death for William and Mary, with the comment from Mary
that I have recorded earlier. It is good, but the question must

arise whether it's any better than the plays she put out under her own name or indeed than its sequel *The Rover, Part II*.

The sub-title of *The Rover* is *The Banished Cavaliers*. Such a subject would of course evoke a certain nostalgia, a remembrance of things past, that, now that the end was gained, might take on a rather rose-tinted hue. What lads we were; how clever, how brave, how irresistible. It was good propaganda too, a rallying for the faithful when the first romance of the King's return had worn thin and the country was again divided into factions.

From Aphra Behn's point of view it was her most outright and positive celebration of those cavalier childhood heroes. Here with the 'masculine' part of her, her poetry as she was to describe it in the preface to *The Lucky Chance*, she could be one of them at last. But as the writer is rarely just one person among a fictitious crowd so I believe, though her identification with the cavaliers is intense, that she was at the same time A B, the courtesan Angelica Bianca. Her trade was words and it was impossible that she shouldn't have noticed those initials. Perhaps that was why she chose the play.

Killegrew had written it as *Thomaso, The Wanderer*, while in exile before the restoration, along with several other plays. In 1664 there seems to have been a move to produce *Thomaso* which never came off.[3] Killegrew owed her a favour and would therefore be unlikely to make a fuss. Indeed since he was master of the revels (he had succeeded Sir Henry Herbert in 1673), his permission must have been necessary. He could have made theatrical life impossible for her if he had so wished. I don't believe the rewriting of *Thomaso* would have been possible without his consent even though she doesn't allude to it in her note to the published edition where she rebuts the by now familiar charge of plagiarism.

She took from Killegrew's play what she wanted at this time, probably having no idea that she would go back to it. She took what was psychologically important to her and what she thought would make a good play. In doing so she left half behind for a sequel. She changed all the names of the main plot except Angelica Bianca. In the apology at the end of the printed edition she says: 'I, vainly proud of my judgement hang out the sign of Angelica (the only stol'n object) to give notice where a great part of the wit dwelt.' She was indeed hanging out the sign of Angelica though not perhaps as her conscious mind supposed.

The names of the cavaliers also have real-life associations though how far she and her audience were aware of them it's hard to say. Wilmore has an obvious similarity to Rochester's family name Wilmot and his father was of course the arch-cavalier, friend and companion of Charles II in the great escape after Worcester. In Colonel Belvile I think there's a contraction of Beville Grenville, the hero of the battle of Lansdowne in which he was killed, a relative of Sir Thomas Gower and of George Grenville, Lord Lansdowne, who was a close friend of Aphra Behn in the 'eighties and perhaps before. His title was taken from the battle. With Ned Blunt, who replaces Eduardo in *Thomaso*, she uses a common English name for character identification. Blunts fought on both sides in the Civil Wars. Sir Thomas was on the Kent committee; Mountjoy fought for the King under the Duke of Newcastle and was eventually captured at Dartmouth. Ferdinando she has replaced with Frederick probably because although the name Ferdinando was quite popular in England it was sufficiently uncommon to lead to identifications and sounds sufficiently Mediterranean to lead to confusion with the Italian characters. The scene is shifted too from Madrid to Naples.

The character of Wilmore contains, I think, some elements of John Hoyle, his physical attractiveness, his total promiscuity and a certain ruthlessness that the original Thomaso, who is presumably based on Thomas Killegrew himself, doesn't have. Once again Aphra Behn converts an earlier main plot with sub-plots structure into the classical two couple form with dependent sub-plots. Wilmore is given the soubrette character Hellena as his partner. The dramatic heroine Florinda is reserved for Belvile. Between them weave the third couple Pedro, Florinda's brother, and Angelica Bianca, his and Wilmore's mistress.

Angelica in both plays, like the Aphra Behn of the poem 'On Desire', is suffering a new experience, that of being in love for the first time and with Wilmore who, having enjoyed her, loses interest in pursuit of new adventures. The character of Hellena, played by Elizabeth Barry, is a new creation. She's described as a gay young woman 'designed for a nun'. She is a match for Wilmore and eventually he is persuaded to marry her while still believing she is a gipsy instead of another sister to Pedro and Florinda. The part is a gift to any actor. It must have been shortly after the opening run that Elizabeth Barry conceived Rochester's child. Perhaps her undoubted charm in this part renewed his appetite for her. He had been out of circulation in 1676, in disgrace with the King, but the opening of *The Rover* must have coincided with a return to court and to the theatrical milieu. If so his presence would have helped to contribute to the play's success. It's likely that he knew who its anonymous author was since the actors themselves must have known and in any case his friendship with Aphra Behn would probably have let him into the secret.

Elizabeth Barry came later to take dramatic rather than comedy roles. The part of Hellena would have suited Nell Gwyn perfectly but she was now retired. It's not impossible of course that as Rochester is said to have coached Barry for tragedy, Nell Gwyn coached her for comedy. The part gave her a chance to appear not only as a gipsy but in drag as a page, and for a great deal of witty exchange with Smith, who became renowned as Wilmore. The Bettertons played Belvile and Florinda.

The cast list gives 'Mrs Gwin' as Angelica Bianca but it's generally accepted that this is a mistake for Ann Quin. Angelica is a heavy passionate part which Elizabeth Barry took over later and was playing as late as 1707, a stretch of thirty years. The last recorded performance was in 1757, though a bowdlerized version was done in 1790 with some success.

Not only did Aphra Behn restructure the plot, she also rewrote the dialogue. *Thomaso* is very pedestrian stuff indeed. *The Rover* is full of wit and poetry. Once again there is an impression of light and elegance in this play as in *Sir Timothy Tawdry*. Nothing is superfluous to the plot. Everything furthers the action. She differs in this from most of her contemporaries who are quite willing to hold up the plot for discussion, a chance for a fireworks display on the manners of the times. Her dramatic singlemindedness has however led to her plays being classified as 'the comedy of intrigue' while those writers most often still performed, Congreve, Etherege, Wycherley and Vanbrugh, are known as writers of 'the comedy of manners'.

Their work has an almost Hogarthian quality about it. Its ancestor is Ben Jonson. Aphra Behn's literary ancestor is the Shakespeare of the comedies and tragi-comedies.

Wilmore's anti-marriage attitude is already there in *Thomaso* but Aphra Behn greatly strengthens it, partly by making Belvile and Florinda so intent upon their own marriage. Their traditional romantic virtue points up his roving unconventionality and Hellena's tomboy wildness. At the end of the scale in the female roles is the coarse Lucetta who fleeces Ned Blunt, while Sancho, her pimp, provides the bottom layer on the male side.

The play is, quite simply, about sex in its several manifestations from prostitution to romantic tenderness. It isn't a vehicle for social criticism although critical comment does form part of its imagery. It's about something much more permanent than transitory fashions of dress or behaviour: human beings in search of a temporary or lifelong mate.

XVI

The Calm

The Rover must have brought her some financial security, for a few months at least. It was licensed for publishing in July and advertised for sale in the *London Gazette* in August. According to the dedication of its sequel the Duke of York took a great interest in it. This must have encouraged her devotion to his interest, a devotion she shared with, among others, Henry Neville Payne, whose last play *The Siege of Constantinople*, produced in 1674, was an allegory in Turkish dress of the contemporary English political situation with the Duke of York in the guise of Thomazo, brother to the emperor, at strife with the chancellor representing Anthony Ashley Cooper, Lord Shaftesbury.

Neville Payne, like others of Aphra Behn's acquaintance, seems to have spent some time in the West Indies, in his case in Jamaica 'intending there to sell coffee, chocolate and popery' as an anonymous and scurrilous biographer wrote of him.[1] Sir Thomas Gower's brother-in-law, the Earl of Carlisle, was appointed governor of the island, whose population had now been increased by the Surinam refugees, in 1677. A tract published in the same year is probably by Neville Payne. It's called *The Present State of Jamaica in a Letter from Mr Nevil to the Earl of Carlisle*. His colonial connections would have further recommended him to Aphra Behn who kept up an interest in those parts and was to produce both a play and a novel with American settings. The events which form the basis of her play, *The Widow Ranter*, took place in 1676 in Virginia (although the play wasn't produced until after her death) during the Indian wars which were made more complex by the intervention of a

Colonel Nathaniel Bacon, whose family had been massacred by the Indians but who eventually found himself in successful rebellion against the government.[2]

1676 saw two further public happenings which touched on her life. One was the publication of a novel in French, and in an English translation, based on the affairs of Charles II, Barbara Villiers and the young John Churchill, called *Hattigé ou Les Amours du Roy Tamerlain*[3] by Gabriel de Bremond. This was the forerunner of Aphra Behn's *Love Letters Between a Nobleman and His Sister* which was to use contemporary events in a similar though much more serious way.

The second was the combination of Buckingham, Salisbury, Shaftesbury and Wharton in an attempt to prove that Parliament was dissolved by a prorogation of over a year. Both Buckingham and Rochester had Whig leanings at this period. Wharton was married to Rochester's kinswoman, Anne, who was herself a poet. All four lords were sent to the Tower. They weren't released until the following year and not restored to the House until their submissions were made in early 1678.

In November 1677 Buckingham stayed with Rochester at Woodstock and while there he visited the city of Oxford of which he was Lord High Steward. It's impossible to guess how often Aphra Behn visited Oxfordshire, apart from the mention of it in her letter to Emily Price, but the presence there of Buckingham and Rochester must have been a great incentive to visits, as well as her acquaintance with several members of the university. Buckingham was allowed out of the Tower in June 1677 for two days to go to oversee the mansion he was building at Windsor.

> At further distance yet on an ascent almost as high as that to the Royal Structure, you may behold the famous and noble Clifdon rise, a palace erected by the illustrious Duke of Buckingham, who will leave this wondrous piece of architecture, to inform the future world of the greatness and delicacy of his mind; it being for its situation, its prospects and its marvellous contrivances, one of the finest villas of the world; at least were it finished as begun; and would sufficiently declare the magnifick soul of the hero that caused it to be built and contrived all its fineness,[4]

she wrote of it nine years later when Buckingham himself hadn't long to live.

Her loyalty must have been strained by the adherence of several of the wits to the Whig side in the late 'seventies when it was still possible to be for reform without revolution. The epilogue to *The Rover* refers to the increasing activity among non-conformists and the growing concern with the doings of Parliament.

> The banisht cavaliers! a roving blade!
> A popish carnival! a masquerade!
> The devil's in't if this will please the nation,
> In these our blessed times of reformation,
> When conventicling is so much in fashion.
> And yet –
> That mutinous tribe less factions do beget,
> Than your continual differing in wit ...
> With canting rule you would the stage refine,
> And to dull method all our sense confine.
> With th' insolence of common-wealths you rule,
> Where each gay fop, and politick brave fool
> On monarch wit impose without control.
> As for the last who seldom sees a play,
> Unless it be the old Blackfriars way,
> Shaking his empty noddle o'er bamboo
> He crys – good faith these plays will never do.
> Ah sir in my young days what lofty wit,
> What high-strained scenes of fighting there were writ;
> These are slight airy toys. But tell me, pray,
> What has the House of Commons done today?
> Then shows his politics to let you see
> Of state affairs he'll judge as notably,
> As he can do of wit and poetry.

In 1676 appeared the first public epitaph that can be definitely ascribed to her, 'On the Death of Mr Grinhill, the famous painter'. This statement, I realize, opens up the whole question of how far the accepted canon of her poems, as included in Montague Summers's *The Works of Aphra Behn*, is complete. He doesn't, for example, include the state poems, although he mentions them in the introductory memoir. He reproduces mainly those which were published in collections, either hers or other people's, and not all of those since he leaves out the biographically important verse letter to Thomas Creech, presumably because he considered it only light verse. Many of her poems were published in broadsheets which may not have survived. Some she didn't have time to collect herself.[5] Others, like the one in *Poems on Affairs of State*, 'Bajazet to Gloriana', which the author of *The Female Laureat* believed was hers, and which I accept, she may have thought it unwise to include.

Her choice of what should go in was perhaps influenced by the appearance after Rochester's death of a pirate collection of his poems, among which were included several of hers attributed to him. The usual date given for this collection is 1680. Her own first collection was four years later. I think in choosing it she will have been anxious to clear up these false attributions. The elegy on Greenhill, as he is usually spelt, is one of them. That it is so shows how well contemporaries thought of it to father it on Rochester.

Greenhill died after an evening at the Vine Tavern at his lodgings in Lincoln's Inn Fields. He is said to have been a pupil of Lely and quickly became much sought after for portraits, his sitters including the King, the Duke of York, Shaftesbury, Locke, Davenant and Cowley. Perhaps he painted Aphra Behn and the elegy is a repayment, or perhaps one of his richer patrons paid for it. It isn't, I think, entirely successful. She hasn't yet discovered the best way of dealing with the expected baroque opening of such a poem and the first six lines are weak in consequence. Once she is beyond the fanfare however the words become more precise. They suggest that Greenhill had indeed painted her.

> The famous Grinhill dead! even he
> That cou'd to us give immortality;

It's always a mistake to be deceived by the high impasto of baroque works into thinking that they have no precise meaning, that all is icing on the cake. I believe that, if she hadn't meant to include herself among those painted, instead of 'to us' she would have said something like 'to men' or 'to all'. There's no record that Greenhill did paint her but the long disapproving silence about her might well have suppressed such a fact. However in 1873 the then director of the National Portrait Gallery Sir George Scharf recorded and drew in one of his notebooks a portrait said to be of Aphra Behn 'in the style of Closterman' which might be a Greenhill.[6]

The poem continues with an interesting description of the Elysian Fields to which the painter has gone, 'those sullen groves of everlasting dawn', and then, as if afraid that she had implied that he was a pagan, she hastens to correct this impression.

> Witty as poets, warm'd with love and wine,
>   Yet still spar'd Heaven and his friend,
> For both to him were sacred and divine:
> Nor could he this no more than that offend.

The mention of wine shows that she knew his reputation for drinking but since she describes him as 'warm'd' by it she isn't suggesting that he was a drunk. The quantities that people drank at this period as a natural adjunct to food would have most twentieth-century people reeling. Few of us now take beer for breakfast to begin the day as we mean to go on.

The next few lines speak of his generosity and gentleness, his faithfulness in friendship. The phrase 'fixt as a martyr' may conceal some contemporary reference, lost to most modern readers, about a specific instance in which Greenhill had suffered for his friendship. The word 'martyr' very quickly called up the image of Charles I to contemporary readers.

The poem is divided into four parts. The second is in some ways the most successful in its evocation of Greenhill's work and its comments on art and nature. The effect of beautiful natural bodies is to create lust; art, that is in this case painting, creates 'in the inamour'd soul a vertuous heat'. She has perceived the difference in psychological effect of art and nature which is at the heart of the argument about censorship. She also gives painting equality of status, among the arts, with poetry.

She doesn't funk the inherent task of such an elegy: the attempt to depict his painting in words.

> So bold, yet soft, his touches were;
> So round each part's so sweet and fair.

> That as his pencil mov'd men thought it prest,
> The lively imitating rising breast,
> Which yield like clouds, where little angels rest:[7]

The sudden evocation of Rubens's putti in an apotheosis, like that she had no doubt seen at the Banqueting Hall in Whitehall, is breathtaking. The third part describes the suddenness of Greenhill's death at the height of his reputation and powers. The fourth reflects on the uniqueness of an artist's talent, that it isn't something that can be passed on. Artistic 'knowledge', unlike scientific, is incommunicable and unreproducible. The poem ends with a return to the traditional formula, very like that which ends Purcell's *Dido and Aeneas* whose libretto was by her friend Nahum Tate. In the Purcell opera the closing chorus brings cupids to strew flowers on Dido's tomb; Aphra Behn's brings virgins for the same office, virgins because Greenhill gave their beauty immortality by fixing it in paint beyond decay.

> For he still gave your charms their due:
> And from the injuries of age and time,
> Preserv'd the sweetness of your prime:

The poem ends with this procession of flower-laden girls but on a slightly wry note.

> And let your eyes a silent sorrow wear,
> Till every virgin for a while become
> Sad as his fate, and like his pictures dumb.

Some time in late 1676 or 1677 appeared a satirical reference to her in a poem called 'A Session of the Poets'. The authorship of this is doubtful but it may have been composed by Buckingham and Rochester while they were together in Oxfordshire. Another suggestion is the playwright Elkanah Settle but if so he has been extremely clever in including himself among those most bitterly attacked. The poem follows an earlier one by Sir John Suckling in imagining the poets gathered together by Apollo who is going to appoint their leader by awarding him the bays which are usually the symbol of the laureate. The verses have the bite and pace of a Buckingham/Rochester combination.

The internal references to plays in the satire date it to post-November 1676.[8] The lines that refer to Aphra Behn are as follows:

> The poetess Aphra next show'd her sweet face
> And swore by her poetry and her black ace
> The laurel by a double right was her own
> For the plays she had writ and the conquests she'd won.
> Apollo acknowledg'd 'twas hard to deny her,
> But to deal frankly and ingeniously by her,
> He told her, were conquests and charms her pretence,
> She ought to have pleaded a dozen years since.

Her 'black ace' graphically refers of course to the female sex organs. The lines can seem very harsh but I don't think they were meant to be particularly so; indeed they can be read as a compliment on her writing. Apollo acknowledges her literary ability. On the other point, her age, he's probably telling no more than the truth. She was now thirty-seven and the age of first charms was the mid teens. 'A dozen years since' she would have been in her early twenties, quite a late age for a beauty at this period although it's true that even ten years later than this she was able to draw compliments from the young George Grenville. The author is telling her quite rightly that her claim must rest on her work. The use of the terms 'frankly and ingeniously' read like quotations from her own work or commendations of her from other people. 'Ingenious' was a word often applied to her.

The next applicant is Ravenscroft. He is followed by Rawlins, whose play *Tom Essence* helps to date the poem, and Durfey. Finally the award goes to Betterton,

> For of all the play scribblers that e'er writ before
> His wit had most worth and most modesty in't,
> For he had writ plays, yet ne'er came in print.

The plays published before this date which are now tentatively attributed to him were clearly not generally known to be his.

To have been left out of such a poem would have been in itself a slight. There is actually a couplet in a later poem in this series, 'An Essay Upon Satire' by Dryden and Sheffield, that indeed speaks of a woman's rage at being left out of a lampoon.[9] It was a mark of her serious pretensions that Aphra Behn should be included among the male poets with Dryden, Shadwell, Wycherley, Otway and the rest. Neither Buckingham nor Rochester is included but their friend 'Gentle' George Etherege is there and the most kindly treated except for a mild accusation of laziness. Wycherley too gets off lightly because:

> No gentleman writer that office should bear:
> 'Twas a trader in wit the laurel should wear,
> As none but a cit e'er makes a Lord Mayor.

I shall have more to say later about this difference between gentlemen and players and its effect on Aphra Behn. On the whole I think the two noble friends were responsible for it. The remarks about her fading charms must have given her pain since she showed herself sensitive to this situation in *Oroonoko* where the aging queen is in the same position, but on balance she was perhaps not too displeased. The lines about her certainly stuck in her mind and emerged again at the end of her life when she was translating Cowley, in a desperate plea for immortality. The images are the same: Apollo, the bays, and the twin appeal on the grounds of her sex and her work.

The reason I believe she wasn't too displeased was that her next two plays are much more her own than those that had gone before, although the first of them, *Sir Patient Fancy*, owes something, obviously, to Molière. Nevertheless she was striking out in this strange career she had chosen for herself and that she was to pursue now until she died through novels, poems, translations and plays, until she had produced more than any writer of her time, Dryden only excepted, and growing more assured in her craft the farther she went.

XVII

Sir Patient Fancy

Several troops of French comedians had visited England since the restoration, performing mostly at court, where they were much appreciated though not without some characteristic mutterings from Englishmen about the superiority of native writers and performers. Molière's plays had already been used by English writers; in particular *Le Bourgeois Gentilhomme* by Ravenscroft as *Mamamouchi*, *L'Étourdi* by Dryden as *Sir Martin Marall*, and *L'Avare* and *Tartuffe* by Shadwell as *The Miser* and *The Hypocrite* respectively. With *Sir Patient Fancy*, then, Aphra Behn joined a respected company. The forerunner she had in mind, as her title shows, was Dryden. He had been given 'a bare translation' by the Duke of Newcastle.[1] She was given *Le Malade imaginaire* 'translated by a gentleman infinitely to advantage'. In both cases this must mean that a printed French text wasn't available since both writers could presumably read French; she certainly could.

Once again she was charged with plagiarism; 'but how much of the French is in this, I leave to those who do indeed understand it and have seen it at the court'. But the worst charge she felt obliged to defend herself against, in the address to the reader of the printed edition, was that the play was bawdy. She hurried it into print in order that people should have the chance to read it themselves and 'find that the most innocent virgins' could have no cause to blush 'but confess with me that no play either ancient or modern has less of that bug-bear bawdry in it'.

The 'most unjust and silly aspersion' had come mainly from women. 'How so cruel an unkindness came into their imaginations I can by no means guess; unless by those whose lovers by long absence, or those whom age or ugliness have rendered a little distant from those things they would fain imagine here', she remarks rather tartly. The book was licensed on January 28th and the play was still running when she wrote this because she offers the critics the choice of either seeing or reading it.

Bawdiness, she says, is 'the least and most excusable fault in the men writers, to whose plays they all crowd, as if they came to no other end than to hear what they condemn in this: *but from a woman it was unnatural*'. She is up against the double standard that was to become ever more rigid after her death until William Acton could positively assert in 1857 that no nice woman enjoyed sex.[2] Oddly enough, as it now seems, it was the same charge that was to be levelled at the anonymous author of *Jane Eyre* when it first appeared: that if it was by a woman she was a disgrace to her sex.

Aphra Behn is however a little unfair in the implication that male writers were never castigated for bawdy. In her defences she is very passionate. They are written with wit and wrath mixed. She is refreshingly unmealymouthed and treats her audience as a much admired beauty might treat an erring lover, with a high scorn which is meant to subdue and dazzle at the same time. There is no trace of the submissive woman about her address to the public. But she sometimes overstates her case as she does here. Many other writers were accused of bawdiness and they reply in their own prefaces. Where the charge against her is different is that it is said to be 'unnatural' for a woman, not merely wicked as it was for a man.

There is, though, something more, I think, behind her vehemence on this occasion and it's related to the satire discussed before. She goes on:

The play had no other misfortune but that of coming out for a woman's: had it been owned by a man, though the most dull unthinking rascally scribbler in town, it had been a most admirable play. Nor does its loss of fame with the ladies do it much hurt, though they ought to have had good nature and justice enough to have attributed all its faults to the author's unhappiness who is forced to write for bread and not ashamed to own it, and consequently ought to write to please (if she can) an age which has given several proofs it was by this way of writing to be obliged, though it is a way too cheap for men of wit to pursue who write for glory, and a way even I despise as much below me.

This last sentence is full of mixed emotions and arguments. It reflects the gentlemen versus players attitude of the satire. She is forced by necessity to be a player, that is a professional. Men of wit who can afford it write for glory. The society she lives in dictates the way it will be pleased and since she is dependent on it for her living she ought to do what it wants and what it wants is bawdy. Yet even so, and in spite of her necessity, she regards herself as above such a lowering of her standards.

Her instincts, her desires were to be a gentleman writer, a wit like Rochester, Buckingham or Orrery. She was forced to be a professional and although she says she isn't ashamed she is worried about loss of literary reputation and standards. The comment about writing for bread and not being ashamed reminds me of some of her pleas for money to pay her debts in Antwerp so that she shouldn't be disgraced, of that uncavalier-like pride and honesty.

The prologue shows the same ambiguity of emotion. It begins by seeming to pick up the image of the professional writer from the satire.

> We write not now, as th'ancient poets writ,
> For your applause of nature, sense, and wit;
> But like good tradesmen, what's in fashion vent
> And cozen you, to give ye all content.

Praise of Dryden takes up the next ten lines, suggesting that even he isn't appreciated any more and again the words seem to glance at the satire:

> ... each small wit starts up and claims his share;
> And all those laurels are in pieces torn,
> Which did e'er while one sacred head adorn.

Satirically she turns on herself:

> Nay, even the women now pretend to reign;
> Defend us from a Poet Joan again!

In case this is thought too palpable a hit against the Roman Catholics via Pope Joan, she next includes the protestant non-conformist 'lay sisters'. Then she shies away from the whole issue to write against those who prefer the jugglers and rope dancers and to say that anyone who writes his best for such an audience is himself a fool. The comment against the jugglers may be a reference to the popularity of the two fairs, Bartholo-mew and Southwark, which showed such novelties, and were in competition with the theatres during August and September.

Elizabeth Barry was still unavailable, of course, to take a part though it's hard to see what she would have had in the play unless it was Lady Knowell. This, it's generally agreed, was played by Ann Quin. The character of Lady Knowell owes something to *Les Femmes savantes* of Molière but I think it owes more to the real-life Margaret Cavendish, Duchess of Newcastle. Both she and her husband were now dead and she could there-fore be safely included as an extra layer of reference in the creation of a female pedant. Sir Patient Fancy himself, I believe, is in the same way partly derived from the Whig alderman Sir Patience Ward, a relative by marriage of the Scots.

Sir Patient Fancy is her first overtly political play. Sir Patient is a non-conformist alderman with hypochondria, who has married a young wife who had been in love with a cavalier, Wittmore, before she was married off for money, because neither she nor her lover had any. It's perhaps a contradiction in terms these days to think of a High Tory as anti-capitalist but this is the only possible interpretation of this play. Sir Patient has the capital and he can buy the lady but the hero is Wittmore who has only his wits and breeding to live by. In the modern world he is what used to be called a bounder and is now called a layabout.

Transposing the political realities of an earlier age into contemporary idiom is hard and unpopular. It can so easily seem cheapjack. But to leave them as they were is often to dodge the issue at least, at most to deliberately mislead. The folk consciousness has consistently picked its heroes regardless of class or political affiliation and I suspect it's usually right, even when it warps the facts. Often the important thing is what these people, acts, struggles have meant in the human psyche, not what they were in fact, if the naked fact can ever be undressed.

There are past times when what we would, many of us, want to ally ourselves with seems to be identified by the wrong political labels. The late seventeenth century, I believe, was a time in which true progress lay elsewhere than where we have since, traditionally, thought it was. What led to the Whig and puritan supremacy of post 1689 wasn't what had animated English radicalism before, or has since. The Whigs themselves had no choice. They were animated by the non-conformity of their fathers which had become conformity and was steadily to atrophy England.

Aphra Behn's political plays trace the progress of the Whigs from democratic opposition to armed rebellion. *Sir Patient Fancy* is the first. Yet even with such political plays she didn't, at least in the beginning, treat her characters without artistic compassion. That she was for a time driven to do so is a measure of the deterioration in the political situation.

At the end of 1677, when, if we allow time for rehearsal, the play must have been written, it was still possible for her to select Sir Patience Ward as a typical figure in the world of city politics and not present him as a monster as she would have felt emotionally obliged to do after 1680. The hypochondria which he suffers from and which is shown to be nothing but fancy at the end of the play is a metaphor for the, to her, imaginary political sickness that obsesses the Whigs and leaves them open to all kinds of deception and false prescriptions for their imagined ills, particularly from foreign doctors. The fact that two of the doctors are from Leyden and Amsterdam is, I think, no accident, for these were still gathering-places for exiled dissidents. She has no better word to say though for the French doctor, Turboon, who lets them in. Pro-French as she was culturally, I find no evidence that she was so politically. She boasted of being 'an Englishwoman' and she chose the English 'whore' Nell Gwyn to make her dedication to, not a French one. Turboon, I think, represents French duplicity in France's meddling in the English political situation and as the mastermind of Europe.[3] The other doctors are impostors. Turboon is corrupt.

Alongside the political implications of the doctors runs a lot of proto-Shavian anti-doctor satire. Some of this is a folk-inheritance. Satire against doctors appears even in mumming plays. But there's a more personal element in it too. Most people in the seventeenth century seem to have suffered terribly from illnesses they could do little about. This didn't of course stop them from trying and I believe they were further encouraged in this by the few real pieces of medical knowledge, like the discovery of the circulation of the blood, and by the fever of scientific enquiry. The remedies they used were largely painful or disgusting and as we know now tended to weaken the patient. Death and sickness were daily hazards. Aphra Behn herself, according to the *Memoirs*, died from the incompetence of her physician and, though I think this untrue, it was a common enough charge and probably a common enough happening.

The one piece of sensible advice the doctors give Sir Patient is to eat less. This comes from the foolish Sir Credulous Easy disguised as 'a High-Dutchman of the town of Collen'. The amounts consumed by the middle and upper classes fill the modern reader with such nausea that it's a relief to read of Hortense Mancini eating bread and cheese. Aphra Behn was interested in the question of diet and wrote a poem commending a book on the subject. The book wasn't published until 1682 but *Sir Patient Fancy* indicates a longer interest in such questions than might have been supposed.

Sir Patient's young wife of course cuckolds him. All she is interested in is his money, which she will give to her lover. But she is herself deceived. Having made an assignation with Wittmore, she is in fact enjoyed by Lodwick who is on his way to a similar, though chaste, assignation with Isabella, whom he is to marry, and mistakes the room. This must have been the episode that upset the women in the audience. Lady Fancy and Lodwick couple in the dark, he realizing the mistake but determined to take advantage of it, she completely deceived. The true moralist considering this episode would have realized that Aphra Behn isn't on the side of lasciviousness. Lady Fancy isn't an attractive character. She's greedy and hypocritical. Her one real virtue is her love for Wittmore and this is betrayed by Lodwick.

It isn't Lady Fancy's fault or Wittmore's that they are as they are. Money and the marriage market have corrupted them, her because she's dowerless and him because he's a younger son. The marriage to Sir Patient was a contrivance to remedy this. Sir Patient himself has a touch of the miser. In terms of the political allegory this reflects Parliament's, and the city's, holding of the King to ransom over money bills. Sir Patient's money is kept, largely in gold, behind the wainscot in his study where it does no one, himself included, any good.

His religious non-conformity lumps the established church and the Catholic church together. 'They say thou art a Papist too, or at least a Church-of-England man and I profess there's not a pin to choose,' he says to his nephew Leander. His family prayers are called 'the exercise', an interesting anticipation of 'methodism'.

Who then is Lady Fancy? I don't think she can be given an exact identification either politically or allegorically but her history is very old. She is surely the descendant of Langland's Lady Meed. She is deception itself. Apart from the foreign doctors it's this that deceives Sir Patient and, by implication, those he represents. She is the victor over Sir Patient because she keeps the money and land he has settled on her. Yet at last she is herself deceived, by his fake death, into showing herself for what she is and Sir Patient is freed of her.

He is capable of reformation. He forgives them all and re-solves 'to turn Spark, they live the merriest lives – keep some city mistress, go to court, and hate all conventicles'. The doctors, his ill-advisers to whose advantage it is that he should fancy himself ill, are sent packing. This is Aphra Behn's formula for political peace: that the Whigs should stop fancying a political sickness which doesn't really exist but is provoked by deception and attempts at cure, and that men and women should get on with the business of life and pleasure. It was a solution her up-bringing had predisposed her to.

She quotes quite deliberately from both *The Merchant of Venice* and *Volpone* on money. Wittmore says when he pulls in the basket which he believes contains Sir Patient's savings:

> Goodmorrow to the day, and next the gold;
> Open the shrine that I may see my saint –
> Hail the world's soul, –

In fact the basket contains only fool's gold in the shape of Sir Credulous Easy who is hidden in it.

Sir Patient's quote is less precise but still unmistakable. 'Oh I am half killed, my daughter, my honour – my daughter, my reputation,' he cries in imitation of Shylock but substituting what the neighbours will say for Shylock's 'ducats'. Money runs through this play and through her introductory preface when she speaks of being 'forced to write for bread'. It sounds as if what she had got from *The Rover* was exhausted and she was in need of another success to survive.

The Duke's Company had produced a political predecessor to *Sir Patient Fancy*, on November 17th 1677, called *Sir Popular Wisdom* and by an unknown author. It was never printed and must have failed although it opened with high expectations. Andrew Marvell wrote to Sir Edward Harley: 'Today is acted the first time *Sir Popular Wisdom or the Politician* where my Lord Shaftesbury and all his gang are sufficiently personated. I conceive the King will be there.'4 Obviously it wasn't enough for a play to be topical and attack the right people (from the court's point of view) for it to succeed. *Sir Patient Fancy* succeeded because it wasn't merely propaganda. No doubt its reputation for bawdiness did it no harm but it's also a splendid piece of dramatic writing with constant pace and variety. Aphra Behn was unequalled in the handling of a complex plot without getting lost or driven to over-contrivance. In this play something theatrical is always happening and yet the dialogue itself is never banal but full of flashes of wit and sense. Lady Fancy, with her lover hidden under the bed and Sir Patient on top, when Wittmore's watch rings, invents a ghostly death-watch that always sounds when someone's dying, making both a dramatic and a verbal pun.

The length of the play and its complexity must mean that she was already writing it when *Sir Popular Wisdom* failed if she hadn't already finished it by then. I don't believe it could have been written in the less than a month there would have been, if rehearsal time is allowed for, had it not been well begun before the other had its first performance.

The epilogue spoken by Lady Knowell is much less ambiguous than the prologue. It's an unabashed claim for the right of women to write plays, and for those plays to be considered equally with those by men. Again Aphra Behn rejects the Jonsonian classical rules, the unities of time, place and action which she calls 'learned cant'. Lady Knowell has made herself pedantically ridiculous in the play because she imitates the least important aspects of masculine prerogative: the learning of the schools and universities. The defence of woman's rights is based however on classical sources.

> What has poor woman done that she must be
> Debarr'd from sense, and sacred poetry?
> Why in this age has Heaven allow'd you more,
> And woman less of wit than heretofore?
> We once were famed in story, and could write
> Equal to men; cou'd govern, nay, could fight.
> We still have passive valour, and can show,
> Wou'd custom give us leave, the active too,
> Since we no provocation want from you.

The hidden references must be to the Amazons and Sappho, and then to the heroines of Ariosto and Tasso who often appear in armour. Drag roles in Aphra Behn's plays weren't merely for variety in plot and sexual innuendo but also to display a more active valour. She herself could claim to have shown the passive kind, at the very least, in her Antwerp episode but she was never able to tell the full truth of this. In this epilogue she is again advancing her claim to be not only equal to but better than her male contemporaries in the hard field of the professional writer. During the next few years she was to show her active courage in taking up the battle on behalf of the Stuart cause and fighting with words, like her childhood cavalier heroes, until the conflict turned again to swords and her cause was defeated.

XVIII

The Popish Plot

The Popish Plot, or the Horrid Plot as contemporaries called it, was first revealed by Christopher Kirkby on August 13th. Kirkby worked in the royal laboratory and therefore had access to the King. The plot was to murder Charles and put his brother James, Duke of York, on the throne in order to bring the country back to the Catholic fold. The authors, or discoverers, of the plot were first Dr Titus Oates who claimed that he had pretended to be a convert to Catholicism and had been admitted to the Jesuit College at St Omers 'where he discovered the whole matter'; the second was the man he reported it to, Dr Israel Tonge, a London clergyman of fanatical anti-Catholic views.

Charles II refused to believe any of it and turned it over to the Lord Treasurer, Sir Thomas Osborne, Earl of Danby, to investigate. Danby realized the danger of such inflammable material and managed to keep the affair quiet for a month while Oates and Tonge were lodged at Whitehall and paid a retainer from the King's secret service money.[1] However, this didn't satisfy the two plotters and on September 26th Tonge went to see Dr Gilbert Burnet. Burnet was a Scottish divine who, having been much in favour, was currently out of favour with the court. He was a prolific writer, a fashionable preacher and much involved in politics.

Burnet reported the matter to the vicar of St Martin's, Westminster, Dr William Lloyd, who relayed it to the Secretary's office where he found the plot was already known about. Burnet next spoke to Sir Thomas Littleton and Lord Halifax. Two days later Oates began his public denunciations. Tonge sent for Burnet to Whitehall. He had met Burnet several years before and Burnet had not been impressed with him then. Oates, whose supposed degree from Salamanca caused him to be frequently ridiculed as 'the Salamanca doctor', Burnet found as unattractive as his colleague.

The public evidence was given before the London magistrate Sir Edmund Berry Godfrey, brother of one of the old Kent interregnum officials. Burnet met him a little after he had taken the depositions and Godfrey apparently told him that he was afraid of assassination. A few days later Godfrey disappeared and was later found in a ditch on Primrose Hill with a sword in his back.

Meanwhile Oates and Tonge had accused Edward Coleman, secretary to the Duchess of York, of being part of the plot. He was imprisoned, his effects searched and, although he had seemingly been warned by Godfrey, with whom he was friendly, that Oates had accused him, he hadn't destroyed all his papers. Among them was an incriminating correspondence with foreign Jesuits which mentioned the Duke of York.

Godfrey's body was found on October 17th. On the 21st Parliament reassembled and the King in his opening speech told the two Houses of the plot. On October 25th five Catholic peers were sent to the Tower, among them William Howard, Lord Stafford. On January 20th, Walter, Lord Aston, joined them. Not content, Oates now accused the Queen of being party to the plot and her physician, Sir George Wakeman, was also imprisoned as a potential poisoner. Charles now sent for Dr Burnet and several secret meetings took place in the back-stairs apartments of William Chiffinch, where the King was accustomed to meet both mistresses and spies. The association didn't last long. The King thought that Burnet wasn't telling him enough about the opposition, although Burnet did warn him in time to prevent it of a Bill in the Commons to raise the militia in November.

On December 3rd Edward Coleman was executed. He had been a friend of Henry Neville Payne, who was himself being watched by the authorities as a suspected person, and on December 16th Payne was seized and searched by a constable called Gill and an elegy for Coleman was found on him. Presumably he had been taking it somewhere to be printed though in his examination he denied this and claimed that it was for his own private use as 'a soliloqui', adding that 'Mr Cowley had formerly said as much of Mr Crawshaw'. Even this appeal to the ghost of Cowley was unable to save him, 'their lordships taking notice of how dangerous it is ... that any person shall presume to style that man a glorified martyr, whom the Law has condemned as a traitor.'[2]

Aphra Behn refers obliquely to this in her dedication to Neville Payne of *The Fair Jilt*. "'Tis true, sir, I present you with a prince unfortunate, but still the more object for your goodness and pity; who never valued a brave man the less for being unhappy.' This willingness to defend the 'unhappy', which she so admired, she herself showed in her defence of Lord Stafford who was to be 'unhappy' in the same way as Coleman. Payne was merely convicted and imprisoned. 'But nothing could press or deject your great heart; you were the same man still, unmoved in all turns, easy and innocent; no persecution being able to abate your constant good humour, or wonted gallantry,' Aphra Behn wrote. It sounds very much as if she visited him in prison.

In his evidence before the Privy Council, Payne claimed to be a good protestant. Perhaps he was at this point and was only converted later. According to Dangerfield he was 'the chief pen-man [for the Catholic cause] and did all that sort of drudgery for a long time' and the Catholic Lords in the Tower were eager to have him arrested again when he was freed the first time 'for as much as when he was formerly in that condition, he had been very industrious about writing of papers in their business, but that being at liberty, he chiefly followed the playhouse'. Aphra Behn in acknowledging her obligations to his 'bounty and goodness' calls him 'patron of the muses' and although this wasn't until 1688 his connection with the Duke's Company may have meant that he was giving her financial support of some kind as early as this. It's not clear where his money came from. He was alleged by his jaundiced biographer to have 'a great house and an upholsterer (who is not yet paid) to furnish it': with 'a tall man at his door with a large silver plate on his breast'. This was before his arrest.

Charles decided to call a new Parliament in January 1679. Lord Danby was impeached but saved for the time being by the dissolution. However, the country party won the election, the first fought on clearly defined party lines, and in March the Duke and Duchess of York left on a judicious visit to their daughter Mary in Holland who had married Prince William of Orange in October 1677. In this atmosphere Aphra Behn's next play *The Feign'd Curtezans* opened in March. By a stroke of genius she decided to dedicate it to Nell Gwyn.

It was Aphra Behn's first dedication; it was Nell Gwyn's third and last. The other two had been by Robert Whitcombe, *Janua Divorum*, 1678, and Thomas Duffet, *The Spanish Rogue*, 1674. The dedication says first that Aphra Behn had asked permission for her dedication and been given it. But it was long overdue and she is ashamed to have delayed so. The words she uses, 'my past ignorance, which suffered me not to pay an adoration long since *where there was so very much due*' (my italics), strongly imply that Nell Gwyn had already helped her with some form of patronage. There are so many ways in which with her constant patronage of the theatre she could have helped a playwright that it isn't necessary to be too specific.

Aphra Behn continues in praise of Nell Gwyn's beauty, good humour and wit. She has been accused of excessive and mercenary adulation in this dedication but this seems to me a total misreading. Nell Gwyn is by popular election one of the folk-heroes of our culture and rightly so. An illiterate but intelligent woman, she raised herself by her skill as an actress to the top of her profession from the very bottom and then left it for a royal bed which by general consent she never betrayed. She retained her good sense, wit and good humour, and a share of royal favour against all comers. There are many stories about her but the best I think is still her swift-witted reply when mistaken in her coach by the Oxford mob for the French, Catholic, Duchess of Portsmouth. She called out, 'Pray, good people, be civil; I am the Protestant whore.'

The picture of her by Gascar, as Venus with her two children as cupids in a masque, makes her physical charm echo Aphra Behn's description and indeed I'm not at all sure that it wasn't this painting that she had in mind when she wrote of the inadequacy of pictures to convey her. In describing people crowding to listen to Nell Gwyn and then returning home to tell their families, I believe Aphra Behn is giving nothing but a factual description of what happened whenever Nell Gwyn went out. In praising her wit she at the same time lays a claim for women in general and herself among them.

The dedication goes on to praise Nell Gwyn's lack of pride and the ease with which she wears her honours, her refusal of titles for herself and her acceptance of them for her children. It ends with a paragraph that claims that the play was 'dedicated yours before it had a being'. This is very important in indicating that the dedication was quite deliberate and long considered, not an impulse after the play had been performed. The play was written with Nell Gwyn in mind and her protégée, Elizabeth Barry, had one of the two female leads.

No one need be surprised that the dramatist should think so well of someone who was acknowledged a consummate performer, nor that a woman who wrote for bread should praise one who had acted for it. They had both pulled themselves up by their own efforts and in Aphra Behn's morality Nell Gwyn in becoming the King's mistress and staying faithful to him had followed the highest canons of love.

There is, however, even more to it than this. In dedicating her play quite deliberately to 'the Protestant whore' she was proclaiming her own protestantism, but in choosing Nell Gwyn she chose someone who never meddled in politics. By specifically mentioning her royal children Aphra Behn dissociates herself from the Monmouth faction which was already starting the rumour that Charles intended to set aside his brother James and substitute his illegitimate son James by acknowledging a marriage to Monmouth's mother Lucy Walters. Strictly speaking, the Duke of Monmouth, except by seniority, had no greater claim to the throne than Nell Gwyn's 'two noble branches who have all the greatness and sweetness of their royal and beautiful stock'.

The two of whom Aphra Behn thought so highly, Buckingham and Rochester, who were both dabbling with the Whig party, would have been unable to take exception to her choice of Nell Gwyn, since they were both close friends of 'Mrs Nelly'. Aphra Behn had sidestepped the ambiguity of her situation as a protestant supporter of the Catholic heir by this dedication. Unlike those who have condemned it as fulsome and ingratiating, her two friends no doubt praised her for her wit and acumen, while admiring the elegance of the language which nevertheless conveys both the charm and the character of its subject as a good portrait would.

The opposite side of the coin from the dedication is the lampoon or satire.

> Of a great heroine I mean to tell,
> And by what just degrees her titles swell,
> To Mrs Nelly grown from cinder Nell,

is the opening of one of them that goes on to present almost point by point the same characteristics of Aphra Behn's dedication but blackened into vices. A reference to the death of her mother, who seems to have drowned while drunk, and to the lavish funeral Nell Gwyn staged for her dates it as after July 1675 when Luttrell records her mother's death.

It also refers to a quarrel between Nell Gwyn and Monmouth, whom she had dubbed Prince Perkin because of his pretensions to the throne. Commentators have been unable to find other references to this quarrel which, the satire says, was because they were rivals in the people's liking but Nell Gwyn was both 'True to the Protestant interest and cause' and 'True to the established government and laws' and for that reason had told Monmouth to 'pack up and be gone'. This suggests a date before his banishment in 1679, since she helped to reconcile him to his father in December when he angered the King by returning without permission. A quarrel between them on those grounds earlier in the year would sit very well with Aphra Behn's dedication. The vicious attacks by the satirists explain why people were eager for flattering dedications to redress the balance and why they were willing to pay for them.

The prologue, spoken by the actress Betty Currer in the character of a courtesan, suggests that at this date Aphra Behn was half prepared to give a little belief to the Popish Plot. A reference to 'new elections' dates it after the proclamation to dissolve Parliament announced in the *London Gazette* on January 25th, but the lack of any reference to York's first exile probably puts it before that event was reported in the *Gazette* on March 3rd. At the end of January a search at Lord Aston's home at Tixall had turned up papers compromising

Lord Stafford and this had probably hastened Charles's decision to send his brother away. The prologue ends:

> Who would have thought such hellish times to have seen,
> When I should be neglected at eighteen?
> That youth and beauty should be quite undone,
> A pox upon the Whore of Babylon.

The 'Whore of Babylon' is of course one of the oldest terms of protestant abuse for the Roman Catholic Church. Betty Currer has stepped out of her role in the play, where she's a nice girl posing as a high-class prostitute, into that of a much lower class of prostitute who says she is still of the religion of her cully,[3] her lover, and that until these dangerous times her principles fixed on no religion but now they're 'something in mere contradiction'. She curses 'this cursed plotting age,/'Thas ruined all our plots upon the stage'. By comparison with the plots and suspicions of real life the actor's is described as an 'honest calling', a subtle hit at those who tried to suppress the theatre for its immorality.

The real-life plot made a deep impression on Aphra Behn and she returned to it nine years later when Sir Roger L'Estrange published the third part of his *History of the Times* which dealt with this period. In the Calendar of State Papers there's a newsletter of February 13th 1679 which describes the burning of 'several books of Popish relics ... in New Palace Yard by the common hangman amongst which was one representing the effigies of our Saviour being so well drawn that some say £50 was offered for it but Sir W. Waller who was present and had that with the other things in his custody could not part with it on that score'. The incident stuck in her mind, emerging in the poem to L'Estrange as: 'The Lord of Life, his image rudely torn, to flames was by the common hangman born.' I suspect it struck so deep because it recalled the destruction of the 'images' in Canterbury Cathedral in her childhood, when Sir William Waller was one of the Commonwealth commanders in the county.[4]

The executions, too, of priests and lesser people than the Catholic lords who were swept up in the plot made their own deep impression.

> At Golgotha, they glut the'r insatiate eyes
> With scenes of blood, and human sacrifice,
> Men consecrate to Heav'n, were piecemeal hew'd
> For sport and pastime to the brutal crowd.
> The world ran mad, and each distemper'd brain,
> Did strange and different frenzies entertain:
> Here politic mischiefs, there ambition sway'd;
> The credulous rest, were fool and coward made.

Those who weren't caught up in the fever were themselves liable to be accused, and

> Honour, as breach of privilege, was detected
> And common sense was popishly affected.

She had voiced this fear in the prologue of *The Feign'd Curtezans*:

> But wit as if 'twere Jesuitical
> Is an abomination to ye all
> To what a pass will poor plays come
> This must be damn'd, the plot is laid in Rome.

As if to prove that only serious matters were worth attention, this was the only new comedy produced in this season. All the rest were tragedies. Dryden transferred his allegiance temporarily to the Duke's Company and Drury Lane seems to have been closed for a while as Aphra Behn remarks in the epilogue. The writers were too busy writing satires for the parties, and against each other, but it was the fault of the audiences for being so taken up with the plot that they had no time for plays.

It's *The Feign'd Curtezans* in which she displays what I called earlier her tourist's Italian but there may be another source for it, and for the Italian song in the play, in the visit of the Duke of Modena's troop of comedians from November 1678 to February 1679. No doubt she both saw them and met them. The setting of the play can be seen as a compliment to James, Duke of York, who like the heroes of the play was married to an Italian, while at the same time the work is dedicated to his brother's protestant mistress.

Since she had decided on the dedication before she wrote the play she took, she says, extra pains in the writing, with the result that she feels she has 'made it less grateful; and poetry like lovers often fares the worse by taking too much pains to please'. Her care shows in three ways. First the play conforms to the Jonsonian rules of unity. The sub-title 'The Mistakes of a Night' quietly boasts its unity of time and there is greater unity of place and action than she has ever restricted herself to before. Secondly no one can accuse the play of plagiarism. No original source has ever been found for it. It copies *The Rover* in several structural ways but the donnée of the two sisters disguising themselves as courtesans is based, I think, on a real-life incident, in which, as the Marquess of Grammont records in his memoirs, two of the maids of honour disguised themselves as orange-girls. They were detected in the end by the quality of their shoes and stockings.

Thirdly the play cannot be accused of being bawdy in spite of its title. No one goes to bed with anyone, at least not success-fully, and all ends in marriage. The nearest to a coupling is between two people who are actually betrothed by their parents but have never met, and even this is interrupted before consummation. On all the grounds therefore on which her plays had been criticized before, she has taken pains to disarm criticism in advance. Such a deliberate effort on a writer's part almost always leads to a slight feeling of dissatisfaction pro-bably because it interferes with the play element in creation. It was this feeling that she was expressing in her doubts at the end of the dedication.

Yet *The Feign'd Curtezans* includes some splendid passages and the plot is handled as deftly as ever. It's almost apolitical, deliberately so I think. The only concession to politics is in the drawing of the tutor, Mr Tickletext, who is chaplain at Buf-foon Hall in Kent and also minister of a London conventicle. He is accompanying the young country knight Sir Signal Buffoon on his tour to make sure he doesn't fall into the snares, religious and moral, of travelling in Roman Catholic countries, especially Rome itself. Tickletext is inclined to cant and to secret whoring but even so the portrait of him isn't entirely un-sympathetic and he is, like Sir Patient Fancy, reformed in the end rather than destroyed.

One piece of dialogue ties up with a letter later in the year from Rochester to his friend Henry Savile who had gone as envoy to Paris. The letter is being carried by Mr Baptist, Rochester's singing valet. Describing him as 'this pretty fool the bearer', Rochester says ' ... the greatest and gravest of this court of both sexes have tasted his beauties; and, I'll assure you, Rome gains upon us here, in this point mainly; and there is no part of the plot carried with so much secrecy and vigour as this.' At the end of *The Feign'd Curtezans* Cornelia, disguised as a boy, claims Sir Signal and Tickletext as two of her lovers to which Sir Signal exclaims 'How, Sir, your lovers! we are none of those, Sir, we are Englishmen.'

By the time of this letter, dated November 1st, Aphra Behn had rejected the 'Horrid Plot'. Her connection with several of the protagonists would have led her to do so but many of the rest of those of 'common sense' had reached the same conclusion. Sir George Wakeman, the Queen's physician was acquitted by a jury and Neville Payne was released from jail. While in there he seems to have used his theatrical talents to help with the construction of a counterplot whose purpose was to discredit Oates and company and shift the hunt on to the protestant non-conformists.

XIX

The Meal-tub Plot

Some time during this year, sickened by what she saw, she wrote or rather paraphrased from the French one of her most famous pieces, *The Golden Age*. I'm able to date it to 1679 because it has strong verbal similarities with both *The Feign'd Curtezans* and the epilogue to *The Young King* which was produced in September or October of the same year.

In the first play Fillamour says:

> Yet charming as thou art, the time will come
> When all that beauty, like declining flowers,
> Will wither on the stalk, – but with this difference,
> The next kind Spring brings youth to flowers again,
> But faded beauty never more can bloom.

The Golden Age repeats these images very closely:

> But Sylvia when your beauties fade,
> When the fresh roses on your cheeks shall die,
> Like flowers that wither in the shade,
> Eternally they will forgotten lie
> And no kind Spring their sweetness will supply.

She was approaching her fortieth year which must have heightened her sense of 'gather ye rosebuds'. I believe the relationship with Hoyle was drawing to the painful end of its erotic phase. Hoyle was an atheist and this is one of her most pagan poems. It ends with no hint of immortality but with 'a sleep' that 'brings an eternal night'. The similarities between the epilogue to *The Young King* and *The Golden Age* are so numerous that they read like two versions of a suppressed original. The epilogue indeed ends with the lines

> Musick and love shall ever bless our swains
> And keep the Golden Age within our woods and plains.

Astrea herself was the goddess of the Golden Age, the last to abandon mankind, when that age was over, by leaving earth. Now it must have been as if Astrea spoke again.

First she described the primal innocence which is common to both pagan and Christian mythology: the plants that cultivate themselves to perfection could come from *Paradise Lost* along with the innocence of the beasts. With almost incredible aptness in a pre-Freudian age, the roses filled with morning dew bend down their heads 'T' adorn the careless shepherds' grassy beds' while the nymphs innocently play with snakes:

> No spiteful venom in the wantons lay;
> But to the touch were soft, and to the sight were gay.

This is the state of sexual innocence.

The poem then considers political and religious innocence, before wars or kings, 'Those arbitrary rulers over men, Kings that made laws first broke 'em,' and before the gods 'by teaching us religion first, first set the world at odds'. Faction had led her to a 'plague o' both your houses' state.

> Each swain was lord o'er his own will alone,
> His innocence religion was and laws.

As for property, that was held in common by general agreement, 'a common sacrifice to all th' agreeing swains'. Property is indeed the wrong word. There was none: 'Right and property were words since made.'

In these utopian conditions lovers too were free:

> Not kept in fear of gods, no fond religious cause
> Nor in obedience to the duller laws.
> Those fopperies of the gown were not then known,
> Those vain, those politick curbs to keep men in,
> Who by a fond mistake created that a sin;
> Which freeborn we, by right of nature claim our own.

It's hard to overemphasize the novelty of what she was saying here. It has taken another nearly three centuries for it to become palatable again. In case anyone suspected that the lines were mere translation or paraphrase and not her own beliefs, she used 'our' to include herself where she could have added distance with another adjective.

She goes on to castigate the whole complex of ideas included under the term 'honour'. In *The Feign'd Curtezans*, Cornelia, the sprightly one of the sisters, had found herself unable at the last minute to yield to Galliard because of her concept of 'honour'. She is, in that incredible seventeenth-century phrase which sums up the whole social mores, 'a person of quality' and therefore she must put honour above everything else. In men the concept led to the duel; in women to passive 'virtues' of rejection and resignation, including, Aphra Behn alleges, even such details as confining your hair in a net in case it should be 'wanton with the air'.

Life is too short for the foolishness of this false honour. Here she is close to a poet whose poetry she must have respected, even though she no doubt deplored his republican politics, Andrew Marvell, who had died only three years before, writing on his mistress's 'quaint honour':

> The grave's a fine and private place
> But none I think do there embrace.

Her last lines bring him very near indeed.

> When snow shall on those lovely tresses lie.
> And your fair eyes no more shall give us pain,
>   But shoot their pointless darts in vain.
> What will your duller honour signify?
> Go boast it then! and see what numerous store
> Of lovers will your ruin'd shrine adore.
>   Then let us Sylvia, yet be wise,
>   And the gay hasty minutes prize.

Marvell's, though the greater poem, is of a more limited philosophical range, a plea for the mistress to give herself physically to him. Aphra Behn's is more universal, a plea for a change in morality though based on the same concept of the fleetingness of life. She extends her concept to religion and politics as well as sexual morals and the instant gratification of pleasure. She is the more far-reaching radical of the two in this poem, though Marvell uses more forceful and immediate imagery. Hers, as so often, is also the more classical edifice, whether tomb or shrine.

She was also making a claim with *The Golden Age* which her contemporaries would have recognized. In Katherine Philips's poem 'A Country Life' she too deals with this theme.

> That Golden Age did entertain
>   No passion but of love;
> The thoughts of ruling and of gain,
>   Did ne'er their fancies move!

> None then did envy neighbour's wealth,
>   Nor plot to wrong his bed:
> Happy in friendship and in health
>   On roots, not beasts, they fed.

> They knew no law, nor physic then;
>   Nature was all their wit!
> And if there yet remain to men
>   Content, sure this is it.

Aphra Behn has rewritten this as she rewrote female drama with her first play. She was doing that most dangerous and necessary thing for a writer, laying a literary ancestor. The contrast of the forms, the pindaric with the quatrain, is bold enough, but it's only an echo of the two contrasting voices and the very different things they have to say.

In May an attempt was made to exclude the exiled James from the succession in favour of his protestant children including his son-in-law Prince William of Orange. An alternative plan was put forward by the more moderate members of the Whig party to limit James's power, or that of any other Catholic heir, without barring him from the succession. What was Aphra Behn's attitude to this vital constitutional issue?

Her later writing and activity would suggest that at this point she was totally opposed to both plans. Certainly she was against the exclusionists and in her dedication of the second part of *Love Letters Between a Nobleman and His Sister* to Lemuel Kingdon, paymaster general of the forces in the 1670s, she praised him for his opposition to them in Parliament. However, I think it's here that her childhood upbringing in Kent shows very strongly and produces that hankering for the Golden Age of innocence which is founded on an unconscious return to childhood. What she is in effect advising James to do in the epilogue to *The Young King* is to give up the crown and retire to the pastoral life. This, though I'm not aware that it was ever put to him, would have been the kindest solution for the country, an act of his own free will which would have done much to modify the effects of a Whig take-over. James himself unfortunately had no choice. As the only Catholic successor his religion obliged him to try to govern and convert the country and he was completely sincere in his religious conviction. There is no suggestion that it was merely a mask for a lust for power, though he was as ambitious as any other heir to the throne of his time.

Her political attitude in favour of James was hardened into passionate support by the efforts to exclude him either by Act of Parliament or by the plots of Shaftesbury to put the Duke of Monmouth on the throne. Both these courses were too reminiscent of 1641. They led to civil war and regicide and she therefore rejected them both. Rochester himself in one of his few recorded speeches in the Lords spoke up against the first attempt at exclusion in 1678, in spite of his Whig sympathies, pointing out that so many people would feel bound by their oath of allegiance to James as the lawful heir that it would lead to civil war. I suspect that she also rejected the alternative of the Securities Bill that would have limited his powers, both on the grounds of impracticability and because limitations placed on a King by his subjects again smacked of 1641. In the ideal world the only competition was for crowns of flowers, property was in common and according to need, men and woman were free and equal. Nothing could have been farther from the England of the late 1670s and James himself wasn't imaginative enough to see the attractions of such a life though some aspects of it were to be forced upon him in his final exile.

Charles prorogued the exclusionist Parliament in May, after the House of Commons had passed the Exclusion Bill by a large majority, but it seemed only a matter of time before both Houses would endorse it. Even this wasn't enough for Shaftesbury, whose aim was to set up Monmouth as King, excluding all the legal heirs to the throne completely. A rebellion in Western Scotland gave Monmouth a chance to act the hero at the head of the troops sent to suppress it. The tale of his mother's marriage to the King continued to spread in spite of Charles's denials, and his victory over the Scots at Bothwell Bridge increased his popularity.

Aphra Behn has two songs about Monmouth in her *Poems on Several Occasions* of 1684 and one on Shaftesbury, 'On The Cabal At Nicky-Nackeys', called after Shaftesbury's mistress. Of the two Monmouth songs the earlier is called simply 'Song To a New Scotch Tune' while the other, which foretells his downfall, is called 'Silvio's Lament – A Song to a Fine Scotch Tune'. Silvio comes from Monmouth's surname Scott and this and his Scottish campaign are reflected in the 'Scotch' tunes so that there shall be no mistake in identification. All three of the songs are meant for popular consumption. The first comes from *The Roundheads or the Good Old Cause*, the others were probably hawked about the streets as broadsides and part of her contribution to the royal cause. Both the Monmouth songs are more in sorrow than in anger. Both speak of Monmouth's charm and popularity, of his dancing and his good looks, and his betrayal by ambition and 'flattering knaves'.

It's possible that they were written in 1679,[1] after Monmouth's June campaign, during the counter-attack on the Popish Plot organized by the Catholic lords in the Tower with the help of Elizabeth Cellier, Henry Neville Payne and Thomas Dangerfield, alias Willoughby, whom Elizabeth Cellier had befriended when he was a prisoner in Newgate for debt.

Dangerfield was given fifteen letters by Lady Powis, wife of one of the lords in the Tower, which he was to plant on a Colonel Roderick Mansell. He took lodgings in the colonel's house and hid the papers behind the head of the colonel's bed. Dangerfield then went to William Chiffinch with information of this new plot, got a search warrant and, on October 22nd, helped to find the papers. He was soon suspected and committed for forging the papers. Elizabeth Cellier's house was searched by Sir William Waller and, at the bottom of a meal tub, papers and a book with the whole scheme of the plot were found. Dangerfield promptly turned King's evidence and began to accuse as many as he could draw in. Among them was Payne.

The plot reads like a comedy of intrigue. Unfortunately for the dramatist he lacked a professional actor for the vital main role. Dangerfield's narrative includes an interesting reference to Payne's daughter as 'like to turn whore'. Payne denied almost all Dangerfield's allegations when he was examined by the Privy Council on November 7th. However he was remanded to prison again although he had been released by March 1680 when Titus Oates declared that a scheme for a penny post for London and the suburbs was 'a further branch of the Popish plot ... the most dextrous invention of Mr Henry Nevil, alias Pain, who is notoriously known to be a great promoter of this way of treasonable correspondence'.[2]

I think Aphra Behn only took part in all this as a sympathetic bystander, though anything that would have saved Lord Stafford without implicating others would probably have had her active support. Payne next appears in 1685 as a friend of the Duke of Buckingham to whom perhaps she had introduced him.[3] Meanwhile other members of his family appear among Charles II's secret service accounts. It's not clear what their relationship to him is but there is first an Alice Neville alias Payne receiving bounty from the King early in 1681 and then, when she dies, her daughter Ursula takes it over for a time. These accounts are usually, in the case of women, for mistress-service but Alice Neville Payne seems a little old for this unless the daughter was very young. It implies, whichever way it's looked at, a closer relationship between Charles II and Henry Neville Payne than has previously been noted. I am reminded again of that curious half-sentence in One of the Fair Sex's *Memoirs* about matters of trust being confided to Aphra Behn which couldn't be spoken of. Certainly, she was once more close to the world of espionage at this time.

Charles II fell ill in the summer although some thought it was only a pretend illness. It was enough for James, the Duke of York, to be sent for home by the more moderate ministers, in order to combat the pretensions of Shaftesbury through Monmouth. He left again on September 24th, some said in order to fetch the Duchess whom he had left behind; others, of course, said it was into a second exile. It was in this second belief that Aphra Behn wrote the epilogue to *The Young King*, which must have been produced during September and October 1679.

The fashion was still for tragedy and she therefore revised this play which, she implies in the dedication, she had begun in Surinam so many years before. The prologue refers to two incidents in June when there had been fighting among the audience at the Duke's Theatre. On the first occasion John Churchill was challenged by Otway for beating one of the orange-women and, although both were wounded, Otway had the better of it. On the second occasion there was fighting between one of the informers, Bedloe, and a novice from St Omers and 'many swords were drawn'.

The prologue is surprisingly and sharply anti-French. Aphra Behn calls Paris 'that sacred Sodom'.

> Well might the French a conquest here design,
> Were but their swords as dangerous as their wine.
> Their education yet is worse than both;
> They make our virgins nuns, unman our youth.

Further on she slashes in passing at the Duchess of Portsmouth:

> ... Your dull forefathers first did conquer France
> Whilst they have sent us in revenge for these
> Their women, wine, religion, and disease.
>   Yet for religion it's not much will down
> In this ungirt, unblest and mutinous town.

It was enough to refer to a Frenchwoman for everyone's thoughts to turn to Portsmouth. The import of French religion is coupled with the French pox. 'Unman our youth' I take to be a reference to homosexuality. Rochester's bisexual singing valet was French and it was at this time that both sexes at court were tasting him. Is there here, I wonder, an added sharpness founded on Hoyle's growing homosexuality and his rejection of her?

About this time too there was circulating in manuscript, if not actually performed, a play called *Sodom* whose authorship was attributed to Rochester.[4] Otway referred to it in *The Poet's Complaint of his Muse or A Satire Against Libels* first printed in 1680.

> The first was he who stank of that rank verse
> In which he wrote his Sodom farce;

> A wretch whom old diseases did so bite,
> That he writ bawdry sure in spite,
> To ruin and disgrace it quite.

Aphra Behn's complaint about Paris looks like another oblique reference to this play. Speaking of wit and wine the prologue says:

> Judgement in both, with vast expense and thought,
> You from their native soil, from Paris brought:
> The drops that from that sacred Sodom fall,
> You like industrious spiders suck up all.

The other suggested author of *Sodom*, of whom nothing else is known, is John Fishbourne 'of the inns of court'.[5]

As well as the two letters to Emily Price which I've discussed earlier which were printed by Tom Brown in his book *Familiar Letters of Love, Gallantry etc.*, there's a third which purports to be from Aphra Behn to John Hoyle which encloses a modified copy of her poem 'The Disappointment'. This poem, which deals with impotence, or rather too early ejaculation, is in content very like one by Rochester called 'The Imperfect Enjoyment'. Both are versions of a French original 'L'Impuissance' but in any case the theme is universal. Aphra Behn's version was attributed to Rochester in the early edition of his pirated poems which can't be much after 1680.[6] She would hardly be likely to send Hoyle a poem already in print and her poem must have been in circulation, at least in manuscript, to be pirated anyway. If there's any credit to be given to this letter then it must have been written before 1680. I'll give it in full.

Pardon me, my dear *Morforio*, for that's the Name I will now call you by, if, among many of your Friends, I have been too hasty in crediting the Report which is generally spread against you. I need not tell you, how nearly I'm concern'd for your Health and Reputation, both which must be lost beyond Recovery, if there be one Word true in what I have heard, with Wonder and Sorrow, so frequently confirm'd. Good God! I am all over Agonies and Confusion; my Heart trembles, and my Hand shakes, when I take the Pen to represent to you the filthy Reflections which the whole Town begins to make upon your past

1 Aphra Behn, attributed to John Greenhill. Virtue records the sale of such a portrait in 1717 and notes that Tom Wright, who was Betterton's 'machinist' at the Duke's Theatre and also a playwright, had a portrait of her by Lely. If this is it, it passed to the Howards of Corby Castle, was exhibited in 1866 and sold at Colnaghi's in 1888. Now in the possession of Mr Arthur Schlechter of New York.

2 St Michael's church, Harbledown, where Eaffry Johnson's baptismal entry appears in the registers.

3 St Stephen's church, Hackington, less than two miles away, where Thomas Culpepper, Aphra Behn's foster brother, and his sister were baptized.

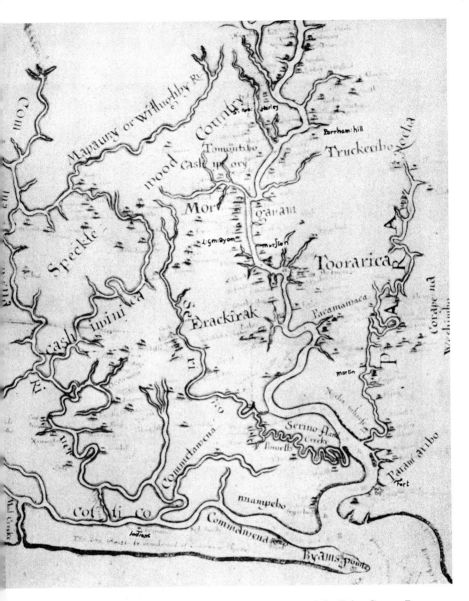

4 A manuscript map of Surinam now in the possession of the John Carter Brown
Library, Brown University. This map perfectly bears out the topography of
Orinooko. It shows the Indian towns they visited eight days' journey away by barge,
the closeness of St John's Hill, here called Sir Robert Harley's, to Parham Hill,
and Colonel Marten's where they fled down river. Although dated 1667 the map
reflects the situation in 1666. Perhaps William Scot provided the Dutch invaders
with a similar map. The plantation here marked 'Thurstons', in a map engraved
in 1671 (John Carter Brown Library, Blathwayt Atlas number 39) has been re-
named Schot, a Dutch version of Scot. Thurston was Eaffry Johnson's grand-
mother's name. It would be a nice irony if the Scots had been given her kinsman's
plantation by the Dutch.

5 The Stowe portrait in an engraving by Fittler in *Effigies Poetae*, 1824, attributed by him to Mary Beale. It shows Aphra Behn in her twenties. The Temple family who owned it were closely re-lated to Sir Thomas Gower.

6 and 7 Two views
of the Duke's
Theatre, Dorset
Garden: the front
from Elkanah
Settle's *Empress of
Morocco*, 1673; the
river view from
an engraving
published in the
*Gentleman's
Magazine*, July
1814. It shows the
theatre in the
years between its
repair in 1703 and
final demolition
in 1709.

8 Bishop Gilbert Burnet

9 An engraving by Masson from Henry Gascar's portrait of Nell Gwyn and her two sons. 'All the pictures, pens and pencils can draw, will give 'em but a faint idea of what we have the honour to see in such perfection . . . Nor can Heaven give you more, who has expressed a particular care of you every way, and above all in bestowing on the world and you, two noble Branches who have all the greatness and sweetness of their Royal and Beautiful stock . . .' Dedication to *The Feign'd Curtezans*.

10 (*above*) An engraving from the vanished portrait by Riley, seen by Virtue in the early eighteenth century, 'the same from which the print is engraved by White'. This version is from Buckingham's *Works*, 1715. It shows Aphra Behn in her forties.

11 Thomas Otway

12 (*below left*) John Wilmot, Earl of Rochester, 'Strephon'. Attributed to Huysmans.

13 George Villiers, Second Duke of Buckingham

14 The Inthronization of Queen Mary of Modena. From Francis Sandford's *History of the Coronation of James II and Queen Mary*, folio, 1687, p. 102. The Queen's Coronation robes were presented to the theatre, and were worn by Elizabeth Barry in the role of Queen Elizabeth.

15 Aphra Behn's tombstone in the cloisters of Westminster Abbey, 'near the door that goes into the church' as Thomas Culpepper described it. An additional couplet was added in the eighteenth century but not included in the nineteenth-century recutting.

Conduct. By Heavens, I cannot believe the Story, and yet my fatal Sympathy seems to confirm it to me. Oh *Morforio*, clear yourself instantly from these black Aspersions, or you'll soon become a Jest or a By-word to all that know you: You begin already to be the Aversion of the Fair Sex, and will quickly be the Scorn of your own too, unless you do something to stop these growing Reflections. I cannot bear to hear you every where reproach'd and vilify'd, and yet I protest, at present, I cannot offer any Thing in your Vindication. Dear *Morforio*, if you have been trying beastly Experiments, which I'm unwilling either to believe or mention, do something speedily that may disengage you from the scandalous Report. You are lost for ever if you delay a moment: Let me beg of you therefore, Nay, let me conjure you in the name of Friendship, and by all our past Endearments, to think of some Remedy to retrieve your sinking Reputation. I have herewith enclos'd to you my short Essay upon *An Imperfect Entertainment*: Read it over with your wonted Candour, and send me your impartial Sentiments. I'm impatient till I see you, that I may know from your own Mouth what Grounds there are for this abominable Rumour; till then, I'll suspend what I have further to say, but that I am, dearest *Morforio*, entirely yours. Adieu.

A. BEHN.

My feeling about this letter is that, if it ever existed (and this raises problems of how Tom Brown could have got hold of it), it has been tampered with. Her attitude to homosexuality in either sex was ambiguous and this isn't. It could be argued that where she herself was involved her attitude hardened, and the prologue to *The Young King* gives some support to this. But the expression 'beastly experiments' doesn't read like her, especially since she had known about his bisexuality for some time. The phrase 'if there be one word true in what I have heard' must be nonsense, since whatever she had heard she had anticipated in 'Our Cabal'. I am inclined to think the whole letter a fabrication though this doesn't mean that there wasn't some letter enclosing something. The original letter may have been against his homosexuality as the prologue to *The Young King* would suggest, and yet she wrote the prologue to Rochester's *Valentinian* which is sympathetic, possibly under the charming influence of Mr Baptist,[7] to the homosexual attraction. Would she have done this, even for someone she loved as much as she did Rochester, if she had totally disapproved of one of the play's strong sentiments? Perhaps. The argument goes backwards and forwards in the biographer's mind and there's no easy answer.

Nor does the letter sit very well with her offer in the winter of 1683–4 to introduce the translator of Lucretius, Thomas Creech, to 'honest Hoyle'. This would mean the letter would have to be later than spring 1684. Yet she herself published the poem she is supposed to have included with the letter in her collection of 1684 and it would have been even more pointless to send Hoyle a copy after this date.

What I think the fake letter reflects is an historical memory-plus-rumour of her association with John Hoyle, and his homosexuality. These two made a sufficient *cause célèbre* for Tom Brown, who was by then very much against her anyway, to write such a letter. Stylistically it has nothing in common with the letters that are known to be hers in the Public Record Office or the other extant letters, one to Tonson and the other to Edmund Waller's daughter-in-law. It has more in common with the Emily Price letters. The Waller and Tonson letters are late in her life and they still have the same ring as the ones from Antwerp. The differences, then, aren't ones of period. The three Brown letters I think have been through Tom Brown's editorial mill and this must make them suspect. In the case of the Emily Price letters it's easier to accept that some prototypes of them existed, since Emily Price herself wasn't well known enough to be an invention. She disappeared from the theatre after 1682 and may well have sold her letters when she was short of money. The only thing in favour of the Morforio letter is that it fits this late 'seventies/early 'eighties period when homosexuality was much in fashion. Then, if ever, is when it must have been written.

There's a touch of Hobbesian doctrine about *The Young King*. Orsames, the lawful heir, has been kept from his throne because the oracles have predicted that his reign will be short and violent. His sister Cleomena has been bred up as an amazon

to rule in his place. Given her loyalism, Aphra Behn has some
unusual things to say about kingship at this time and mainly
she says them through the mouths of the rabble of citizens. It's
they who insist on a King even though they have little idea
what one is. They are the 'mutinous town' of the prologue.

> *1 Cit.*:   Is that the King, neighbour, in such mean clothes?
> *Gorel*:   Yes, Goodman Fool, why should the Colonel kneel
> else.
> *2 Cit.*:   Oh, pray, neighbour, let me see a little, I never
> saw a King in all the days of my life ...
> *3 Cit.*:   Good lack-a-day, 'tis as a man may say – 'tis just
> such another body as one of us, only he looks a
> little more terrably.

This sounds to me like an oral memory from the return of
Charles II in 1660 through Kent to Canterbury. By contrast
the other characters are less impressed by kingship. Their
reason for having a King is to satisfy the citizens and to lead
them into battle. Only a King can do this and this is a doctrine
of Hobbes's. The other characters, although personally devoted
to their monarchs, have no real need of government because
their reason and sensibility are too developed. Their happiest
life would be the pastoral. The rural peasantry are contrasted
with the town rabble in an image of contemporary politics,
where the London mob was particularly volatile and easily
played upon by Pope-burnings and such-like propagandist
practices backed by free drink and handouts.

Contemporary politics appear obliquely again when the
Queen confesses that she has kept Orsames from the throne

> Through what she thought her duty to the gods
> But now repents her superstitious error.

Orsames is equated with James, Duke of York, who could also
be kept from the throne by the superstitious error of anti-
Catholicism which prophesies that his reign will be brief and
violent. Orsames himself has been bred in ignorance and
mirrors Miranda in *The Tempest* in his amazement at women
and indeed the whole of human society. In his first trial attempt
at reigning he does indeed show himself a tyrant, at which they
all despair and he is sent back to his confinement believing

that his hour's reign was a dream. Aphra Behn isn't so besotted a royalist that she believes Kings are allowed to behave as they please after the French way.

Her other great concern is with women, with their ability to govern, to act and to fight. The idea of the Amazons deeply appealed to her,[8] again I think from childhood when men fought for the King while women on the whole showed a more 'passive valour'. Cleomena is the epitome of her own problem. She can rule; she can fight. She it is who perceives that the only political solution is for Orsames to become King, and she defeats the oracles with reason. She organizes his return to power. She commands the army. She can't beat Thersander, the hero she is in love with, but then neither can anyone else. She is a warrior queen from Tasso[9] or Spenser and there is nothing hard about her though she is passionately jealous and is prepared to kill the man that, she thinks, has killed her lover. The character of Cleomena is a plea for equality without the sacrifice of what Aphra Behn thought of as the feminine virtues which she believed men should have as well, if they weren't to be coarse barbarians, and which she covers by the term 'softness'. Her heroes are 'charming', 'gay', and 'soft', words which she used with totally bisexual approbation. There's nothing butch or tough about Cleomena yet she is the entire equal of Thersander in everything except fighting, and this he negates by his total submission to her. Men are physically stronger on the whole, particularly when they have had a military training, but the truly civilized man will counter this himself by making the woman indeed his mistress.

The god of love o'ercomes the god of war.

XX

The Death of Rochester

The rivalry between the two Jameses, uncle and nephew, continued. The elder asked the King that, if he was to be exiled from him again, it should be to some place within the royal dominion and accordingly he and the Duchess set out for Scotland on October 27th. This was a wise move, for Monmouth had been gaining popularity there since his victory at Bothwell Bridge. Parliament was prorogued again until January 26th and Shaftesbury was turned out of all the councils. Monmouth, feeling his chances were slipping, returned secretly from Flanders in November. Charles was very angry that he had come back without permission and refused to see him. Nell Gwyn, no doubt with some urging from Buckingham, who was still supporting Shaftesbury, acted as intermediary between father and son but Charles was very angry at being disobeyed and Monmouth was deprived of all his commands.

All these political comings and goings affected and interested Aphra Behn, but the most important events of all, to judge by their appearance in her work, must have been Lord Stafford's continued imprisonment and Rochester's breakdown in health. Rochester was still in London and at court during this winter but he was already being visited once a week by Gilbert Burnet and it was at this time that their conversations took place which are recorded in Burnet's account of his death. Their first meeting seems to have come about through the Mrs Roberts with whom Henry Savile had cheered up his stay in Leather Lane while taking the cure for venereal disease. She had died in remorse six months earlier, charging Burnet to warn the King whose lover she had been as well as Rochester's, against the evils of a dissolute life. Burnet had written a long letter to Charles on January 29th and left it at seven o'clock in the evening at William Chiffinch's lodging. Charles read it twice, looked back again to the beginning, which contained the political part, and then threw it into the fire.

Rochester had been impressed by Burnet's *History of the Reformation*, the first part of which appeared in 1679, and apparently suggested to the King, who was, not surprisingly, angered by Burnet's letter, that he wondered why Charles 'would use a writer of history ill; for such people can revenge themselves'. The King replied that Burnet dared say nothing while he, Charles, was alive and when he was dead he would be no worse off for what Burnet said.

Rochester had obtained a formal introduction to Burnet in October and their discussions continued until Rochester left London in April for his Woodstock Park residence. Although not an atheist, Rochester was not 'arrived at a full persuasion of Christianity'. He wanted to believe, seeing that those who did were given a great deal of emotional support in times of crisis, particularly sickness and death, by their belief. Rochester's objections were rational and scientific. Burnet's replies are to a modern reader often extremely distasteful and totally unconvincing. His argument against promiscuity, for example, is that women are the property of men, either fathers or husbands, and it's wrong to spoil another man's property or rob him. What must have convinced Rochester in the end was his own desire to believe, his great weakness and his approaching death.[1] It could surely not have been these specious arguments. A great poet himself, he must have been particularly susceptible to the constant and comforting reading of the King James Bible by those about him and indeed it was during such a reading that 'God touched his heart' and his conversion struck deep into his emotions.

He tried to convert William Fanshawe, too, during one of his visits. Fanshawe was so shaken by Rochester's appearance and behaviour that, when he returned to London, he put about the story that Rochester's mind had gone and his mother was forced to deny it. It was only to be expected that such a sensational sinner should become an equally sensational saint. His repentant letter to Burnet was published as a broadside and so was his *Dying Remonstrance*. He summoned Burnet to his bedside on June 25th but Burnet didn't reach Woodstock until July 20th. He stayed until the following Saturday, the 24th, and left at four o'clock in the morning without daring to say goodbye. Rochester died on Monday July 26th, aged thirty-three. The funeral sermon preached by his mother's chaplain was equally sensational and immediately printed.

Early in 1680 appeared a volume of translations from Ovid's *Heroides*, edited by Dryden and prefaced by his *Essay on Translated Verse*. The list of authors includes most of the names of those with serious literary pretensions who were friends of Dryden. Among them were Aphra Behn, Otway, Nahum Tate and several other friends of hers, Mr Wright, who must be James Wright, a lawyer who had contributed a song to *The Young King*, John Cooper who described himself in his adulatory verses to her a few years later as 'of Buckden', and Thomas Flatman,[2] the great friend of Nathaniel Lee who was to write her a moving elegy. Perhaps Dryden's new intimacy with the Duke's Company had brought her into close touch with the laureate whose work she had always admired and praised, as she was to continue to do even when he grew cold towards her.

Dryden's preface is a justification of his way of translation which he calls paraphrase to distinguish it from the other two kinds, 'metaphrase' which is strict, word for word, and imitation which is very loose indeed. As examples of this last he instances Cowley and Sir John Denham. His example of paraphrase is Waller's *Aeneid IV*; of metaphrase Jonson's *Ars Poetica* of Horace. Cowley's imitations of Pindar and the Horatian *Odes* are cited. The main argument was between the paraphrasers and the imitators. These, among whom Dryden includes Aphra Behn, to add to the confusion often called their translations paraphrases and hers appeared as such in this volume. 'That of Oenone to Paris is in Mr Cowley's way of imitation only. I was desired to say that the author who is of the Fair Sex understood not Latine. But if she does not, I am afraid she has given us occasion to be ashamed who do,' Dryden wrote.

No compliment could have pleased her more. Honesty, pride and the knowledge that attack is better than defence in such things had caused her to desire him to say. She couldn't help her lack of a classical education but she could regret it. The very earliness of a boy's grounding in Greek and Latin would have made her feel it was too late to try those languages. She therefore had to rely on someone else's translation on which to base her own. In this case it was John Cooper whose translation of the same verse letter precedes her own in the book.

Once again she has turned the work she was doing to mirror her own concerns: there's no other explanation of the similarity between this, *The Young King* and *The Golden Age*. Paris has rejected Oenone and the pastoral idyll to be a King. Love is honour; only the breaking of love is dishonour. Aphra Behn has made and enunciates her own code of morality.

> I lov'd, and all love's dictates did pursue
> And never thought it could be sin with you ...
> 'Twas thou wert honour, glory, all to me:
> Till swains had learned the vice of perjury,
> No yielding maids were charg'd with infamy.
> 'Tis false and broken vows make love a sin,
> Hadst thou been true, we innocent had been.

Again she contrasts court and country.

> What stars do rule the great? no sooner you
> Became a prince but you were perjur'd too.
> Are crowns and falsehoods then consistent things?
> And must they all be faithless that are Kings?

Helen who has supplanted her Oenone says:

> Whilst she with love has treated many a guest
> And brings thee but the leavings of a feast ...
> And still the rape hides the adult'rous deed.
> And is it thus great ladies keep entire
> That vertue they so boast, and you admire?
> Is this a trick of courts, can ravishment
> Serve for a poor evasion of consent?

Behind the portrait of Helen lurks some real-life figure: Cleveland or Portsmouth. 'On her dang'rous smiles fierce war must wait with fire and vengeance at your palace gate.' Oenone in an exquisite piece of word-painting has climbed to the top of a rock to watch for ships. She sees a vessel pass with purple sails and Paris lying in Helen's lap under a gold and silver canopy while her fingers play with his 'perjur'd lips'. The ship is a 'glorious scene of state'. As with all good allegories this shouldn't be pinned down too precisely but the effect of it is to voice an uneasiness with England's affairs and a concern about betrayal that has nothing to do with Monmouth and Shaftesbury, though at a deeper emotional level it may have something to do with Hoyle.

In February *The Rover* was given a performance at court. The Duke and Duchess of York returned shortly after and Charles, who was delighted to see his brother, swore he would never part with him again. March saw another court performance; this time of *The Feign'd Curtezans*. These would both have brought her some money but she seems to have produced no new plays this year unless the anonymous adaptation from Marston's *The Dutch Courtezan*, which was produced in July at the Duke's Theatre as *Revenge or A Match in Newgate*, is hers. Once again it's one that's often attributed to Thomas Betterton and maybe they collaborated in it.

I think that the reason that she produced nothing of her own was that she was very low in spirits and possibly ill as a result. The fluent couplets of *Oenone to Paris* must have been produced late in 1679. Now she had three things to depress her: Hoyle, Rochester and Stafford. Together, for a time, I think they broke her heart.

Their importance for her can be gauged by the amount she wrote about them. Hoyle obviously has first place but Rochester comes very close behind. Her first response to his death was probably the formal elegy, though even that may have taken some time to emerge since in it she speaks of the loss of inspiration that has followed his death. It's a piece that has to be seen in terms of funeral monuments of the period, decorated with swags of sculpt flowers, with the winged heads of putti, all surrounded by a marble frieze in one of the decorative orders and with a maiden or two reclining in tears on a classical urn. Below will be the verses in that script that's two thirds of the way to the eighteenth-century classic English but yet keeps a touch of renaissance Italian, is in fact English baroque.

The elegy is in eighteen-line stanzas with a choral opening and ending to each to contain the grief, and because she wanted it to be worthy of him, not just a shapeless outpouring. She draws him as poet, satirist, lover mourned by women and then love itself and last as the great Augustan, the Ovid of his age. It is totally pagan.

Other literary mourners hadn't been idle. Thomas Flatman, Samuel Holland, John Oldham, Samuel Woodforde all produced elegies and so did his cousin Anne Wharton. She was married unhappily to the Whig Marquess of Wharton who has the great distinction in English letters of having written the words to Purcell's tune of Lillibullero. I think she was more than a little in love with Rochester. Most people were. But her love was accentuated by the coarseness of Thomas Wharton and her own artistic sensibility. She was only twenty-one when Rochester died. Her husband was nearly the same age as Wilmot. She wrote about his penitence and his reception into heaven.

A curious contest now developed, as if the struggle was over Rochester's body or soul. Anne Wharton wrote a poem: 'To Mrs A Behn on what she writ of the Earl of Rochester' and sent it to her.

> Fame, Phoenix like, still rises from a tomb;
> But bravely you this custom have o'ercome.
> You force an homage from each generous heart
> Such as you always pay to just desert.
> You prais'd him living, whom you dead bemoan
> And now your tears afresh his laurel crown.
> It is this flight of yours excites my art,
> Weak as it is, to take your muse's part,
> And pay loud thanks back from my bleeding heart ...
> May yours excel the matchless Sappho's name;
> May you have all her wit without her shame:
> Though she to honour gave a fatal wound ...
> Scorn meaner themes, declining low desire,
> And bid your muse maintain a vestal fire.
> If you do this, what glory will ensure,
> To all our sex, to poesy, and you?
> Write on, and may your numbers ever flow,
> Soft as the wishes that I make for you.

No doubt Aphra Behn read this over several times when she received it, as no doubt too Anne Wharton had worked it over several times before she sent it even though she told Burnet she found rewriting impossible.

Aphra Behn was in a very difficult position. Anne Wharton was young, nobly born, married, and probably beautiful and she was the new idol of the aged Waller, who was praising her elegy all over town and had written a short poem commending it but begging her not to melt in tears. It's very hard to establish exact dates but certainly the whole episode went on much longer than might have been expected, on into 1682 in fact. Anne Wharton's elegy on Rochester had dealt almost exclusively with his conversion. God, she says,

> Gave him a penitence so fixt, so true,
> A greater penitence no saint e'er knew.

At the end he goes to heaven. Now she is asking Aphra Behn to reform her verse. She is to leave out sex, write with a virginal flame and avoid the shame of Sappho.

Aphra Behn had translated a poem from Sappho, the 'Ode to Anactoria'. It sounds from the reference in Anne Wharton's poem as if it was already in circulation. Aphra Behn didn't include it in any of her own collections, but it was published after her death by Charles Gildon and it also appeared in an early edition of *Poems on Affairs of State*, wrongly titled as 'On Madame Behn', and in the works of the Duke of Buckingham where she is alleged to have written it to Buckingham in 1681. I doubt if it was written to Buckingham but 1681 seems the right date.

Whether Anne Wharton is specifically censuring Sappho's homosexuality it's hard to be sure. She may have been condemning her for passion generally rather than a 'vice' specifically. I don't think, either, that her lines can be taken as concrete evidence that Aphra Behn was known to be bisexual. But the poem had to be answered in some way without offending either Anne Wharton or the powerful literary coterie that was supporting her. The answer is called 'To Mrs. W. On her Excellent Verses (Writ in Praise of some I had made on the Earl of Rochester) Written in a Fit of Sickness'.

> Enough kind heaven! to purpose I have liv'd,
> And all my sighs and languishments surviv'd.

> My stars in vain their sullen influence have spread,
>   Round my till now Unlucky head:
> I pardon all the silent hours I've griev'd,
> My weary nights and melancholy days
> When no kind power my pain reliev'd ...
> Sad as the grave I sat by glimmering light,
> Such as attends departing souls at night.
> Pensive as absent lovers left alone,
> Or my poor dove when his fond mate was gone.
> Silent as groves when only whispering gales,
>   Sigh through the rushing leaves,
> As softly as a bashful shepherd breathes,
>   To his lov'd nymph his amorous tales.
> So dull I was scarce thought a subject found ...

It's an opening which disarms completely until it reaches the
lines that bring in the lovers, which make it clear that she's
totally unrepentant. The description of her pain and misery I
think are nothing but the truth. The poem goes on to say that
Anne Wharton's verses have so totally recalled Rochester that
it seems as if he is really present. Even in its correcting of her it
is the same voice that 'obligingly ... school'd my loose neglect'.

> Through the known paths of my glad soul it flew;
> I knew it straight, it could no others be,
> 'Twas not alied but very very he.

The last line is an echo of Waller where he describes Anne
Wharton as 'allyd in genius, as in blood' to Rochester; indeed,
the whole conceit of Aphra Behn's poem is based on a line of
Waller's: 'Shews that still in her he lives.'

By taking this device she makes the correcting of her faults
Rochester's and therefore acceptable as from an old friend and
patron. The faults themselves are made, by the mention of 'my
muse', literary, not moral, ones and this makes their correction
doubly acceptable. The rest of the poem is taken up with two
long similes: the first of a shepherd who hears the music of the
spheres and grows discontented with his rustick sounds until he
hears just one heavenly note that recalls all the divine music he
heard before; the second of the gods coming down to live awhile
in disguise as shepherds and being kind enough to praise the
simple rustick songs.

Aphra Behn betrayed nothing by this poem but she disarmed a potentially dangerous situation. It was written before December 1682 when Gilbert Burnet referred to it in a letter to Anne Wharton. The letter is very important, for it wasn't the last time he was to appear in Aphra Behn's life. He wrote:

> Some of Mrs Behn's songs are very tender; but she is so abominably vile a woman, and rallies not only all religion but all virtue in so odious and obscene a manner, that I am heartily sorry she has writ anything in your commendation. As I am glad, I had almost said proud, that you have honoured me as you have done; the praises of such as she is are as great reproaches as yours are blessings.[3]

Burnet is useful because among other things he makes it clear that her 'songs' were in circulation before 1682 as well as the longer poems. One of them, the song about Monmouth beginning 'Young Jemmy was a fine lad', was pirated in a collection called *'Female Poems on Several Occasions,* Written by Ephelia'. This had first appeared in 1679 but it was republished in 1682 with several extra poems, among them this one and a poem by Ephelia to Aphra Behn. Ephelia's name was to be coupled with hers later in a satire by Robert Gould. According to Gould and to her own words, Ephelia had a group of literary admirers. Ephelia's poems aren't very good but her very existence is significant, for what Aphra Behn had done was to open up the whole field of literature for women and there were now many of them where there had before been only two or three.[4]

Ephelia's eulogy speaks of her amazement, on first reading Aphra Behn's poems, that a woman writer should be capable of things that might be 'envied by the wittiest men' and of the 'rare connection of strong and sweet' in her writing. By the end of the century a few brave women were even following her into playwriting.

She had now been working for over a decade. Anne Wharton herself had grown up during Aphra Behn's literary lifetime. In 1682 Burnet was worrying about Anne Wharton's soul, for she was unhappy enough for it to be rumoured that she was on the point of leaving Thomas Wharton and her poems showed signs of a Rochesterian unrepentant deism if not of atheism. Burnet picks particularly on a phrase in one of her poems – 'endless night' for death – as evidence of atheism in Anne Wharton's work and this is actually a phrase which she has taken from Aphra Behn as Burnet probably knew. He was by implication accusing Aphra Behn of being an atheist but this was untrue. Anne Wharton wasn't entirely convinced by Burnet's arguments nor did she break with Aphra Behn, unless 'The Despair' published in Aphra Behn's *Miscellany* in 1685, the year of Anne Wharton's death, was done without her permission.

These poems were only part of Aphra Behn's mourning for Rochester whom she never forgot. Her longest elegy of all, however, wasn't sad at all. It was a celebration of his vitality, of his invention, and even of his affair with Elizabeth Barry. Perhaps Burnet knew of it and it was this in particular that he had in mind when he called her 'vile' and a mocker of all religion and virtue. Perhaps it was his own book, published in the autumn of 1680, *Some Passages of the Life and Death of the Right Honourable John Wilmot Earl of Rochester who died 26 July 1680*, which caused her to rouse from the stupor of misery she was in and begin work on a new play, *The Rover, Part II*. Certainly she knew what Burnet thought of her and she never forgot it.

XXI

The Rover's Return

Stafford was finally brought to trial on November 30th 1680. He conducted his own defence better than had been expected and the trial lasted seven days before he was found guilty and sentenced to be hanged, drawn and quartered. The voting had been fifty-five to thirty-one and amongst those against him had been all the lords of his own family except Lord Mowbray, Henry Howard of Arundel. They included Sir Thomas Gower's brother-in-law, Charles Howard, Earl of Carlisle. The King commuted the sentence to beheading and Stafford was executed on Tower Hill on December 29th, maintaining his innocence to the last.

> Calm as a dove, receiv'd a shameful death,
> To undeceive the world, resign'd his breath;
> And like a god, died to redeem our faith.

The attempts to exclude the Duke of York, who was now in Scotland, from the succession had gone on all through the year with unabated violence. Shaftesbury and his followers had kept the populace in a constant state of excitement by continuing to exploit the Popish Plot until the country was dangerously near civil war. But as so often in English history, their violence began to turn the more moderate against them. Nevertheless the Duke was still in voluntary exile when Aphra Behn dedicated *The Rover, Part II* to him claiming that he had taken a personal interest in this sequel to her earlier success.

It's generally been assumed that when she came to write this play Aphra Behn merely gathered up what was left over from

her first rewrite of Killegrew's *Thomaso*. This consisted of a
sub-plot about a mountebank who is to cure two rich female
'monsters', one big and one small, so that Edwardo and
Ferdinando can marry them for their money. The double
marriage takes place and the monsters are put into the bath
that is to change them but the arrangements go wrong, other
characters fall in too and there's a magical mix-up in which
some change size and others sex.

In *The Rover, Part II* there's no magic and no mountebank
but only Wilmore in disguise, though the giant and the dwarf
remain. Many of those in the audience will have known, indeed
their memories had been refreshed by Burnet himself, of
Rochester's disguising himself as the mountebank Alexander
Bendo during one of his periods of being out of court favour,
during which escapade he not only prescribed medicines but
told fortunes as well, as Wilmore does. 'He disguised himself so
that his nearest friends could not have known him and set up in
Tower Street for an Italian mountebank, where he had a stage
and practis'd physick for some weeks not without success,'
Burnet writes. A later account by Thomas Alcock who had been
a servant of Rochester's at the time gives details which leave no
doubt that Wilmore's impersonation is modelled on Rochester's.
In particular they both claim to restore old women to beauty.
'Here's that will give you auburn hair, white teeth, red lips
and dimples on your cheeks,' cries Wilmore in his patter while
Bendo's bill offered 'to cleanse and preserve your teeth, white
and round as pearls, fastening them that are loose; your gums
shall be kept entire and red as coral, your lips of the same
colour, and soft as you could wish your lawful kisses'.

Perhaps it was reading Burnet that made her see the opportunity to capitalize on the success of *The Rover*, Part One, and at
the same time pay her tribute. The Wilmore of *Part II* is even
more Wilmot than in Part One. Hellena, whom he married at
the end of the first part, has died and he is now in Madrid and
in pursuit of a famous courtesan, La Nuche, played by Elizabeth
Barry. This too couldn't have escaped many in the audience.
Rochester's affair with Elizabeth Barry was well known. Here
she was in effect playing herself. Appropriately in the end she
agrees to go away with Wilmore without the benefit of marriage,
which he describes as 'formal foppery'.

La Nuche: Nay, faith Captain, she that will not take thy word as soon as the parson's of the parish, deserves not the blessing.
Wilmore: Thou art reform'd, and I adore the change.

I believe it was this in particular that had angered Burnet for if it's Rochester speaking it is a complete rejection of the death-bed repentance. This is Rochester as Aphra Behn and Elizabeth Barry had known and loved him in their different ways. Wilmore's last words, the last words of the play, are an extraordinary way to end a comedy but not when once the identification is made. Speaking to Beaumond, who is to marry Ariadne, Wilmore says; 'You have a hankering after marriage still but I am for love and gallantry':

> So tho by several ways we gain our end
> Love still, like death, does to one centre tend.

This was her mocking at religion and virtue.

The play was also a vindication of Elizabeth Barry, and she must have been magnificent as the tempestuous La Nuche who defends herself brilliantly in the verbal battles and is Aphra Behn's greatest dramatic creation, a complete rebuttal of Burnet's concept of women as property. Many of the exchanges between Wilmore and La Nuche foreshadow those between Mirabel and Millamant in Congreve's *Way of the World*. Both plays of course owe a lot to Shakespeare's Beatrice and Benedict.

Both prologue and epilogue protest against the public neglect of the theatre. Aphra Behn accuses the public of only coming to see Whig plays, striking particularly at Elkanah Settle, the City Poet, and his play *The Female Prelate*, which had had an enormous success in the early summer of 1680. There's also a reference to the Bartholomew Fair entertainments, which had been particularly lavish this year, and to Settle's involvement in the Pope-burning in November, when the effigy was stuffed with firecrackers which went off as it burnt. On one occasion live cats were used instead to simulate diabolic howls of anguish.

The Rover, Part II wasn't the only play to mention Rochester. Nathaniel Lee refers to him as Count Rosidore in *The Princess of*

Cleve. The date of first performance of this is uncertain as is that of *The Rover, Part II*, except that references in the epilogue of *The Rover, Part II* which uses the calling of Parliament to vote money for the King as a metaphor for audience and poet suggest a date between October and January, though it could be later. It was certainly acted on April 4th. The last lines of the epilogue have what I read as a puzzling reference to Dryden as 'our King of poets' and asking the public not to let this 'glorious monarch want'. This may refer to something specific or may just be a general complaint against a falling box office. Dryden was now writing regularly for the Duke's Company and the King's was in a very bad way. He had just had a great success with *The Spanish Fryer* so it seems unlikely that he could be in want.

Aphra Behn wrote of Rochester at least twice more. His death had left an emotional and intellectual gap in her life which she found it hard to fill. Otway was a possible candidate. Intellectually they were very close during this period. Both dedicated plays to the Duke of York and supported the Yorkist cause. But if Otway is the author of *The Poet's Complaint* written about this time he was as unhappy as his disappearance a few years later would suggest. His unhappiness seems to have been caused by that dread of writers, the writer's block, and by an unhappy love affair with, it's usually supposed, Elizabeth Barry.

Nathaniel Lee was a friend and fellow writer at the Duke's Theatre but he was reputed to be an alcoholic and had fits of insanity. One fierce but rather magnificent satire on the poets describes him in Bedlam.[1] Both these poets are traditionally said to have been helped by Aphra Behn. Neither of them was in a position to help her, either financially or emotionally, although Otway was to write her a prologue and they were clearly close friends.

To fill the gap, and because the ambiguity of Rochester's own position was removed by his death, she threw herself into the political battle and wrote 'madrigals and doggerel on the times'. None of these has ever been identified among the mass of propaganda that was poured out during these years, except for the three songs I've already mentioned on Monmouth and Shaftesbury, though the last of these wasn't written until after this comment, which occurs in the prologue to her next play called *The False Count*. The 'doggerel' must be satires like those collected in *Poems on Affairs of State* of which, of course, the greatest example, which rises far above doggerel, is Dryden's *Absalom and Achitophel*.

It's because neither she nor her work has been taken seriously that Aphra Behn has never been identified among the great flock of male satirists. This attitude of condescension is well demonstrated by the modern editor of these state poems when he refers to her as 'that notable female worthy'. I don't intend here to enter into which may or may not be hers in any great detail but only to suggest a couple and to mention that she herself provides some clues. She has, she says, in the prologue to *The False Count*, charged the Whigs with their fathers' crimes, said that the Popish Plot was an imposture and spread tales about them eating young Tories. Though these may be exaggerations or generalizations, they give some idea of the 'doggerel' she intended and it ought to be possible to identify some of her contributions.

From the volume that runs from 1678 to 1681 I tentatively suggest two pieces merely on internal evidence. One begins very like the Shaftesbury song: 'A pox on the factions o' th' City.' The other is called *The Waking Vision*. I can only say of both of them that they sound like hers in their choice of words and manipulation of the verse line. The second one also takes up the moderate position which the prologue to *The False Count* suggests she was adopting at this time, where she refers to the hissing by the 'popish crew' of Shadwell's popular *Lancashire Witches or Teague O'Divelly* a few weeks before.

Charles had dissolved the latest exclusionist Parliament, which he had summoned at Oxford in March, and had issued a royal declaration which, together with the violence of the Whigs, had swung the people once more behind him. In June events were running sufficiently in the court's favour for Shaftesbury and Lord Howard of Escrick, one of those members of his family who had voted against Stafford, to be sent to the Tower, and in September the city chose a pro-court Lord Mayor to succeed Sir Patience Ward.

All this affected her choice of a new play for the winter, and its prologue. The epilogue was written by 'a person of quality' who claimed that Aphra Behn had written the play in five days.

The prologue is later than November 23rd since it refers to Shaftesbury's release, by a verdict of *ignoramus* from the grand jury, which was greeted by the city with bonfires and general rejoicing. The play, although set in Cadiz, deals with a milieu which she hadn't touched since *Sir Patient Fancy*, that of the wealthy citizens. Its basic theme is money. I suspect that at this time she was short of it and therefore quickly wrote this play to make some, though the five days of the epilogue may be a satire on those writers who often claimed to write their plays in a week.

It's hard to know what money she made or how much she needed to live on; two problems that must have been among the most frequent concerns of her life. Burnet, when he was trying to raise money from Anne Wharton to provide a living for a 'gentlewoman', thought that £40 a year would be enough to 'subsist' on. A writer might get as much as £100 for the third day's performance. Shadwell is recorded as having received the highest up to that time: £130 for *The Squire of Alsatia* in 1668. But in 1681 the box office receipts were very low, often barely covering the cost of production. Southerne in 1694 had £140 from a performance, £50 from noblemen and £36 from the publisher.

The publisher's fee seems fairly standard, since Aphra Behn was bargaining around the £30 mark for a book in 1684-5 with the publisher Jacob Tonson. For this year, 1681, she can be reckoned to have had £30-£40 for the book of *The Rover, Part II*, something from the Duke of York, though royalty possibly expected a dedication for nothing, and perhaps £50 or more for her third night; a total income of about £150 since there had also been at least two court performances of her earlier plays.

However, Burnet's 'gentlewoman' was obviously living a more retired life than a well-known playwright who would be expected to entertain, go herself to the theatre and be dressed à la mode, hire a coach to go about in, and have at least a couple of servants, her 'people' of the letter to Lycidas. The portraits of her show just such a person as her life would lead one to expect, with dark eyes and brown hair, a 'black' woman as Charles II was a 'black man'. She wears the fashionable low-cut dress to show off neck and shoulders and, in the Fittler engraving, a row of pearls and a flowing robe over her dress.

The False Count is her clearest statement about both money and class. It's unwise to deduce an author's views from what the characters say but I think it's legitimate to make such deductions from plot and structure. Isabella is the vain, jumped-up daughter of Francisco, who has made his money as a cordwainer in England and turned gentleman in Spain. She refuses to marry Antonio, a merchant's son, and is holding out for a count. A false count is provided from among the chimney sweeps and she is tricked into marrying him. Antonio is married to Clara while her sister Julia, who had been married off to old Francisco, is reunited with her previous lover Carlos.

Guiliom, the false count and chimney sweep, makes ten thousand pounds out of the deal. Carlos advises his father-in-law to take him home to Seville. 'Your neighbours know him not, and he may pass for what you please to make him; the fellow's honest, witty and handsome.'

Carlos is highest on the play's social ladder but he has only just become so through the death of his father. Before that he wasn't high enough for Balthazer, the father of Julia and Clara, and that was why Julia was married off to rich old Francisco. Now that he has gone up in the world he is intended by Balthazer to marry his other daughter Clara.

Antonio, who's a merchant's son, is Carlos's friend and by the resolution of the play they will be brothers-in-law. Carlos is now marrying beneath him, though it's not clear whether, when Francisco hands over his wife to her old lover at the end, there is to be a divorce and a marriage or whether the two will simply be lovers. The crux of the social comment comes when old Francisco, believing they have all been captured by the Turk and that he is to be killed, begs his wife to buy his life from the Grand Seignior with her body.

Even though the play was confessedly written very quickly, there is one bit of dialogue in it which shows that Aphra Behn never lost sight of what she was doing. Carlos's servant, disguised as a Turk, reports to him that old Francisco has gone into a trance at his fake capture. *Carlos:* 'Whatever you do, have a care you do not overfright the coxcomb, and make a tragedy of our comedy.' This play within a play is an effect like the false perspective of painted scenery or like Chinese boxes.

The comment applies equally to the author's view of this comedy in particular and her understanding of comedy in general.

Francisco is the least appetizing of her elderly husbands who have bought themselves young wives, yet even he isn't to be frightened to death and there is hope for his partial reformation since he surrenders Julia in the end. The political turn-around enabled Aphra Behn to stage a play in which the social classes have complete mobility. It isn't money or rank which 'maketh man' in *The False Count* though they make him in the eyes of the world. A chimney sweep may be a count and is better than a proud beauty who derides 'th' industrious noble citizens'.

It's an appeal to reason beyond party politics. It's also a rejection of the Whig concept of property which was coupled with liberty. Liberty is just as important for women who shouldn't be bought and sold like property. The real value of money is to ensure liberty to everyone to realize their potential. This seems to be the antithesis of her pastoral ideals but in fact it isn't, only another mode, social comedy, for expressing the same values, which are above formal laws and social codes alike. Not only sexually but socially, she goes further in the direction of freedom than the next two centuries were to find admissible.

The False Count wasn't successful enough for Aphra Behn to ask permission to dedicate the play to anyone when it was published the following year. It looks as if whatever sudden need had caused her to write it so quickly wasn't allayed, and another soon followed, though it's difficult to decide when its première must have been. It was a rewrite of a 1660 play, *The Rump*, by John Tatham. As a play or as a vehicle for ideas, it's nowhere near as good as *The False Count*, yet it was an unqualified success because of the royalist faction which must have packed it from the beginning, since she says in the dedication it 'was carried in the House nomine contra dicente, by the Royal Party'. It must have been acted very late in 1681 or in January of the next year, only two months after *The False Count*.

The Roundheads or the Good Old Cause is a return to the years of her childhood, for it's set in the last months of the interregnum when the republican leaders were squabbling among themselves for power. As usual she's opened up the whole play and enormously improved upon the original, this time by introducing two cavalier heroes to seduce the republican wives. Not surprisingly one of them is called Loveless who is in love with the Lord General Lambert's wife. The other, Freeman, loves Lady Desbro. The cast includes Corporal Right, 'an Oliverian commander, but honest and a cavalier in his heart', and Ananias Goggle, a canting lay elder. If money is the main theme of *The False Count*, hypocrisy is that of *The Roundheads*.

By presenting the old rebels she drew a parallel with the new, and reminded people of what life had been like under the old dispensation, with its reintroduction of capital punishment for adultery and for incest within the forbidden degrees for marriage, while for simple fornication the penalty could be three months' imprisonment.

An Act for suppressing the detestable sins of incest, adultery and fornication had been passed in 1650. Among its other provisions was a penalty for being a bawd and keeping a brothel, of public whipping and branding on the forehead with the letter B, to be followed by three years' imprisonment. But perhaps worst of all were the powers given to justices to 'enquire of all and every crimes aforesaid'. At the same time brothels had flourished and the great had been rumoured to carry on sexual affairs like that of Cromwell and Mrs Lambert and some, Harry Marten among them, had kept virtual harems of mistresses.

There was hypocrisy too in the greed with which they made themselves rich in sequestrated property both private and ecclesiastical while extolling simple virtues and unostentatious living. The success of the play depended largely on the political situation but there is a strongly nightmarish quality about it which comes, I think, from the remembrance of things long past. The characters have the oversimplicity of terror-filled fairy tale, of the gossip of the adult world overheard by a child and only half understood. Appropriately the prologue is spoken by a ghost.

Her next play, which she had produced at the end of March, *Like Father, Like Son*, has vanished. It must have been a complete failure and only the prologue and epilogue remain, published in broadsides. The reasons for its failure were there on the first night and are embodied in her prologue. The King was at Newmarket for the races and the Duke of York had come from

Scotland to join him there. As the contemporary diarists back her up in saying, all the world had gone to pay its respects to James. It was the court party that supported the theatres and with them away it was a 'thin' house. She seems to have tried to provide against this by writing a play that, whatever the title suggests, wasn't, she claimed in the epilogue, anti anybody. It had a good cast but her previous assessment of the city was right: they only came to plays by Whig writers and even then they were shy about it.

Her allegiance to the court could, it might be argued, have been purely mercenary. The Commonwealth had closed down the theatres as wicked and no doubt another puritan government would do the same. There must have been an element of this in her unconscious if not her conscious thinking. She had made herself a way of life and a living both of which would be destroyed if the theatres closed, but her attitude to her art wasn't merely mercenary: that would have made her another face of the whore she despised. She believed that poets were in some sense sacred and she instanced, to back up her belief, the value set on them by classical civilizations; if she had read Plato she thought he was wrong. In the dedication to *The Lucky Chance* she claims of plays, quoting the Abbot of Aubignac: 'the philosophy of Greece, and the majesty and wisdom of the Romans did equally concern their great men in making them venerable, noble and magnificent'.

The False Count and *The Roundheads* were both published in 1682, so she must have picked up some money there. She would have got something too for the prologues and epilogues which were published separately and bought by Narcissus Luttrell, that avid collector, hot from the presses, and for a prologue she wrote for a revival of *The Jealous Lovers*. But her biggest coup must have been the dedication of *The Roundheads* to Charles II's natural son by Barbara Villiers, Buckingham's cousin, Henry Fitzroy, Duke of Grafton, one of the most promising and popular of the King's children who had recently been made colonel of the first regiment of foot guards.[2]

Once again it was a careful protestant choice. She could make in her dedication a comparison between this young son of the King and Monmouth without quite saying so, though she came very close indeed. The fact that he was Buckingham's cousin also helped, since Villiers hadn't yet abandoned the Whig party and I don't think she wanted to fall out with him. She warns Grafton against the vain ambition of wanting to be a King, with all the cares that state would entail, but she's really warning Monmouth. She says that the play has 'drawn down legions upon its head for its loyalty – what, to name us cries one, 'tis most abominable, unheard of daring cries another – she deserves to be swing'd cries a third'. Describing the state of the three kingdoms, as she calls them, in the days before the restoration, she writes: 'How they were govern'd, parcell'd out, and deplorably enslav'd, and to what low, prostituted lewdness they fell at last: ... and such mean (and till then obscure) villains rul'd and tyranniz'd, that no age, nor time, or scarce a parish book makes mentions or could show there was any such name or family.' It's ironical in the light of this last statement that her own entry in a 'parish book' has taken such finding. But the emphasis on their obscurity suggests to me that, for whatever reason, she had undergone some emotional change between the writing of *The False Count* and *The Roundheads* which had hardened her political attitudes. Perhaps, although the prologue and epilogue are immediately contemporary, the main body of *The False Count* was written a couple of months earlier before Shaftesbury's verdict of *ignoramus* which set him free. This would be consistent with a month's rehearsal and a première in November.

By April she had had three plays produced in six months and another was in rehearsal. This was another success; it 'had the luck to be well receiv'd in the town', Langbaine recorded in his *English Dramatic Poets* of 1691. It was successful enough for a dedication and one that she had had in mind for a long time, to the Howard family in the person of Henry Howard of Arundel and Mowbray, who would one day succeed as Duke of Norfolk.

XXII

Daphnis

The success of *The Roundheads* angered Shadwell, as did the combination of Otway and Behn, for Otway had written the prologue to *The City Heiress*.

> Such stupid humours now the gallants seize
> Women and boys may write and yet may please.
> Poetess Afra though she's damn'd today
> Tomorrow will put up another play;
> And Otway must be pimp to set her off,
> Lest the enraged bully scowl and scoff,
> And hiss, and laugh, and give not such applause
> To th' *City Heresie* as the *Good Old Cause*.

The words 'though she's damned today' must refer to the failure of *Like Father, Like Son*. It sounds as if Shadwell's verse was written immediately before the production of *The City Heiress*,[1] in anticipation. Shadwell was in dispute with Dryden in 1682 and their verse insults were flung back and forth like paper darts. His lines show the kind of prejudice she was still facing and added no doubt another personal layer of anger to her anti-Whiggery.

The City Heiress was still running on May 17th, when the Moroccan ambassador attended a performance. The court was in London and the play was skilful and political enough to get the audience. Once again the dedicatee is a protestant royalist. Henry Howard had abandoned the Roman Catholicism of his family for the Church of England when he had publicly taken the sacrament. It's in this dedication that Aphra Behn speaks of being brought up with the praises of the Howards and of seeing them praised by foreign crowds. 'This I have seen with a joy that became a true English heart ... and join'd my dutiful respects ... but never had the happiness yet of any opportunity to express particularly that admiration ... ' It sounds as if she hadn't spoken personally to Lord Stafford unless she doesn't count him as specifically a 'Howard of Norfolk and Arundel'. If that's so, then she must have someone else in mind, possibly Cardinal Philip Howard, as I've suggested earlier, or even the Duke of Norfolk himself, Thomas, when on a foreign visit.

She praises Henry Howard for voting for Stafford but at the same time very subtly suggests her approval of his own religious position. She also mentions the success of the play and the changed political temper of the country to which she attributes the play's good reception.

The City Heiress is a brilliant unflagging piece. Wilding is the young male lead; another successor to Wilmore. All the women are in love with him but in particular Lady Galliard, a rich city widow, and Charlot, the city heiress who finally gets him. Wilding himself is a nephew of a city knight, Sir Timothy Treat-all, but he has taken up with a group of young Tories and become corrupted in his uncle's eyes.

Wilding advances the strongest arguments to get Lady Galliard into bed of any of Aphra Behn's characters.

Wilding:	Beauty should still be the reward of love,
	Not the vile merchandize of fortune,
	Or the cheap drug of a church ceremony.
	She's only infamous, who to her bed
	For interest takes some nauseous clown she hates:
	And though a jointure or a vow in public
	Be her price, that makes her but the dearer whore.
Lady Galliard:	I understand not these new morals.
Wilding:	Have patience I say, 'tis clear:
	All the desires of mutual love are virtuous.
	Can Heav'n or man be angry that you please
	Your self and me when it does wrong to none?

Wilding gradually destroys her with argument and emotional blackmail until she agrees to go to bed with him and he leads

her off into the bedchamber, exulting with the power of a
Faustus.

Wilding: All Heaven is mine, I have it in my arms,
                  Nor can ill fortune reach me any more.
                  Fate, I defy thee, and dull world, adieu.
                  In love's kind fever ever let me lie,
                  Drunk with desire, and raving mad with joy.

So powerful is this scene, and indeed all the exchanges
between Lady Galliard and Wilding, that it was used in one of
the most savage satires against her, equating her of course with
the character of Lady Galliard.

What though thou bringst (to please a vicious age)
A far more vicious widow on the stage,
Just reeking from a stallion's rank embrace
With rifled garments, and disorder'd face;
T'acquaint the audience with her slimy case?
What can the surly critics urge from hence,
When thou shalt rise up in thy own defence,
And plead impenitable impudence?[2]

A 'stallion' was a slang term for what would now in America be
called a stud.

Sir Timothy Treat-all himself is modelled on Shaftesbury,
and the whole strange episode in 1675 of Shaftesbury's delusion
that he was going to be offered the crown of Poland is ridiculed.
Otway also refers to it in the prologue to his last complete
tragedy *Venice Preserv'd*, which was first produced a little before
this, and Dryden, as well as various unidentified satirists, makes
play with it in *The Medal*, published in March of this year.

The City Heiress isn't, however, an unequivocal play. There's
a strong hint that Wilding and his friends incline to Roman
Catholicism, and Wilding although so physically attractive is in
the end subdued by the virtuous Charlot. He marries her partly
out of pique, because Lady Galliard has married his friend
Charles, but there's a strong suggestion that Charlot, who has
shown great enterprise and pertinacity throughout the play in
her efforts to get him, will tame him. The real loser is Lady
Galliard, who was played by Elizabeth Barry, and hers is a
complex character, not the merely lecherous bitch that the

satire suggests by the phrase 'lewd widow'. She truly loves Wilding and she loses him.

Henry Howard remained Aphra Behn's patron for at least the next three years, although there's no record of further payments from him, but in her coronation poem in 1685 she calls him 'Maecena of my muse, my patron lord'. This must rest on something more than just one payment for *The City Heiress*. She also wrote a prologue for a revival of *The Jealous Lovers*[3] as I've said so that by the spring of 1682 she should have been in a reasonable financial situation. The emotional problem of a successor to Rochester was also a little alleviated by the arrival on the literary scene of a new poet, Thomas Creech, with his translation of Lucretius' *De Rerum Natura*.

Creech was twenty-three and, like Rochester and Sir Thomas Gower, a product of Wadham. The *De Rerum Natura* was a work that fascinated the collective intellect of the period, particularly those who had leanings towards atheism and a scientific explanation of the world. Creech's translation first appeared in 1682 and her poem in praise was dated January 25th 1682.[4] She had written it in London. She didn't know the young man, who had been published anonymously, but she knew he was from Wadham. Waller, Otway, Tate, Duke and Evelyn among others also wrote commendatory verses which were prefixed to the second edition the following year. Aphra Behn's must have been some of the first and it's quite clear she was trying to use the Unknown Daphnis, as she calls him, to heal the wound of Rochester who inevitably appears in the poem.

This dedication led to a friendship, intense at first, though it's hard to decide how long it lasted; certainly till 1685. The commendatory verses when she didn't yet know him are a vehicle for several things she wanted to say, in particular about the education of women.

The kind of education they could expect and that was thought suitable for them can be deduced from an advertisement in the *London Gazette*, for March 18th–22nd 1680. A boarding school at Holywell, Oxford, offers 'dancing, music, vocal and instrumental, writing, works and what other qualifications belong to young gentlewomen'. Defoe at the beginning of the next century was to make a strong plea for the improved education of women on the grounds that it would make them better companions for men. Defoe had an enormous respect for Aphra Behn and included her among the 'giants of wit and sense' of the previous generation in his poem 'The Pacificator'.

Women like Anne Wharton and those ladies to whom Dr Burnet was busy showing her poems in late 1682 had obviously some degree of learning but Aphra Behn felt it wasn't enough. In particular the classics were closed to them. Prior in a *Satyr On the Modern Translators* was to attack her on exactly this point, calling her 'our blind translatress Behn, the female wit'. The young Prior was, like Shadwell, a protégé of Charles Sackville, Lord Buckhurst, a supporter of the Whig party. The first attack on the Dryden collection had come in May 1680, shortly after publication, with a volume advertised in the *Gazette* as *The Wits Paraphrased, a burlesque on the several late translations of Ovid's Epistles.* Although she had tried to prevent this kind of attack by getting Dryden to admit her ignorance of Latin in his preface, she had obviously failed and this early burlesque may also have attacked her in the same terms as Prior. Her defence is in her praise of Creech.

Creech's great achievement, for which she must be particularly grateful, is that he has made Lucretius accessible. The 'scanted customs of the nation' forbid 'the female sex to tread,

> The mighty paths of learned heroes dead.
> The god-like Virgil, and great Homer's verse,
> Like Divine mysteries are conceal'd from us ...
> The fulsome jingle of the times
> Is all we are allowed to understand or hear.

The god who first advanced human beings from their primal savage ignorance and made them gentle and civilized was adored himself next to what he taught. Creech has advanced women from their state of ignorance by his translation, making them equal to men, and therefore they should adore him.

Lucretius' own aims in writing his immense work were to remove the fear of the gods and of death from mankind and to provide rational explanations for natural phenomena which, like thunder and volcanoes, gave rise to superstitious interpretations. He also put forward the atomic theory of Leucippus according to which the world was created by the coming together of elemental particles following certain simple laws.

What excited Aphra Behn about the work was Creech's
fluency in expressing even the most difficult concepts, and
Lucretius' appeal to reason.

> ... reason over all unfetter'd plays,
> Wanton and undisturb'd as summer's breeze;
> It pierces, conquers and compels,
> Beyond poor feeble faith's dull oracles.
> Faith the despairing soul's content,
> Faith the last shift of routed argument.

These lines must have angered Burnet if he read them, which I
expect he did since he tried to keep up with literary developments. He was on visiting terms with Waller, who was now in
his old age turning to religious verse, and he had read and
praised the Earl of Mulgrave's verse 'Essay on Poetry'.

In his correspondence with Anne Wharton Burnet accuses
her of leaning towards atheism because she suggested that
'eternal night' followed death and that God was uninvolved in
human affairs. This last was also a doctrine of Lucretius. In
Aphra Behn's comments on faith he must have seen another
rejection of Rochester's deathbed repentance. He wouldn't
have been pleased, either, with the lengthy praise of Thomas
Sprat which follows the praise of Wadham as a nursery of poets
who are 'born not made by dull religion and necessity'. Sprat
Burnet saw as a rival. They had both preached at St Margaret's,
Westminster, before the Commons on December 22nd 1680,
Burnet in the morning with the applause of the Commons,
Sprat in the afternoon to the approval of the King. Sprat, as
well as being Buckingham's friend and chaplain, was the friend
and biographer of Cowley, an historian and founder member
of the Royal Society and, since 1680, a canon of Windsor. In
1683 he was made Dean of Westminster and the following year
Bishop of Rochester. Aphra Behn refers directly to his afternoon's preaching when he was 'above the thanks of the mad
senate-house' and calls him a 'noble ornament of the sacred
gown'.

She wasn't, then, setting up for an atheist. Inevitably she
turns next to praise Rochester, Strephon the great, 'for whom
the muses mourn – the cupids flag their wings'. Had Wadham

never produced any other poet it would have been enough but
now

> Daphnis rises like the morning star
> That guides the wandering traveller from afar.

She is 'the wandering traveller' herself, needing his guidance
since Rochester's death. In return he called her 'Love's great
Sultana'.

Two events of 1682, however, threatened her livelihood just
when she seemed at the height of her success. The first was the
merging of the two theatrical companies into one. This took
place in May under the management of Betterton and Smith.
The first result was that the number of new plays produced
dropped drastically. Betterton preferred to stage old plays and
the combined total of new works fell below that for a single
company before the union. His preference may have been based
on economy or on the number of problems of censorship that
had arisen during the hottest part of the political conflict.

Nathaniel Lee's *The Duke of Guise* was banned on July 15th
when the Duke of Monmouth complained that it vilified him,
and 'though his Majesty's pleasure is to be dissatisfied and angry
with the Duke of Monmouth, yet he is not willing that others
should abuse him out of a natural affection for him'.[5] Unfortunately the warning didn't reach Aphra Behn in time to
modify the prologue and epilogue she had written to an anonymous play called *Romulus and Hersilia* which was produced on
August 10th. Two days later the Lord Chamberlain ordered
her arrest together with the actress who had played Tarpeia
and in that character spoken the epilogue, Mary Lee, now Lady
Slingsby.

Once again Monmouth was involved. But the arrest seems to
me an accumulation of Whig rage rather than for this particular
offence. The Lord Chamberlain's warrant runs:

> Whereas the Lady Slingsby comedian and Mrs Aphaw
> Behen have by writing and acting at his Royal Highness
> Theatre committed several misdemeanours and made
> abusive reflections upon persons of quality, and have
> written and spoken scandalous speeches without any
> license or approbation of those that ought to peruse and
> authorize the same, these are therefore to require you to

take into your custody the said Lady Slingsby and Mrs Aphaw Behen and bring them before me to answer the said offence, and for so doing this shall be your sufficient warrant. Given under my hand and seal this 12th day of August 1682. To Henry Leggatt Messenger of His Majesty's Chamber etc.

The warrant was reported in the *True Protestant Mercury* and in the *Newdigate newsletters*. Unfortunately there's no record of what happened. This suggests that they got away fairly lightly and there are two other reasons for thinking so. The Lord Chamberlain was none other than Lord Arlington who, of course, owed Aphra Behn a favour, and she had further compounded this by her dedication to the Duke of Grafton, since he was married to 'a princess of such indisputable charming beauty, as if Heaven, designing to take a peculiar care in all that concerns your happiness, had form'd her on purpose to complete it': Arlington's daughter.

The prologue and epilogue had been printed before the première so the opposition had had plenty of time to prepare itself and indeed to stop the epilogue being performed. It looks as if the idea of having them taken into custody came later and indeed the words complained of sound far less offensive than many others. Tarpeia says:

> And of all treasons, mine was most accurst
> Rebelling 'gainst a King and father first ...
> 'A pox of fathers, and reproach to come
> She was the first and noblest Whig of Rome.'

The complaint was against 'speeches' in the plural but presumably, since Charlotte Butler who spoke the prologue wasn't arrested, that wasn't included although it's good swinging stuff, calling the Whigs rats and weasels that gnaw the lion's beard and then hide behind packed juries.

Whether it was coincidence or not, or whether it owed more to the union of the companies than to their arrest, the facts are that Aphra Behn produced no more work for the theatre until her prologue to Rochester's *Valentinian* in February 1684, and Lady Slingsby was soon to retire from the theatre completely.[6]

There is a possibility that Aphra Behn was involved in yet

another theatrical work in this year which was probably performed at court. The suggestion is very tentative but I put
forward the idea that she may be the anonymous author in part
if not of all of the libretto to John Blow's opera *Venus and
Adonis* whose manuscript is dated 1682. In Charles Gildon's
Miscellany of 1692 there's a piece of dialogue between Venus
and Cupid that's obviously intended to be set to music and is
very much in the style of the exchanges between Venus and
Cupid in the opera. Perhaps it was a discarded section or a first
draft. It wouldn't be the only time Blow had set her words to
music since he was responsible for the music to 'O love that
stronger art than wine' in *The Lucky Chance* in 1686. Nor would
it be the only time she had written for 'an entertainment at
court' since she has two such pastoral dialogues, one in *Poems
on Several Occasions* and the other in her *Miscellany* of the following
year, both presumably meant to be sung like the pastoral
dialogue in the masque from *Dioclesian* set by Purcell.

Many of the songs from her plays were published in the
contemporary collections of 'choice' songs and airs which were
so popular. Nothing is known of her relationship with any of
the composers, who seem to have included everyone, except the
greatest, Henry Purcell, whose only known setting of her work
was after her death. But her friendship with Daniel Kendrick
may have come about through music and through him, as I've
said, she probably knew the Purcells.[7]

If the libretto of *Venus and Adonis* isn't by her, then it can
truly be described as 'school of':

> She who those soft hours misuses
> And a begging swain refuses
> When she would the time recover
> May she have a feeble lover.

XXIII

Love Letters

At the end of 1682 Shaftesbury, realizing that his life might be in danger in the changed political climate, fled overseas to Holland, only to die in his bed in the new year. At the same time Dryden's patron and friend John Sheffield, Earl of Mulgrave, was deprived of his offices and forbidden the court for renewing his suit to the Duke of York's second daughter Princess Anne.

The princess was now seventeen, Sheffield thirty-four. The year before proposals had been made for her marriage to Prince George of Hanover but these had fallen through. Sheffield seems to have been in love with her for some years[1] and the Duke was probably afraid that she would begin to respond if left unmarried and approachable.

Rochester had hated Sheffield and there had been a long feud between them. What now happened would, I believe, have been impossible while Rochester was still alive. Sheffield commissioned Aphra Behn to write a poem of vindication and pleading, as from himself to Anne. It appears in the original *Poems on Affairs of State* entitled 'Bajazet to Gloriana'. There's no mistaking her style in this and indeed it was recognized and attributed to her by the author of *The Female Laureat* who, as I've suggested above, was almost certainly Robert Gould.

The title of Gould's riposte to the Bajazet poem is a reflection of the relationship between Sheffield and Dryden as well as of her own standing at this time. It comments on Sheffield's abortive visit to Tangier when he was what Rochester described as a 'Tangier bully'. But the real invective is kept for Aphra Behn herself and her work, in particular *The Golden Age* and

The City Heiress. Gould calls *The Golden Age* 'so fam'd a piece/It has at once outdone both Rome and Greece' and satirizes its permissiveness. Then he suggests that if Anne won't have Sheffield he should have Aphra Behn and describes this happy pair 'He kind as lovely, you as good as fair'. Finally he describes her plays, saying her heroes are 'sworn foes to sense' and 'affect bombast, noise and insolence', her loyal men are 'lewd and vain,/Ridiculous, impertinent, profane' and her virtuous women hate virtue while her virgins 'curse their virginity'.

All this was only to be expected and, although it no doubt hurt her, as criticism always does, she can't have been surprised. What is particularly interesting to consider is why Sheffield got her to write the poem rather than Dryden. Perhaps it was her reputation for handling the theme of love. Perhaps Dryden refused the job. Did Sheffield send Anne a copy of the poem? Was it printed or merely circulated in manuscript? What indeed did the court think of what could be described as her interference in this affair so soon after her arrest? Once again she was hitting at Monmouth, for Bajazet in the poem asks what's so wrong about aspiring to be a King by love and marriage when others aspire with their 'vain pretensions' and there are several lines about Monmouth's mixed parentage, a favourite stamping ground of the Tory writers who claimed another father for him than Charles II as Aphra Behn was to do again in her verse letter to Creech.

It's possible she wrote the poem partly to have her own back on those who had had her arrested. In any case it further supports her claim to be a writer of popular satire. There is of course a possibility that she wrote the poem not on Sheffield's commission but with her tongue in her cheek and I have looked at the lines from this point of view. But against this it has to be said that Gould or whoever was the author of *The Female Laureat* didn't think so.

The changed conditions at the theatre must soon have made it clear to her that it was going to be increasingly difficult for her to make a living and she probably undertook this commission mainly for the money, though the concept of the slave being raised to equality by love certainly appealed to her. It could only have brought her a small sum and she must have looked round rather desperately to see where more was to come from. Neville Payne could perhaps have lent her something, for he was still in good favour with his friend Sir Ellis Leighton and visiting him in his lodgings in Whitehall, which suggests that Payne himself was flourishing.

Prior in his harsh lines on her as a translator, which date from after the union of the companies, had also referred to the 'ruin of her face'.[2] She was forty-two and in the seventeenth century that was an age for a woman when it was hard for her to trade on her physical charms any longer. She could only write for a living, but what? She was an avid reader of the *London Gazette* and her eye was no doubt caught by an advertisement late in September 1682. 'Whereas the Lady Henrietta Berkeley has been absent from her father's house since 20th August last past and is not known where she is nor whether she is alive or dead', a reward of £200 is offered to anyone who will bring her back to her father. She is 'a young lady of a fair complexion, fair haired, full breasted and indifferent tall.' This is Sylvia, the anti-heroine of *Love Letters Between a Nobleman and His Sister*. The advertisement was run twice more in the following weeks but leaving out 'full breasted' which had probably caused a lot of ribald comment. The *London Gazette* continued the story on October 3rd. 'Whereas in Benskin's *Domestic Intelligence* published on Monday 2nd it is said that the Lady Henrietta Berkeley hath in a letter to her father given an account of her departure and that she is married etc. It is thought fit to give notice that this is a false report and in all probability spread on purpose to hinder the discovery of her ...'

In fact it was impossible for her to be married to the man she had eloped with because he was already married to her sister. He was Forde Grey, Lord Grey of Werke, who appears in Aphra Behn's novel as Philander. The idea of using these real-life people in a novel was undoubtedly founded on *Hattigé* which I mentioned earlier, the epistolary novel by Bremond based on Charles II. As well as Lord Grey and his 'miss', as reports in the state papers frequently call her, *Love Letters Between a Nobleman and His Sister* also has a character called Cesario who is Monmouth and an Octavio whom I identify as Mynheer Hermanus de Bressaw. Robert Ferguson, Monmouth's Scottish plotter, is easily recognizable as Fergusano, Hermione is Lady Wentworth, Monmouth's mistress, and so on. With patience all the characters can be identified and the plot follows their move-ments including a fake marriage to a man called Turner by Sylvia/Henrietta which is recorded in the state papers. The novel was published in three parts over a period of four years. When she began she can't have known the ending. Dryden had been in a similar position with *Absalom and Achitophel* and in his preface had said that he preferred to leave an open end. *Love Letters Between a Nobleman and His Sister* is Aphra Behn's *Absalom and Achitophel* but for some reason critics, perhaps daunted by its length of over 200,000 words, have been slow to see this.

The first part takes the story up to the end of June 1683. The book appears in the Stationers' Register on October 26th. Either she had written some 70,000 words in about three months, which isn't impossible, or she was writing it as events developed. From the dedication to the second part it's clear that she intended to continue with the story. Meanwhile she had stopped it with Philander/Grey's escape from the coach that was carrying him to the Tower.

In the novel it's the Bastille that he's being carried to, for the fiction is that Sylvia, Philander and the others are French and the setting is, at first, France. The dedication of the first part keeps up this fiction. The anonymous author claims that 'having when I was at Paris last Spring met with a little book of letters called *L'intrigue de Philander et Sylvia*' he has Englished it because of its similarity to recent events. The dedication is to Thomas Condon about whom I've been able to find out very little, except that later he appears as a Captain in Ferdinando Hastings's regiment. He was obviously a royalist and a devotee of James, who ordered him to stand for Parliament after Charles II's death when James was trying to pack a Parliament in his favour. He may have been a Roman Catholic.

Presumably he was in Aphra Behn's own little plot and had agreed to it. Meanwhile the real Rye House Plot had been dis-covered, a plot to murder the royal brothers at Newmarket the year before, when *Like Father, Like Son* was failing for lack of a London court. Several people had been sent to the Tower, including Lord Russell and Algernon Sydney. A warrant was out for Monmouth's arrest. Grey, as I've said, escaped on his way to the Tower and fled overseas to Holland where his sister-in-law, Lady Berkeley, joined him.

Woven round these events are the erotic happenings that made the novel run into at least sixteen editions by the end of the eighteenth century. Some of these must also have an historic element since the couples concerned were lovers, the elopement did take place and so did the seduction by Grey of his sister-in-law for which he was tried and found guilty on November 23rd 1682.[3]

It's hard to guess how much the publisher Joseph Hindmarsh paid her for the first part. In the same year she decided to publish her first play *The Young King* and dedicated it to 'Philaster', who must be the 'Philly' of the letter to Lycidas. In February an adaptation of Fletcher's *Philaster* was put on. The prologue and epilogue were by Buckingham. The main body of the play may have been too. In the preface to the 1711 edition of Buckingham's works it's said that Buckingham spent some time altering the play and took it with him when he retired to Yorkshire in 1686. Significantly it concludes: 'I am very well informed it was since the Revolution in the hands of Mr Nevil Payne.' I believe that Aphra Behn's Philaster is Buckingham.

'Wit, good nature and beauty at first approach she found in Philaster,' she says in the dedication, speaking of her 'virginmuse', and 'since she knew she could not appear upon the too critical English stage without making choice of some noble patronage, she waited long, look'd round the judging world, and fix't on you'.

This dedication raises all sorts of problems for the biographer. If, as she implies, *The Young King* was Aphra Behn's first play and begun at Surinam, why wasn't it performed before 1679, let alone published before 1683? I can only suggest a hypothesis: that she was worried that it wasn't good enough and therefore kept it back, and this is the waiting long, and that she intended to dedicate it to Buckingham and the dedication was indeed written but that his identification with the Whig cause made this impossible. Now, however, he had abandoned the Whigs and was back with the theatre after his long involvement with politics, and, by 1685 certainly, a friend of Neville Payne.[4] He wasn't involved in the latest plot and there was no warrant for his arrest. His play *The Chances* was produced again in late 1682.

The publication of *The Young King* could also mean a performance this year, and so could a reference in the Stationers' Register on June 27th to a song, 'as it is sung at the Duke's theatre, The Faithless Lover or Amintas' Complaint'. This sounds very like the song[5] in *The Forc'd Marriage*, her first performed play. Perhaps, as well as the plays of the previous generation, Betterton was reviving earlier ones by contemporary playwrights. No play is recorded for June so a production of *The Forc'd Marriage* would fit in very well.

Aphra Behn's dedication to Philaster is 'unpermitted'. It implies that, as seems likely from all the other evidence, he too with Rochester helped her to make her debut. She speaks of his kind and generous nature and of his wit, the quality she was to celebrate in her elegy for him. If they had been estranged by politics this dedication should have brought them together again, which makes more sense of the elegy than if it was written in a vacuum.

I'm inclined to think that *Love Letters*, Part One was her first sustained piece of prose writing. It was a field she was to make particularly her own, where the great shadow of Dryden didn't already lie although his critical essays in prose are magnificent pieces in themselves. For some reason, presumably mere tidiness, it's generally supposed that the English novel 'began' in the eighteenth century; yet the developments in the novel after 1700 couldn't have taken place without the earlier prose writers and chief among them must be reckoned Aphra Behn. Among other things, she must be credited with the invention of the anti-hero, for that is what Sylvia and Philander are. The hero of *Love Letters* is Octavio and the heroine Calista who is destroyed by Philander.

This isn't the place to embark on a lengthy history of the novel form in English but Richardson's work, in particular *Clarissa*, must be seen in its historical context as a puritan and middle-class reply to the enormous popularity of *Love Letters Between a Nobleman and His Sister*, even in its use of the same epistolary method. I believe the name of Aphra Behn's virtuous heroine Calista, who retires to a convent in the end, is reflected in Richardson's choice of name for his heroine: Clarissa. It's curious that Richardson's rape fantasy has been thought somehow more real than Aphra Behn's much more clear-eyed presentation which is largely based on fact. Perhaps it's because, as is often the way of the world, Philander and Sylvia survive.

There are several prose pieces among her posthumous works which are difficult to date accurately, but one or two can be dated before the death of Charles II in 1685 by the nature of their references to him. These are two short stories called *The Court of the King of Bantam* and *The Unfortunate Happy Lady*. Neither, I think, comes before *Love Letters* but my reason for this is only the tricky matter of judging by style. *Love Letters Between a Nobleman and His Sister* seems to me much closer to poetry and to romance in its verbal handling, whereas the other two are unmistakably prose. A note to the posthumous 1698 edition which contains *The Court of the King of Bantam* says that if the reader thinks this is unlike her usual style it's because it was written for a bet about whether she could write in the style of Scarron, which is heavily facetious.

The story is supposed to take place at Christmas 1682 and was written between then and February 1685. The ambassador from the real King of Bantam had been in England in 1682 and had gone several times to the theatre, and Ravenscroft's *The London Cuckolds* was being performed about Christmas time as it says in the story. It's very good for an account of a semi-fashionable seventeenth-century Christmas with roasting oranges, cards, Christmas games and the Twelfth Night revels of choosing the mock king and queen by who gets the bean and pea when the cake is cut. There's a very real sense in which it can be said to be a forerunner of Thackeray's and Dickens's Christmas stories in its tone and atmosphere even though the subject it deals with is the more adult one of marriage and money: Mr Would-be King is tricked out of £3,000 to provide a dowry for Philibella so that she can marry Goodland. It must have been a valuable exercise in developing her prose style but Aphra Behn didn't intend to publish it although she kept it and presumably circulated it among friends. During the next four years she developed her prose talent by translation, short stories and two more parts of *Love Letters*, until it reached the perfect instrument of *The Fair Jilt* and *Oroonoko*.

Meanwhile she kept up her end in the satirical struggle. Once again none of the satires that appeared in 1683 has been attributed to her but a reference in the poem to Thomas

Creech written early in 1664[6] makes it indisputable that she continued to write propaganda for the court and to be paid for it. My suggestions are only tentative as before, but poems that could be hers are 'Shaftesbury's Farewell', which apart from its form contains references which appear in other works of hers, 'The Elegy on The Earl of Essex' and 'Algernon Sydney's Farewell'. This isn't the place to argue the pros and cons of an attribution to Aphra Behn of these particular poems but if they aren't hers they nevertheless give a good idea of the sort of thing she must have been writing. All three are slightly equivocal in their approach, not merely pieces of ranting polemic as many of the others are.

There's an interesting note about how these verses were distributed, in cases where they weren't printed, that's attached to one called *A New Ballad*.

> Momentum. I had this ballad of a bookseller at the Miter in Fleet Street next the Devil Tavern (whose name I know not) on Friday afternoon 6th June 1684, and returned it to him again next morning by my coachman, sealed up under a covert, wherein was written: 7th June 1684. I here enclosed return you the paper I had yesterday from you, which I do not think on second reading to be so witty as I thought it at first: and in some places I can't make sense of it.

He had nevertheless copied it without payment either to author or bookseller.

At the same time as she was writing political verse she must have been gathering her own poems together for her first collection and translating *A Voyage to The Island of Love*. She was still feeling the effects of the union of the theatre companies and was desperately short of money. One of her rare letters belongs to the end of 1683 when she was bargaining with Jacob Tonson, the publisher, for more money for this book. Dryden's own struggles with Tonson are an interesting comment on this letter of Aphra Behn's.[7]

Dear Mr Tonson
   I am mightily obliged to you for the service you have done me to Mr Dryden; in whose esteem I would choose

to be rather than anybody's in the world; and I am sure I never, in thought, word, or deed meritted other from him, but if you had heard what was told me, you would have excused all I said on that account. Thank him most infinitely for the honour he offers, and I shall never think I can do anything that can merit so vast a glory; and I must owe it all to you if I have it. As for Mr Creech, I would not have you afflict him with a thing cannot now be helped so never let him know my resentment. I am troubled for the line that's left out of Dr Garth, and wish your man would write it in the margin, at his leisure, to all you sell.

As for the verses of mine, I should really have thought 'em worth thirty pound; and I hope you will find it worth £25; not that I should dispute at any other time for 5 pound where I am so obliged; but you cannot think what a pretty thing the Island will be, and what a deal of labour I shall have yet with it: and if that pleases, I will do the second voyage, which will compose a little book as big as a novel by itself. But pray speak to your brother to advance the price to one £5 more, 'twill at this time be more than given me, and I vow I would not ask it if I did not really believe it worth more. Alas I would not lose my time in such low gettings, but only since I am about it I am resolved to go through with it though I should give it. I pray go about it as soon as you please, for I shall finish as fast as you can go on. Methinks the Voyage should come last, as being the largest volume. You know Mr Cowley's David is last, because a large poem, and Mrs Philips her plays for the same reason. I wish I had more time, I would add something to the verses that I have a mind to, but, good dear Mr Tonson, let it be £5 more, for I may safely swear I have lost the getting of £50 by it, though that's nothing to you, or my satisfaction and humour: but I have been without getting so long that I am just on the point of breaking, especial since a body has no credit at the Playhouse for money as we used to have, fifty or 60 deep or more; I want extremely or I would not urge this.

Yours A.B.

Pray send me the loose papers to these I have, and let me

know which you will go about first, the songs and verses or that. Send me an answer today.

This letter is so stuffed with intriguing detail that it's all the more frustrating that so few of her letters are extant. In the first place there's the part about her relations with Dryden. Some gossip has told her something that Dryden has said or is supposed to have said about her or her work. Tonson is acting as mediator and Dryden has promised, what? The likeliest is either some commendatory verses to preface the volume or a poem of his own for inclusion or a recommendation to someone influential. She reaffirms her admiration for Dryden. It sounds as if someone had told Dryden first that she had said something about him, he had reacted and his reaction has been reported to her. Tiffs among the poets were frequent. In a small society there were always people delighted to stir things up. It could be, however, that Dryden was put out that she had written the poem for his patron Mulgrave and had made some disparaging remarks about the lines. Tonson has healed whatever breach there was.

Is there any poem among the several commendatory verses at the beginning of her *Poems on Several Occasions* that could be ascribed to Dryden? I believe there is. It's entitled 'Upon these and other Excellent Works of the Incomparable Astrea', and it's quite the best of the set, with Thomas Creech's next. The form of the poem is that of Dryden's homage to another woman artist, poet and painter, who died in 1685, Anne Killegrew, Thomas Killegrew's niece. The opening two lines are very similar in form indeed; the same length and the same invocation. 'Ye bold magicians in philosophy', the poem to Astrea begins, and that to Anne Killegrew, 'Thou youngest virgin daughter of the skies'. No one else, I think, could have handled the ode so masterfully or sustained it so well. There are three precise poetic references in the poem and all are connected with Dryden. The poet praises at length Aphra Behn's translation of *Oenone*, which was done for Dryden's book, he also speaks of her lines in praise of Creech, in which, according to Antony Wood, Dryden joined, and there's a specific reference to *Absalom and Achitophel*.

Whoever the poet is, his praise is unstinting and precise.[8] He rebuts the suggestion that she is helped to write by anyone. He speaks too of her faded beauty and her inevitable death in a last magnificent stanza giving her immortality in her work:

> When towns inter'd in their own ashes lie,
> And chronicles of Empires die,
> When monuments like men want tombs to tell
> Where the remains of the vast ruins fell.

It's hard to see what she objected to in Creech's poem unless it is that it concentrates on her as a love poet, emphasizing the erotic almost to the point of making it pornographic or as if she were merely supplying a kind of delicate literary voyeurism:

> In the same trance with the young pair we lie,
> And in their amorous ecstasies we die.
> She poisons all the flood with such an art,
> That the dear philter trickles to the heart ...

This was no doubt what many people read her for but she must have grown very tired of being told what a good writer of erotica she was and how that was a special female gift. Creech's praise may have been too close to the picture of her work and person presented by the lampoonists. If this was her objection to Creech's poem, the poem was written and was 'a thing cannot now be helped'. In its way it's a small erotic masterpiece itself. Creech is said by Giles Jacob in his *Poetical Register* to have been of a 'morose temper' and easily offended, which also accounts for the bit in Aphra Behn's letter about never letting him know her resentment.

The letter and poems can be dated roughly together by a poem by John Cooper in the set of commendatory verses which has November 25th 1683 affixed to it by its author.[9] As well as writing the other translation of the epistle of *Oenone*, he was a contributor to Dryden's *Miscellany*, together with John Adams who also supplies some lines in praise of this collection. Adams, like Henry Crispe, Thomas Culpepper's kinsman, was a fellow of King's College, Cambridge. He too had complimented Thomas Creech. The poets were almost incestuous in their intertwinings. The presence of Adams, Creech and Cooper makes Dryden's own presence even more likely.

She found a patron for her volume in the new Earl of

Salisbury, James Cecil, a distant relation of Sir Thomas Gower. Cecil's father's death in 1683 had given him the earldom. The old earl had supported the Whigs and she refers to this in her dedication. The young one she praises for his loyalty maintained even against the influence of his father. The dedication also has one interesting lie. She refers to her book as 'this little piece, which lazy minutes begot and hard fate has oblig'd me to bring forth into the censuring world'. Unless she means only the poems and is excluding *A Voyage to the Island of Love* this statement is clearly untrue since she had told Tonson that the translation would take a 'deal of labour ... yet'. This is a theme she was to pursue increasingly and I shall come back to it later. It put her close to the gentlemen writers.

The satirists of course immediately suggested she must be bedding with the Earl of Salisbury, particularly since it was an isle of love she had dedicated to him. She had described it to Tonson as 'a pretty thing' and so it is. But it's much more than that and here Creech's evocation of her work is so true. This, and the sequel which she had promised Tonson in her letter if the first pleased, but which wasn't published until three years later under the title of *Lycidus or The Lover in Fashion*, are both explorations of the psychology of love, the voyage to and the inevitable, it seemed, return from Cythera that Watteau re-created for the next generation in exquisite painting,[10] that Baudelaire was to return to and find the pleasure garden all despoiled. Aphra Behn greatly expanded the original, adding among other things the consummation and the death of Aminta which the original simply ascribes to 'le Destin qui enlever Amynta d'entre mes bras'. There's no suggestion that she is dead and indeed the ending is completely unexplained.

The French original was written by a literary priest, Paul Tallemant, and first published in 1663. In 1667 it was re-published in Cologne in *Le Recueil de pièces galantes*, which links it with the whole tradition of the galante in French art. The most recent edition before Aphra Behn's translation had been in Paris in 1675. In the dedication of the first part of *Love Letters Between a Nobleman and His Sister* the author had claimed to have been in France 'last Spring'. This may be sheerest fiction to support the idea of a French original or it may contain a grain of truth. It was certainly imaginatively true, since the translation of French works was to play an increasing part in her attempts to earn a living over the next few years.

The copyist of the manuscript book of *Satyrs and Lampoons* has glossed the lines on Aphra Behn and the Earl of Salisbury: 'Mrs Aphra Behn a poetess writ several fine plays and volumes of poetry. James Earl of Salisbury to whom she dedicated her fine book called the Island of Love'.[11] The gloss rejects the criticism of the lines but once again no doubt she was glad to be included in the satirical catalogue of poets, all the rest of whom are men. It was a kind of laureateship in itself.

XXIV

James II

The great frost which closed that year and went on until February 1684 has become part of our history. Everyone knows that there were frost fairs on the frozen Thames which included an ox-roasting, puppet plays and coach and horse races. Thomas Creech came up from Oxford to London for Christmas bringing a friend and they were all merry together for Twelfth Night just like in the story *The King of Bantam*. Aphra Behn was to meet him again before he went back at Tonson's bookshop and had promised him a billet doux the last time they had met. She set out by coach with it in her pocket, going first to Whitehall to dun the King,

> Who oft in debt is truth to tell
> For Tory farce and doggerell.

The streets were full of ice and slush, which must mean that the thaw had just begun, and her coachman, driving too fast, over-turned the coach. She wasn't badly hurt but bruised and her writing wrist was sprained. She was forced to go home instead of going on to meet Creech and introducing him to John Hoyle. She was deeply disappointed but asks his forgiveness. The bio-grapher can only be grateful for the accident since in the verse letter she wrote explaining there are some of the most intimate glimpses of her.

She makes a joke of the accident and herself saying she looked like 'brawn in sowsing drink'. Presumably as well as being bruised she was soaked in freezing and filthy water. Regulations had been issued by Act of Parliament for cleaning the streets of Westminster but the accident had happened near the Temple outside the tavern called the Scarlet Whore. Coach accidents, which were quite common, could be fatal and even the royal coach wasn't immune.

She has written the letter because she doesn't want Creech to think she had merely forgotten, since the last time they had met they had been drinking wine and she had been in that state of mild drunkenness where you feel wittier and wittier after every glass. Tories drank alcohol; Whigs drank coffee. Oldys in a manuscript note says that John Bowman, an old actor who had joined the Duke's Company as a boy in 1673, told him that Aphra Behn was the first person he knew or heard of to make milk punch. This might encourage the idea that she was a great drinker but I think that would be untrue. She drank beer and wine as everyone did in the days when breakfast was beer and bread. I doubt if she drank spirits, not at least in any quantity or unless heavily diluted with something like milk.

I don't think she smoked and she ate very little, if any, meat. The basis for this is her endorsement of Thomas Tryon's regimen for healthy living by a controlled diet, without meat and spirits, which he expounded in a book called *The Way to Health, Long Life, and Happiness* published in 1682. Her poem in which she says she lives by his rules was written by 1685 when he prefixed it to *The Way to Make all People Rich* and she included it in her *Miscellany*.

The verse letter to Creech shows that she was still on very friendly terms with Hoyle in 1684, though, as I've said before, the passion seems to have gone from the relationship. He hadn't met Creech so he couldn't have been at their Twelfth Night revels. At the end of the letter in a postscript she praises Creech's friend and asks to be remembered to him. Unfortunately she gives no hint of his name, though he may be J. Barnes of Emmanuel College, Cambridge. Barnes in his verses calls him 'my Creech'. He is a loyalist as Aphra Behn describes the friend in her verse letter. Given that they were to meet John Hoyle, I wonder if there's some hint here that Creech too was bisexual.

Such a thought would have been in her mind for she had just written the prologue to the first day's performance of Rochester's *Valentinian* which was finished not later than February 11th when the play was done at court. Her prologue is written for the theatre, which means there must have been a performance before the court one which can't therefore have been the première. It also refers to the great fair on the ice. *Valentinian* makes an unequivocal plea for the pleasures of homosexuality and in Rochester's lines they become acceptable to her: 'eternal music dwelt upon his tongue'. Her praises of him here are some of her best and saddest.

It's hard to judge how long she took to finish *A Voyage to the Island of Love*. It's over two thousand lines long and has a seemingly endless variety of verse forms, narrative and lyric. It has to be read as the baroque version of *Le Roman de la Rose*. Creech had already seen part of it when he wrote his poem but not all, to judge not only by her letter to Tonson but also by the fact that Creech shows no knowledge of the sting in the end of the poem when Aminta dies and Lysander is left to grieve alone.

I can't help feeling that the emotional motivation which made her choose to translate or rather recreate this erotic work is somehow seated in her relationship with Hoyle. Once again she fiercely rejects the false concept of honour which in the poem prevents final physical consummation until love himself persuades Aminta to yield and the lovers go to the Spenserian Bower of Bliss where after a temporary impotence on Lysander's part they at last enjoy each other. After a short period of happiness, however, Aminta dies in Lysander's arms.

In real life of course the situation was reversed. It was Lysander who died to Astrea though remaining to physically outlive her. She was still sufficiently involved with him in 1685 to dedicate the second part of her *Miscellany*, *Seneca Unmasqu'd*, a translation from the French of La Rochefoucauld, to him as Lysander with a stinging preface that makes it clear that he is one with the Lycidas of the letters and Mr J. H. of the poems. She accuses him again of 'an abundance of gravity to the loss and destruction of many an honest hour which might have passed more gaily if you had pleased to lay by that (sometimes necessary) humour and that face of dull business'. She speaks of his 'grave silence and scarcity of speaking' that drives her to chatter too much and of his 'wise reproofs' of her which always have a contrary effect on 'the temper of a woman of my humour'. His virtue she believes is really only a form of self love, indeed self love is the basis for and runs through all human behaviour, even the temperance of the stoics. She signs herself 'your real

friend and servant' but clearly no relationship could survive
such public disagreement for long.

I don't know how she made her living in the rest of 1684.
The Earl of Salisbury's money might have been enough to see
her through but I doubt it. She probably wrote *The Unfortunate
Happy Lady* but since it doesn't seem to have been published it
can't have earned her anything. A performance of one of *The
Rovers* in January 1685 may have brought her something. She
should have been working on the second part of *Love Letters* and,
given the speed at which she wrote, she could have finished it
but she was 'oblig'd to lay it by for other material business'. She
intended to dedicate it to Lemuel Kingdon, who was now in
Ireland as commissioner of the revenue. She had sent him the
first part and, in return for the favours she had received from
him, she wanted 'to make an acknowledgement where I cannot
pay a debt.' What that 'material business' was I find it hard to
reconstruct. There was less need for Tory song and doggerel.
The nation was calmer.

What she could be referring to was the event which shattered
the whole nation at the beginning of February 1685, the sudden
death of Charles II, which plunged her into a flurry of public
verse, first an elegy for Charles, then a poem of sympathy for
Queen Catherine and finally the great coronation ode for James
and Mary. There were no fewer than seventy funeral poems
for the death of Charles, including Dryden's monumental
'Threnodia Augustalis'. The poems were sold as broadsheets or
bound up in books of elegies. Several of them were by friends of
Aphra Behn: Sir Francis Fane, who had been a friend of
Rochester and on whose play *The Sacrifice* she wrote a poem,
Nahum Tate and Edmund Arwaker, M.A., who contributed to
her *Miscellany*.

Augustus was dead but a good Tory had to help to ensure
that Caesar would succeed. There is a sense in which the two
poems on the death of Charles are practice pieces for her
pindaric on the coronation of James, which took place on
April 23rd. The poem to Queen Catherine is much more
successful than the elegy which is rather pedestrian. The idea
of the mourning queen has produced the image of the pietà
which is depicted like a piece of sculpture by Bernini. She was
evolving her own style for public verse, rich, formal and heavily

PINDARICK POEM
ON THE HAPPY
CORONATION
Of His most Sacred
MAJESTY
JAMES II.
AND
His Illustrious Confort
QUEEN MARY.

By Mrs. B E H N.

L O N D O N,
Printed by *J. Playford* for *Henry Playford,* near the
Temple-Church : 1685.

Figure 6   The Coronation Ode, printed as a pamphlet for quick sale.

pictorial. There was a long account of the coronation in the *London Gazette*, on which she could have based the poem. The whole ceremony was also eventually done in pictures, like a comic strip, by Francis Sandford. Aphra Behn realized that this was the greatest poetic task of her life and she deliberately summoned all her talents in the opening invocation.

Ever since Dr Johnson did his demolition job on the greatest of the English baroque writers, Dryden, and accused him of want of feeling, particularly in his elegy for Charles II, we have found it almost impossible to understand and appreciate this mode in English literature while admitting it in St Paul's Cathedral and, just, in Purcell's *Dido and Aeneas*. Aphra Behn's coronation pindaric is nearly a thousand lines long in the same unfashionable idiom. It is unashamedly baroque where *The Voyage to the Island of Love* was equally unashamedly rococo.

She sets a deliberately slow pace to the poem because she knows it has a long way to go. James is her muse's 'godlike patron'; Mary is Laura, after her mother and Petrarch. The poem proceeds by a series of pictures using all the baroque devices of cherubs on pillows of yielding air making celestial music, of streets thronged with courtiers, the royal pair bedded like Mars and Venus; James driving the sun god's chariot and Mary arrayed for the ceremony.

This particular section I think influenced Pope in the dressing of Belinda in *The Rape of the Lock*.[1]

> And now the nymphs ply all their female arts
> To dress her for her victory of hearts;
>   A thousand little loves descend!
> Young waiting cupids with officious care
>   In smiling order all attend;
> This decks her snowy neck, and that her ebon hair.
> The Trophies which the conqueress must adorn,
>   Are by the busy wantons born;
> Who at her feet the shining burdens lay,
>   The goddess pleased to see their toils,
> Scatters ten thousand graces from her smiles;
> While the wing'd boys catch ev'ry flying ray.
> This bears the valu'd treasure of the East,
> And hugs the golden casket on his breast;

Another's little hand sustains
The weight of oriental chains;
And in the flowing jetty curls
They weave and braid the lucid pearls;

At this point she voices a complaint that she was beginning to feel more strongly: her own exclusion from the court, her 'silent dull obscurity' that sets her at distance. She speaks of it as a 'scanted bliss' and says her stars destined her for 'the humblest portion'. It was a thought that was to grow on her in the next years and returns in a different form in the preface to *Seneca Unmasqu'd* when she praises the ease and naturalness of the gentleman writers by contrast with the 'trading poets'. She was tired and a little envious.

The next picture is of the journey by royal barge with James as Neptune while the sullen seagods 'Dress their blue locks and flounce along the sea', and then of the landing at Westminster with the shouting crowds. Again Aphra Behn breaks off for a personal comment of sadness and exclusion at her own 'toil for life all day'. I can only conclude that she hoped by these lines to get something in the way of an official appointment or pension.

Next comes the procession with the emblems of state, the Duchess of Norfolk carrying the train, Dorset, the 'Lord of Hearts' and the King, followed by other lords, among them Grafton, her sometime patron, and Henry Howard, 'Maecena of my muse, my patron lord.' The next picture is a kind of living apotheosis of the throned pair with bishops and angels and the poem ends with a pair of separate but matching portraits: Mary, doubly endowed from a line of poets and kings, and James, an equestrian portrait like that of his father by Van Dyck.

It is a magnificent achievement, superb propaganda, and a televisual recreation of the sumptuous occasion for those who couldn't be there. James should have been enormously grateful for it. No doubt he paid her something but there's no evidence to suggest that it was much. A few months later she was back 'to starve more securely in my own native province of poetry'. One of her admirers, in a poem about the coronation pindaric, suggested that James should reward her with a house in the country:

Not with a short applause of crackling bays
But a return that may revive thy days ...
Mayst thou be blest with such a sweet retreat,
That with contempt thou mayst behold the great;
Such as the mighty Cowley's well known seat.

I think Aphra Behn deliberately included these not very good
verses in her volume of 1687, *Lycidus*, as a gentle hint. Princes,
however, are notoriously bad at rewards and she had besides
one great thing in her disfavour, her religion.

The temptation to change, for someone who relied so heavily
on court patronage, must have been very strong. Instead,
characteristically, she produced a paraphrase of the Lord's
Prayer. It gave her a chance to set out her religious position,
which is as rational as a pre-Freudian age could allow. Many
people will find it disappointing for exactly this reason. Sin and
guilt are so much more exciting to the romantically minded
than reason. If God is a father there's no need to fear, she says.
If he is holy, wise and just we should obviously submit to his
will. Her one sin has been through love and she is sure God will
forgive that of all sins because love is the earthly thing that most
resembles heaven. She has looked in vain for any enemy 'whom
with the least revenge I would pursue'. Forgiveness is a 'grateful, little charity'. Once again she repeats her plea for love 'if
without some sin we cannot move'. Finally she lists the evils she
would be delivered from, ending with a plea for guidance and
against 'blind' guides who might mislead her. The influence of
Hooker is strong. Her religion is rational, unsuperstitious and
not at all guilt-ridden. She was a very unlikely candidate for
Roman Catholicism except as a piece of self-interest which she
would have recognized as such and despised.

This paraphrase is in her *Miscellany* of 1685 and as if to
underline it there's only one poem in direct praise of her, except
for a reprint of some old lines by Edward Howard. The poem
in praise is, I believe, by Henry Crispe, who had just taken up
the living of Catton, in Yorkshire, and was among 'clod pate
souls who talk of sheep'. England has a nobler task for her
which is to subdue 'the brute Whigs' but, in case this should
seem too partisan the other way, the 'fond Catholicks' also come
in for their share of stick: 'no other saint shall know the winged

passions of our souls' but Astrea, 'while we are bards or lovers militant'. She is identified with the Anglican and rationalist cause by this poem, and this would have seriously affected her chances of royal favour. Burnet had gone abroad just after James's accession; Dryden became a Catholic. These were the extremes. Her upbringing shows again in her middle way in religion, in her support for the established church, partly because it was established but also because it laid fewer psychological burdens on the individual than the other versions of Christianity open to her.

No doubt too she had been influenced by John Hoyle's more radical position as an atheist and by her discussions with Buckingham and the pre-conversion Rochester. Her patron Henry Howard had even greater problems. On one occasion he declined to carry the sword of state before James into his Catholic chapel but waited at the door. 'Your father', said James referring to the Catholic Duke of Norfolk, Thomas Howard, 'would have gone farther,' to which Howard replied, 'Your Majesty's father was the better man and he would not have gone so far.'

Dryden's conversion seems to have been real, not mere expediency. Inevitably it provoked a great number of verses, on Mr Dryden renegate, among which is a set attributed to Aphra Behn. I don't believe they are hers. It was against her nature to produce such a thing but I think Dryden may have thought, if only for a time, that she had written them. They are skilful enough to be hers but since she continued to praise him in public, in *Seneca Unmasqu'd* and in the later *Aesop's Fables*, I don't think they are and in any case they are too personally bitter. *Seneca Unmasqu'd* has a positive encomium on Dryden which, though it was probably written before his conversion, would be very hard to deny even in retrospect.

The *Miscellany* is dedicated to Sir William Clifton, loyalist and friend of her friend Charles Cotton. Sir William had a large fortune and various proposals were made for his marriage. A satire says that all the London mamas trundled out their daughters when Sir William came to town. There had been proposals for him to marry into the family of the Duke of Newcastle which also came to nothing, and he eventually died unmarried. In spite of living mainly on his own estate in the county of Nottingham, he was also a literary patron and this, I think, is how Aphra Behn came to solicit him. At the same time he stirred in her some childhood remembrance. Her childhood was in any case, to judge by various small indications, close to the surface of her consciousness at this time. She praises him specifically for his English virtues against 'the follies ... we import from France'. These virtues are hospitality and treating the 'underworld about you', instead of pulling down his great hall, retrenching his servants and confining himself to scanty lodgings in the city while starving the poor of his parish and racking his tenants 'to keep the tawdry jilt in town a hundred times more expensive'.

There speaks, or rather writes, the Kentish gentleman of 1640. The good landowner is the monarch of his own county-country, instructing his peasantry who will otherwise run wild like brutes. All will be well if only everyone will be quiet and respect his superiors, she says, who had no respect for anyone when she had decided not to respect them. She, who was so brave and clear-sighted when it came to religion, morals and what we should now call women's lib, was in politics the kind of high Tory that Disraeli would have been in total agreement with. There are psychological reasons for this. Everything she says about fathers leads me to deduce a great fondness and respect of her own. This was reinforced by her birth into and upbringing in a society which would kill its father-king, and by the tenets of her local Kentish society. At the same time, however much the forerunners of liberté, égalité, fraternité, are to be applauded, the horrors of violence and civil war must be admitted, especially when it becomes clear that the 'glorious revolution' led to the gradual descent into the miseries, repressions and exploitations of the nineteenth century. Aphra Behn couldn't possibly have foreseen where the pursuit of liberty and property would go but she knew it in her bones and in the criticism levelled at her.

The dedication to Sir William Clifton speaks of her borrowing poems from 'my friends' to make up the *Miscellany*, all of whom are agreed in their praise of him. The author list, then, gives us a good idea who her friends were at this time. The Earl of Dorset and Sir George Etherege represent the older wits, with a song by the dead Rochester whose ghost still presides over this collection. Anne Wharton is here with her poem 'The Despair', which Burnet had shown to several ladies one of whom had expressed herself sorry to see her 'quarrelling with her god'. Anne Wharton died in the year of this *Miscellany* but not until after it was published and her inclusion shows that she hadn't accepted Burnet's estimate of Aphra Behn. It may have been partly her influence that had caused Aphra Behn to write her paraphrase of the Lord's Prayer, since Anne Wharton had done one too, which Waller admired. There's a poem by Nahum Tate, 'Old England or New Advice to the Painter' which puts the case for the moderate position in politics and religion, and a send-up of the Dutch by Mr Neville, who must be Henry Neville Payne.

There are a great many poems by Henry Crispe. There are three poems by Mrs Taylor, some by J. W., who I think must be James Wright, a couple by R. A.[2] and one by Otway.

When she was dead, in the preface to the 1702 edition of her plays, the editor wrote: 'Those who had the happiness to be personally acquainted with her were so charmed with her wit, freedom of temper and agreeable conversation that they in a manner ador'd her,' and goes on to speak of 'her acquaintance and intimacy with the more sensible part of mankind and the love she drew from men of all ranks'. The list of friends in the *Miscellany* bears out part of this since it does include men if not of all ranks from several different spheres although united by their poetry.

There's also a poem by 'Mr J. H.' who may be Hoyle or may be the Honourable John Howard since her long poem in praise of him also appears in this collection. It gives her a chance to recall her Antwerp days and to lament Stafford again. I think by now she was lying about her age since she says that her Antwerp commission, at Charles II's command, was 'unsuited to my age'. Yet she had been about twenty-six, by no means a child.[3] She praises Howard's lack of court ambition. He had bought himself a house, Hawley Hall in Kent, so in a very real sense he had joined the shepherds. But the shepherds here are the poets as distinct from courtiers and politicians. The 'rural sports' are love and literature, a more 'solid happiness' than jockeying for position or scheming for place.

Howard had translated the Camilla episode from Virgil in

Dryden's miscellany, *Sylvae*, Part Two, as well as other pieces by Virgil and Horace. Camilla is one of the heroic fighting women and typically Aphra Behn picks on this one of his translations to praise him for, since he has shown how to be 'at once hero and woman too'. Earlier in the poem she has lamented the fickle ravishers among men who deceive and seduce one woman after the other, leaving each in turn soiled and made miserable. Howard suggests how women, while remaining themselves, can become more heroic and, by implication, less vulnerable and dependent. He is the first who has made 'fighting in our sex a charm'. In this he has outdone Creech and even Dryden's 'mighty self'. Perhaps she had fallen out with Creech at this date. He published two translations in 1684, of Horace and Theocritus, which perhaps absorbed all his poetic time but it's, I think, significant that he has nothing in this *Miscellany*.

Finally in the *Miscellany* there are six poems by Mr T.B. and from the inclusion of one of them 'On Flowers in a Lady's Bosom' in his complete works he can be identified as the young Tom Brown. Among his collected poems there is also one to Creech on his *Lucretius*. The inclusion of so many poems of his in her *Miscellany* shows that at this time she thought of him as a friend and was moreover helping him to establish himself as a literary figure and to earn some money by writing which he was badly in need of when he first came to London from the university of Oxford. It makes his later treatment of her in *Letters from the Dead to the Living*, when she was dead and could no longer defend herself, all the more unpleasant. He alleges there, using Anne Bracegirdle as a mouthpiece, that Aphra Behn lured young men straight from the university to her bed when they came poet-struck to her door. There would be no great harm in this *Chérie*-like situation if it were true but although she enjoyed the company of young men and women there's no evidence at all that she went to bed with them. Tom Brown was simply making money by using her for quasi-pornography. His early biographer says that what made his reputation was his series of poems on Dryden's conversion.

Aphra Behn had been at work on the second part of *Love Letters* but her dedication to Lemuel Kingdon, who had come back from Ireland to stand as M.P. for Bedwyn in James's first Parliament, says that she hadn't completed it until after the

Monmouth rebellion, which finally collapsed when Monmouth was captured trying to escape on July 8th. The second part is much less political than the first, though based on Lord Grey's real-life trip to Cologne in 1684. It mainly consists of a very long letter from Philander to Octavio relating his seduction of Calista, the young wife of a rich old don. She is actually Octavio's sister and the narrative is therefore particularly bitter to him. In a wicked piece of literary Chinese boxes, in the manner of Cervantes, Philander/Grey says of this letter that he has written Octavio more of a novel than a letter and this is exactly what it is, a short story set within the framework of the novel.

She had set a fashion with the first part of *Love Letters* that was rapidly followed.[4] The Stationers' Register begins to show such titles as *The Innocent Maid Betray'd*; *The Gallant − a novel in two Parts*; *The History of Nicerotis*; *The Serasquier Bassa, a historical novel of the times done out of French*; *The Gallant Ladies, a novel*; and so on. It looks as if the term 'novel' was itself in process of change from the original meaning of a short story to the modern one as successor to the romance. A novel in two parts can hardly be a short story though it might be that genre we have no name for in English, the novella.

The inclusion of Otway's song in her 1685 collection was one of the last things Aphra Behn was to do for him. By the time she included his elegy on the death of Charles II in her *Lycidus* volume, he was dead. Otway, the greatest tragedian of his generation, had himself become a tragedy. After all that he had done for the Tory cause and his own personal devotion to James, it seems too ironic that he should die in want within a few weeks of James's accession. The story of her assistance to him persisted into the eighteenth century: 'He had now no recourse left but to apply to Mrs Behn for the loan of five pounds which she generously advanced.' She also read through what he had written of his new tragedy and advised him to show it to Betterton but he refused until he had finished it. Aphra Behn however apparently told Betterton of the interview and he made enquiries after him until, about a month later, he was told of Otway's death at his lodgings at a poor woman's in Tower Hill. Betterton went there looking for the unfinished play, only to be told that on the night Otway died a man who used to come and visit him had taken away all his papers and books.[5]

The story is partly borne out by an advertisement in the *London Gazette* of November 1686: 'Whereas Mr Thomas Otway some time before his death made 4 acts of a play whoever can give notice in whose hands the copy lies either to Mr Thomas Betterton or Mr William Smith at the Theatre Royal shall be well rewarded.' As she had commemorated Rochester in *The Rover* so, I believe, she commemorated Otway in *The Lucky Chance*.

XXV

Farewell to Love

It must be said to James II's credit that he didn't always allow his poets to starve. Wycherley had been seven years in the Fleet prison for debt until in December 1685 his friends got a performance of *The Plain Dealer* put on at court, which led to his debts being paid and his being discharged. According to George Grenville, James also gave him a pension of £200 a year.

Both Aphra Behn and Otway had had performances at the end of 1685. *The Rover* was played at court in October and Otway's *The Soldier's Fortune* was given at the Inner Temple in November. Yet she was still in want of money. On August 1st she had had to write a promissory note for a certain Zachary Baggs.

> Whereas I am indebted to Mr Baggs the sum of six pound for the payment of which Mr Tonson has obliged himself. Now I do hereby empower Mr Zachary Baggs, in case the said debt is not fully discharged before Michaelmas next to stop what money he shall hereafter have in his hands of mine, upon the playing my first play till this aforesaid debt of six pound be discharged. Witness my hand this 1st August, ——85
>
> A Behn

Zachary Baggs, as the watch rate books show, lived next door to the Dorset Garden Theatre. His father, Zachary senior, at the time of his son's birth in St Saviour's parish, Southwark, in 1658, was a gold merchant. His son probably followed the same trade and it sounds as if he was involved in the finances of the theatre. Perhaps the court performance of *The Rover* brought her enough to pay him off or perhaps he had to wait till the following spring.

If there is any truth in the story of Otway's applying to her for money it must have been about the end of February, since he died on April 14th. She could have begun her play at once since it was licensed for printing on April 23rd. She wouldn't have known the end of Otway's story when she finished *The Lucky Chance*. It appears in the Stationers' Register under a completely different title as '*The Disappointed Marriage or The Generous Mistress* a comedy by Madam Beane'.

Gayman, one of the pair of heroes, is living in disguise in Alsatia, the cant name for the poorer part of Whitefriars where rogues and debtors hid out. When we first see him he is wearing 'an old campaign coat'. Otway had gone to the Flanders wars in the late 'seventies and from this had his title to captain. Although the locations, Tower Hill and Alsatia, are different I believe Gayman is based on Otway. It's too close to his death in these circumstances for it to be merely coincidence, particularly since this wasn't a theme she had handled before. All ends happily for Gayman and he is restored to fortune and mistress, played once again by Elizabeth Barry as the spirited Lady Fulbank. Elizabeth Barry's influence on Otway's heroines has been often mentioned, but it was just as important in forming the strong-minded, witty women of Aphra Behn's comedies. Among the best scenes in *The Lucky Chance* is one between Gayman and his landlady in which he soft-talks her into getting him his clothes out of pawn so that he can emerge from Alsatia. I can't prove it but I think this scene is based on some anecdote Otway may have told her since 'the poor woman' with whom he was lodging appears in the accounts of his death and Betterton's search.

The Lucky Chance is a very good play indeed, full of invention and with a splendid exchange between Lady Fulbank and her husband in which she defends her right to love. It was an immediate success, had a very good third night and ran at once into fierce criticism, so that she was forced to write a hasty preface to the printed edition. The criticism was again on the grounds of the play's immorality because it was written by a woman. Her defence is both reasoned and impassioned.

She had taken the precaution of having the play vetted by

many private people, women and men, and by the master of the revels, Charles Killegrew, Thomas Killegrew's son, who had succeeded his father in 1680, Dr Davenant, Sir William's eldest son, and Sir Roger L'Estrange, the official censor. She instances many contemporary plays which are similar in content to her own and have scenes which show sexual activity either about to take place or just over. These, she says, are all by men and for this reason they are thought acceptable. But in all cases they are justified, as her scenes and language are, by their relevance to the play and its donnée. Finally she threatens that if she isn't to be allowed the same freedom to write as male writers she will give up altogether since she's as concerned about her literary reputation as she is about the money.

> All I ask is the privilege for my masculine part the poet in me, (if any such you will allow me) to tread in those success-ful paths my predecessors have so long thriv'd in, to take those measures that both the ancient and modern writers have set me, and by which they have pleas'd the world so well. If I must not, because of my sex, have this freedom, but that you will usurp all to yourselves; I lay down my quill and you shall hear no more of me.

What has hurt her most is that the attack has come partic-ularly from 'brothers of the pen' although she says that she excuses them since they are merely envious of the play's success. Unfortunately little of this ephemeral criticism has survived except in verse and most of that by one person, Robert Gould. From her preface it's clear that there were others. She would never have embarked on such a piece of self-vindication for one critic and that an extremely biased one whose criticism of women writers stems partly from his having been jilted by one.

Aphra Behn also puts forward a claim which she says she's unwilling to do because it has 'a vanity in it', to have written 'as many good comedies, as any one man that has writ in our age'. Were she a man this would be recognized 'but a devil on't the woman damns the poet'. Criticism of the so-called immorality of the stage was growing and was to culminate in Jeremy Collier's famous attack on it.[1] The puritans had thought the stage sinful and closed the theatres, but now the clergy of all persuasions were taking up the same cry. Art shouldn't reflect life but should be a hypocritical watering down of it. Restoration comedy is essentially realistic in its choice of subjects. People have sex in their millions every day. To pretend that they don't is merely hypocritical and the results can be seen in the vapid writing for the stage of the next two hundred years, which produced brilliant players and not one worthwhile dramatist. Even Sheridan and Goldsmith are soft-centred adulterations of their predecessors.

A woman writer provided an easy target to begin the more general attack. As if in further defiance she had managed to get the patronage for this play of one of the most powerful men in England, James's brother-in-law, Lawrence Hyde, now Earl of Rochester since John Wilmot's young son had died the year after his father. Once again she has chosen an Anglican, thereby quietly proclaiming her own position. This was a luxury, however, that she wouldn't always be able to afford.

Who were 'the poets of the town' who had attacked her? I think it not impossible that Dryden was among them. At the end of her defence she refers to Will's coffee house, which was known to all to be Dryden's favourite and which she also used. In his poem on the death of Anne Killegrew, published in 1686, Dryden makes a great deal of the chastity of her verse, laments the contemporary prostitution of poetry and calls it a 'lubrique and adultrate age' that has increased 'the steaming ordures of the stage'. Many readers would have seen his lines as a direct cast at Aphra Behn in several places. At one point he refers to Anne Killegrew's writing on love as 'but a lambent flame that played about her breast' and he also says that she is Sappho reincarnated and compares her to Katherine Philips. This was to deny Aphra Behn's supremacy and to rob her of what had become almost a second pseudonym used by her admirers for her: Sappho.

Dryden was by now a convert to Catholicism and the satire which was attributed to Aphra Behn had probably appeared between the publication of the *Miscellany*, in which she praises him, and the production of *The Lucky Chance*. The two things, the conversion and the satire, could have turned him against her at this date and put him among those who criticized *The Lucky Chance*. This seems even more likely in view of his later letter to Elizabeth Thomas. Criticism from him would have wounded Aphra Behn deeply.

Hyde's acceptance of the dedication with all its implications suggests to me that she had renewed her connection with the extended family of Sir Thomas Gower, since his granddaughter who appears so charmingly in the Gower household accounts in such items as 'a muff for Little Miss' had married Hyde's son. Her mother had been a Granville, daughter of the Earl of Bath, whose nephew George Grenville became about this time one of Aphra Behn's admirers.

> Some for your wit, some for your eyes declare;
> Debates arise which captivates us most
> And none can tell the charm by which he's lost ...
> Poets such emblems to their gods assign,
> Hearts bleeding by the dart, and pen be thine.

He also has a poem to Lady Hyde, *née* Leveson Gower. Her father William, under the influence of his uncle the Earl of Carlisle, had become a supporter of the Whigs and was one of Monmouth's bail in his first disgrace. Perhaps it was through these connections that Aphra Behn got such good inside information on Lord Grey and Lady Berkeley for *Love Letters Between a Nobleman and His Sister*.

As well as *The Lucky Chance* she also published in August of this year *La Montre or the Lover's Watch and the Case for the Watch* which is dedicated to an unknown young lawyer, Peter Weston. It may be coincidence but in the congratulatory verses at the beginning are some by George Jenkins which seem an echo of Dryden's comment on Anne Killegrew:

> Nor can thy soul a fairer mansion find,
> Than was the beauteous frame she left behind:

Jenkins says:

> Never were soul and body better joyn'd;
> A mansion worthy so divine a mind!

And these hark back to a couplet in a poem on her I believe to be Dryden's[2] which is identical except for two words.

Aphra Behn's dedication, which could have brought her very little in the way of money, uses the charming and virtuous young Peter Weston for other purposes. One is to comment on the fickleness of other men, and here I think she is getting at another lawyer, John Hoyle, and the other is to advance her claim to be writing about virtuous love, thereby rebutting the critics who had been crying out that she was obscene. *La Montre* is a piece of gallantry that doesn't end in bed. It's about the love game and is as pretty as one of those ceramic watches that have young lovers painted on them. She describes it very accurately as a 'little unlabour'd piece', translated from the French of Bonnecourse. Was it her French translations, in particular *The Voyage to the Island of Love*, that Dryden was aiming for when he wrote of Anne Killegrew's poetry as 'unmix'd with foreign filth, and undefiled'?

Towards the end of this year she fell ill. What the illness was it's hard now to diagnose. It was variously described as, inevitably, 'the pox', gout and sciatica. It sounds like a form of arthritis which made her lame, distorted her limbs and affected her hands so that the very act of writing was painful. Her illness sounds of physical origin but it must have been compounded by the malice of the critics, John Hoyle's loss as a lover, her need to earn a living and the political situation, any one of which could have been enough to make her ill.

> Doth that lewd harlot, that poetic queen
> Fam'd through Whitefriars, you know who I mean,
> Mend for reproof, others set up in spight,
> To flux, take glisters, vomits, purge and write.
> Long with a sciatica she's beside lame,
> Her limbs distortur'd, nerves shrunk up with pain,
> And therefore I'll all sharp reflections shun,
> Poverty, poetry, pox, are plagues enough for one.[3]

There's no indication what side she took in the controversy over James II's moves towards toleration for all sects which, beginning in 1685, exercised the talents of Buckingham and Neville Payne in a series of pamphlets in their favour. Buckingham's came first with a defence of natural religion which soon drew in others on both sides. As a member of the established church she should have been against her two friends in this but I doubt it. Her commitment to James was too strong and her reasonableness would have found it hard to support any form of intolerance that couldn't be shown to be for the real national good. Intolerance on both sides had led to civil war. I think she supported Neville Payne in his claim that James was the only physician on earth who could heal religious dissension by letting all religions coexist peacefully.

The dismissal of Lawrence Hyde from his office of Lord High Treasurer at the beginning of 1687 must nevertheless have shaken her, especially since it was specifically because he had refused to change his religion. At the same time as the decision to dismiss him was being made in December, *The Rover* was given another court performance. It would be interesting to know which part and whether James asked for the one that was dedicated to him.

Her chronic lack of money must have been made worse by doctor's bills. She felt very ill indeed and described herself as 'dying'. Yet she had to earn if she wasn't to end up like Otway. The theatres were in a shrunken condition with a series of old plays, and the foreign opera usurping one whole playhouse. She managed to get a play put on in the spring of 1687. It was an earlier work that she had intended for Charles II and that had been cut off by his death. She remembers him with something close to nostalgia in the dedication to Charles, Marquess of Worcester, but hastily adds a commendation of James. *The Emperor of the Moon* offended no one and charmed all.[4] It proved one of her longest-running plays. It's based on the Italian *commedia dell'arte* characters, like Otway's *The Cheats of Scapin* which, however, was only a short interlude. Aphra Behn's is the first full-length use of this convention in English. It was chosen, I believe, instead of a much tougher, more exciting play that was eventually produced after her death: *The Widow Ranter or The History of Bacon in Virginia*.

The dating of this later play is very difficult since it's set during the happenings in Virginia of ten years before. But it's obviously not too far removed from *Oroonoko*, and it's hard to see among the enormous number of works in her last two years when else she would have had time to write it unless in the very last months of her life when she no longer cared whether she was to be accused of obscenity or not. It's very much of a piece with *The Lucky Chance* and so I suggest a date for it of 1686–7. The other posthumously performed play, *The Younger Brother*, she refers to in *Oroonoko* as 'my new comedy'. It's certainly later than 1684 since it refers to the rhinoceros that was exhibited in that year. Again it's probably to be dated in 1687.

Is there any indication that she kept up her writings of political satire in these years? I've found no comment from her that suggests it, but there is a poem in *Poems on Affairs of State* that could very easily be hers and indeed has all her ring and favourite turns of phrase. This is 'A Poem on England's Happiness', dated by the modern editor to 1686. There's nothing in it that doesn't accord with her moderate though loyalist position, and in its praise of James it not only uses her favourite adjective 'godlike' twice but also repeats her sun image of him from the coronation ode.

On April 16th 1687 Buckingham died at Kirkby Moorside. He had retreated to his estate in Helmsley, Yorkshire, in 1686 where he lived in the half-ruined castle busying himself with his laboratory. His death was very sudden with Buckingham refusing to believe in its onset for several hours, during which time he was hounded by one of his heirs to make a will and by others to reconcile himself to God. The will he refused: the reconciliation he made a half-gesture towards, clearly to quiet the argument. He was lucid enough to have no intention of ending as Rochester had done. His estate was largely wasted. James II paid for his funeral. I believe he also paid something for Buckingham's elegy by Aphra Behn which was sold in broadsheet. But I don't believe it was written for money. Its defence of Buckingham would have been too unpopular among the poets. She calls him 'wit's great reformer', and says that when he was accused in satires of 'roving change' it was out of a misunderstanding of his nature.

> Thy wit, a torrent for the banks too strong,
> In twenty smaller rills o'er flowed the dam,
> Tho the main channel still was Buckingham.[5]

She praises the lightness of his concern as a politician, remembers his embassy to France, where his English rose made Louis's fleur de lis faint with envy, and commends even his prodigality.

> Let grovelling minds of nature's basest mould
> Hug and adore their dearest idol gold ...
> What others borrow, thou canst there to lend ...

She ends with a lengthy image of the phoenix, that favourite mythical beast of the seventeenth century, but says that he has outdone even her in leaving no successor to rise from his blaze of heaped generosity. This praise of childlessness, which would have seemed a rejection of the accepted values, must be based on her own lack of any other children but her books.

Her courage shows in this elegy, in her defence of the seemingly indefensible. She doesn't dodge the criticism of Buckingham. She confronts it straight on and explains, out of her knowledge of a man who was a ridiculed enigma to his contemporaries. To her even his eccentricity was great; he was the last of the renaissance princes and she couldn't but admire his style. What also comes through is the defence of a friend although nowhere in the poem does she claim his friendship. That would have seemed to her impertinent on such an occasion but she hints at it when she pictures not only the muses weeping but time himself, Buckingham's debtor since time borrowed new life from him:

> Whilst thy gay wit has made his sullen glass,
> And tedious hours with new born raptures pass.

Beneath the baroque image are hidden evenings when the wits met to talk and drink together.

They were all dying. The following November Nell Gwyn was also to die of an apoplexy at thirty-eight. Aphra Behn was nearly ten years her senior and this death of someone she had admired must have depressed her. In the poem on Buckingham she had written of the muses 'whom misery could never tire/ But chirp in rags and ev'n in dungeons'. Yet ill health, she thought, was affecting her own writing. Still she managed to bring out the last volume of *Love Letters Between a Nobleman and His Sister* and, in May, the second part of the Tallemant translation *Lycidus or The Lover in Fashion*.

Lycidus is a bleak work which ends in the young man's renouncing love in favour of glory. Although she had promised Tonson that she would do the second part of the *Voyage to the Island of Love* book, the fact that it came out now must also be related to the trial of John Hoyle at the Old Bailey, for buggery, in March 1687. Luttrell records in his diary, March 23rd–29th, that 'Mr Hoil of the Temple had a bill preferred against him

(Old Bailey) to the grand jury for buggery which the jury found ignoramus; so he was discharged,' and the London Sessions record, Newgate Gaol Delivery, shows two counts against him, one by William Bistow of Gracechurch St, poulterer, and one by Thomas Archer.[6] In the state papers for 1683 a 'Mr Hoyle' is shown as being himself on the Grand Jury for that year and involved in some business over L'Estrange's newspaper the *Observator*. This might have stood him in good stead when his own case came up. Although he was discharged the world believed him guilty and he is included with his 'he-mistress' in *A Faithful Catalogue of Our Most Eminent Ninnies*, usually attributed to Charles Sackville.

As well as *Lycidus* the volume contains a grieving poem on Amintas's faithlessness, some lines in a poem to Damon about having said goodbye to love 'since Amintas proved ingrate' and 'To Amintas upon reading the lives of some of the Romans', which the *Muses Mercury*, in its 1707 reprint, glossed as *To Mr H——le being belov'd by both sexes*. It also contains her by then famous poem 'On Desire' and a long pastoral on the marriage of Charles Sackville to the Lady Mary Compton. Significantly it also has the final poem by her, 'To the Fair Clarinda, who made love to me, imagin'd more than Woman'.

The rest of the volume is made up by a collection of biographically fascinating poems by a group of her friends, most of whom are unfortunately unidentifiable under their pastoral soubriquets. The best poem as poem is Otway's elegy on the death of Charles II, followed by Daniel Kendrick's commendatory verses in which he claims she has outdone all other female writers. He renews the old metaphor of Daphne in flight from Apollo and then specifically disposes of Katherine Philips's literary claim:

> If we Orinda to your works compare,
> They uncouth, like her country's soil appear,
> Mean as its peasants, as its mountains bare:
> Sappho tastes strongly of the sex is weak and poor ...

Sappho may mean the original Greek poet or Kendrick may be using it for the equally anonymous Ephelia whose work is indeed weak and poor. Aphra Behn was herself often known as Sappho to both her enemies and friends. Kendrick's last lines refer to her reputation as an elegy writer, mentioning in particular her ability to inspire 'Greenhill's clay with living paint'. Her pen is the wand which calls the dead to life.

Other poems in *Lycidus* speak of a visit to Tunbridge Wells in what must have been the previous summer. If she was already ill she would have gone to take the waters there. She was accompanied by 'Eliza' and she has another close friend 'your Gloriana'. Two poems refer to this visit and another poem is written by Strephon to his three mistresses: Astrea, Gloriana and Eliza. It sounds very much as if she was plastering over the wound made by John Hoyle with the company of women. Having said farewell to love but being of a deeply erotic nature she was naturally led into equivocal semi-erotic situations with them and with young men who admired her poetry.

The unknown Strephon who can make no impression on 'Astrea always airy, witty, gay' has several poems to her and I'm inclined to wonder if he is the sender of the verses which, in 'To Damon', she says have given her such disturbance though she has renounced love. If so this may be the first appearance of George Grenville. He would need to be of some standing to usurp the dead Rochester's pseudonym. Rochester is still present in poems by his friend, and apologist in the preface to *Valentinian*, Robert Wolseley, and in a verse comment on that preface by 'a lady of quality'. He's also present in an elegy on Anne Wharton whose pseudonym was Urania.

Of all the earlier wits only Etherege remains, with one song. The poems, except for one on Henry Clarendon going to Ireland with some praise of the Duke of Ormonde, are pastoral and apolitical, with titles speaking of gifts backwards and forwards between the friends: a bottle of orange water from Astrea to Strephon, Cowley's works and a basket of fruit for Astrea. One woman, abandoned by her faithless lover, begs only to devote herself to Astrea, another pleads for a house for her where she can be without 'toil or pining want perplext/Thy body easy and thy mind at rest'. It's all a bit hot-house, like the last years of Colette in a darkened room among her neophytes, but there was reason enough for it.

Waller died on October 21st and she wrote to his daughter-in-law enclosing an elegy which she excused for any weakness it might show. 'I can only say I am very ill and have been dying this twelve month, that they want those graces and that spirit which possible I might have dressed 'em in had my health and dulling vapours permitted me, however madam they are left to your finer judgement to determine whether they are worthy the honour of the press among those that celibrate Mr Waller's great fame, or of being doomed to the fire.' In the postscript she adds: 'I humbly beg pardon for my ill writing madam for tis with a lame hand scarce able to hold a pen.'

The poem wasn't of course doomed to the fire but published at the beginning of 1688 along with others mostly by relations of George Grenville, Beville Higgons, Sir Thomas Higgons and Sir John Cotton,[7] with two by Thomas Rymer, the Yorkshire antiquary, and one, significantly, by the Duchess of Mazarine's devotee Monsieur St Evremond. Hers is, not surprisingly, the best. Biographically the most interesting parts are where she describes her present illness:

> I, who by toils of sickness, am become
> Almost as near as thou art to a tomb?
> While every soft and every tender strain
> Is ruffl'd, and ill-natur'd grown with pain.

and the lines on his early influence on her which I have discussed before.

Both she and George Grenville speak of Waller's private fortune which put him above the customary concern of poets, poverty. Good as it is in comparison with the others the poem can't compete in scope with her elegy on Buckingham. Only the last couplet comes close to her best:

> Yet, sullen with the world, untir'd by age
> Scorning th' unthinking crowd, thou quit'st the stage.

This image of quitting the stage ties in with one she had used earlier in the year in *The Emperor of the Moon*, which appears in the Stationers' Register as 'a fars by Mrs Blune', one of the more bizarre variations on her name. The influence of Shakespeare on her work hadn't waned and the play ends with Dr Baliardo bidding farewell to his lunar studies with strong echoes of Prospero drowning his books. In her case I think the moon has its significance as an aspect of Venus and that her farewell is to love.

On August 21st James resolved that the recently appointed governor of Jamaica, Christopher Monck, the second Duke of Albemarle, should proceed on his voyage to the island and this gave Aphra Behn the chance to earn a little money and also to renew her interest in colonial affairs. It's in line with the theme of *Lycidus*. Glory has awakened him from the enchanting dream of love and he breaks the lazy chains. This is a complete *volte-face* from her poem on Celladon going to Ireland and is a measure of how badly she had been hurt. Monck had been raising treasure ships near the coast of Hispaniola and she refers to this in the poem and then describes his imagined arrival in Jamaica. That it is Jamaica makes me wonder if Henry Neville Payne had some part in her taking on this theme.

The farewell to love continues in her dedication of the last part of *Love Letters Between a Nobleman and His Sister* to the young son of the Earl of Sunderland and of Waller's Sacharissa and Thomas Culpepper's aunt, Dorothy Sydney, Robert, whom she castigates quite sharply for wild and profligate behaviour. It's hard to see that the young man would have paid her anything for this so perhaps his father, at the height of his power, did. The last part takes the book to beyond the death of Monmouth, with hints of the subsequent careers of all the protagonists. Its most striking passage is the taking of the veil by Calista in the nunnery of the Augustines in Brussels, where her aunt is abbess, which could almost be modelled on a real-life account among the Tixall letters. It's full of the kind of counter-reformation magnificently gloomy camp that you don't expect to find until Horace Walpole and the gothick. A story not published till after her death, *The Nun or The Perjur'd Beauty*, is in the same tone and I would therefore date it about the time she was writing the last part of *Love Letters* although it's almost incredible that she could have fitted in anything else in a year already so prolific.

Even so she wrote some commendatory verses to a translation by a Yorkshire lawyer, Henry Higden, of Juvenal's *Tenth Satire*, in company with Dryden, and Settle who had now changed political sides. Shortly after Higden's translation Shadwell produced one of his own. Higden's was a paraphrase and indeed he calls it 'a modern essay on'. Shadwell's was very much close to the original. 'My friend Henry Higden',[8] he

writes in his introduction, which is mainly directed against
Dryden and his *Macflecknoe* where Shadwell is savagely ridiculed, 'has made an ingenious version of this satire but in other
numbers and in a different way so that we shall not interfere
one upon another.' Aphra Behn always preferred paraphrase to
a close translation and disagreed strongly with Dryden on this
issue. Her lines on Higden's translation which begin 'I know
you', adding another to the list of her friends at this time,
imitate the wit and pace of the work she is praising with a
sentiment that Pope was to take up.

> Wit is no more than nature well exprest;
> And he fatigues and toils in vain
> With rigid labours, breaks his brain,
> That has familiar thought in lofty numbers drest.

She carries on this thought to consider the vices under
seeming virtue, including the judge who reviles the criminal
before him because 'old age's ice / Has chill'd the ardour of his
willing vice.' But her best lines are kept for the hypocrisy she
so disliked in women

> ... whose knack of cant
> Boasts of the virtues that they want:
> Cry *faugh* – at words and actions innocent,
> And make that naughty that was never meant.

She has said farewell to love but she doesn't betray her earlier
beliefs, though she does, and this reflects the curious admonitory
dedication of the third part of *Love Letters* to Robert Spenser,
speak of 'mad infected youth' wasting 'their fortunes, health and
reason'. Robert Spenser's debaucheries even get into the state
papers at this time. Perhaps he was trying to relive the earlier
exploits of Rochester and the wits but lacked their style and
brilliance.

There was yet one more work in this year: a set of verses to
some charming engravings by Francis Barlow. There's something odd about this book. It first appears in the Stationers'
Register in July 1686 as '*Esops Fables*; the English by Thomas
Philpot Esqre, the French and Latin by Robert Codrington
M.A., sculptures by Francis Barlow'. Yet the first edition is
usually dated 1687 and in his preface Francis Barlow says the

English versions are by Aphra Behn and that that will sufficiently commend them to anyone of understanding. The true
explanation may be that he was dissatisfied with many of the
original English versions and got her to redo them. The result
is that, though many of them are very good and sound like hers,
several of them are of a clumsiness that was unnatural to her.
In writing the lines of Aesop's statue she pauses to pay tribute to
Dryden, and many of the concluding moral couplets are unmistakably hers in sentiment.

> Women do oft those heights of glory reach,
> Which even the schools have wanted power to teach.

One of them in particular shows that however much everything
may have seemed against her she hadn't given up:

> Though rack'd with various pains yet life does please
> Much more than death which all our pressures ease.

XXVI

Oroonoko

The new year began with Tory bonfires, for the Queen was at last pregnant again and all those who wanted it to be so predicted a son. James had announced the pregnancy just before Christmas and a form of prayer to be celebrated in January was prepared by three bishops, among them Thyrsis, Thomas Sprat. Aphra Behn must have got out her poem of prediction very soon after. It was needed to counteract the scepticism of the opposition. History has tended to concentrate on this opposition but her poem ran into two editions, which is some indication that not everyone had turned against the King.

Daringly she painted the expected royal birth in terms of a new nativity, as usual confronting the critics who were making satirical allegations that the Virgin Mary appeared to Mary of Modena 'and declared to her that the holy thing that shall be born of her shall be a son. They say likewise that the Pope has sent her the Virgin Mary's smock and hallowed bairn clothes.'[1] There are references in Aphra Behn's poem to the Magnificat and the Hail Mary which could have caused her enemies to cry that she too was a convert to Catholicism. That they didn't, as far as can be judged, must be because she was known to be an Anglican still, presumably by observed attendance at church. The poem ends with praise of James and support of his right to reign. At first glance the last couplet looks like a statement in favour of the divine right of kings but there's another possible interpretation when the two preceding lines are taken with it. It's her old theme of uniting the factions under one unarguable head, in fact it's Hobbes's doctrine again, given a slight twist. The birth of the prince settles all the arguments about the succession and precludes civil war. That is why she celebrates it. Now that there's no peg to hang faction on it should fade away.

It must have been the rough criticism given to *The Lucky Chance* that made Aphra Behn unwilling to hazard another play this year, although I believe she had one written and another partly so. Instead she concentrated on translations and prose stories for her bread and butter. I imagine she was paid between £5 and £10 apiece for such works, augmented by a similar sum for the dedication. Establishing the date of composition for a piece that hasn't some recognizable contemporary starting point is often impossible, particularly where the date of licensing isn't known, and publication often followed several months after the licence was granted.

Her first original prose work with a licence date in 1688 is *The Fair Jilt* in April. But probably in early March, when its publication is advertised in the *London Gazette*, she wrote a poem to mark the publication by Sir Roger L'Estrange of his *History of the Times*, Part Three, relating to the death of Sir Edmund Berry Godfrey, some of which I quoted earlier. L'Estrange was, with Dryden, the most fiercely attacked of the Tory propagandists. The opposition called him Towser. He was both a propaganda writer and a manipulator through his running of a succession of news sheets and his official position as censor.

L'Estrange's purpose in publishing this part of his history at this time must have been at least two-fold. The world knew that Burnet, now in voluntary exile at The Hague, was also writing a history. By publishing his in parts as he went along L'Estrange must have hoped to defuse Burnet, from whom a steady stream of pamphlets was directed across channel against popery, James II and toleration. In 1687 he had produced thirteen such pieces, and included among his objects for attack was Henry Neville Payne. L'Estrange had said before that Sir Edmund Berry Godfrey had committed suicide. He repeated it at this time because the Tories needed once again to deny the Popish Plot, now that the King was running into increasing criticism because of his advancement of Catholics, particularly in the army, which he was building up. If there had never been a plot, by analogy there wasn't one now to reimpose Catholicism on the country.

Aphra Behn's function was as back-up to the original. L'Estrange was also an Anglican, though he was of course accused of being a proto-Catholic. Her poem rehearses the madness of those times and praises him for pouring calm truth on the hysteria. It was printed in broadside for rapid distribution. She must have sensed that the temperature was rising again while the Whigs waited to see if the Queen would miscarry or the child would be another girl and therefore only third in line of succession after the two protestant princesses.

Whatever she was doing for money or as her political contribution, she must also have been writing for what she must have seen as fame, for Nahum Tate had decided to put into English the revered Cowley's great Latin work *On Plants*. Once again, as with *Aesop's Fables*, there's an oddity. The first mention of it is in the Stationers' Register of April 5th 'newly made English by several hands' yet the date of publication is 1689 and it was advertised in the *London Gazette* for that year in July. The advertisement particularly mentions her translation: Book Six, 'Of Trees'.

To be asked to translate the venerated Cowley must have given her immense pleasure even though her other translators, apart from Tate himself, were comparatively unknown. Tate says his motive in undertaking the translation is so that all Cowley's works shall be available to every Englishman whether he has any knowledge of the classics or not. No doubt Aphra Behn would have added Englishwomen too or perhaps the term still sufficiently comprised both sexes. Nahum Tate also remarked that the last book 'o'ertops the others'. This was the one he had asked her to do.[2]

She had never written so flowingly as for these over fifteen hundred lines. Not only is hers far and away the best of the translations, it's a remarkable achievement in itself. The poem encompasses the whole of the Civil War and the restoration up to the victory over Opdam in the first Dutch war. Ironically, as perhaps it seemed to her remembering William Scot's appointments, one bit deals with the uprooting and sale of the royal forests. It's when she comes to Laurel, Daphne, however that she suddenly breaks from her original and utters a plea that becomes almost a cry. Here it says down the side of the text, 'the translatress in her own person speaks'.

And after monarchs, poets claim a share
As the next worthy thy priz'd wreaths to wear.
Among that number do not me disdain,
Me the most humble of that glorious train.
I by a double right thy bounties claim,
Both from my sex and in Apollo's name:
Let me with Sappho and Orinda be,
Oh ever sacred nymph adorn'd by thee;
And give my verses immortality.

It is the old image from the satire *The Session of the Poets For the Bays* which she uses, confronting criticism as usual, and making a plea for that immortality that the childless have a special hankering after. Unfairly one critic describes her in this translation as straining a little in this mighty work and then wisely dying. Nothing could be less true. The lines, whatever other criticism could be levelled at them, are almost liquid in their sense of ease and confidence. It was a style which she had developed as distinct from that of Dryden as possible so that she could never be accused of mere imitation or conversely of aiming too high, of ambition. And yet this plea, although it confines itself to the female hierarchy, is deeply ambitious. She would not have believed that there would be so few women poets among whom she might be numbered in the next two centuries. I am convinced she saw herself as forerunner to dozens of women writers within a very short time.

In the same month she had licensed *The Fair Jilt* which was published in that year with its dedication to Henry Neville Payne. The dedication may be for recent or many years of favours. The style of this story is like an early precursor of Jane Austen. For example, of Miranda, the heroine, she says: 'To this she had a great deal of wit, read much, and retain'd all that served her purpose.' Of Alcidiana, her sister, she writes:

All her senses were eternally regaled with the most bewitching pleasures they were capable of: she saw nothing but glory and magnificence, heard nothing but music of the sweetest sounds; the richest perfumes employ'd her smelling; and all she eat and touch'd was delicate and inviting; and being too young to consider how this state and grandeur was to be continu'd, little imagined her vast fortune was every day diminishing, towards its needless support.

The full weight of the whole sentence falls on that perfectly inserted needless, as in the first example all Miranda's virtues are undermined by the triplet construction that ends in the deadly clause 'that served her purpose'.

She was at the peak of her prose powers. *The Fair Jilt* had gone back to Antwerp. Now she went further back as though her illness was causing her to remake all her life in the more lasting form of art. She must have begun at once on *Oroonoko* though she claims to have 'writ it in a few hours' and never rested her pen a moment for thought. It was a story she had often told and therefore it flowed easily, but at the same time the act of creating, of working, for an artist begins before he takes up whatever are the tools of his trade. *The Fair Jilt* carries a trailer for it as 'now in the press'. In between that and its publication, however, the new prince, who was to be the Old Pretender, was born. Both she and Dryden were among the rush of literary congratulations. Dryden's is a good sinewy poem. Aphra Behn's flags.

I suspect there are two main reasons for this though renewed illness may have been another factor. She had been on a prose stint and the switch to verse was too difficult. The birth was early. Though no doubt she always intended to produce a poem, she wasn't prepared for it at that moment when she was seeing *Oroonoko* through the press. The second reason, I think, was that she was beginning to find difficulties in maintaining her political position. Dryden through his conversion had no qualms.

There's a hint of her worries in the poem itself. Her praise for the father is still unstinting and she can even add a touch of I told you so for having foretold 'your glorious fate and fortune' and how his stars would triumph 'o'er Great Charles's Wain'. She counters already spreading rumours that the birth was a fake, because, among other things, it took place at St James's not Whitehall, by pointing out that both Charles and James were born there. Then she considers the appropriateness of the lessons for the day and, following the image of the winnower,

finds herself about to say, having indeed said, that the young
prince will make all of one faith and scrambles out by adding
'at least one soul'. Is this a clumsy slip retrieved or is it deliberate? There's a great deal of political difference between a
nation being all of one soul and being all of one faith. Only one
verse seems to me up to her usual standard:

> Methinks I hear the Belgic lion roar,
> And lash his angry tail against the shore.
> Inrag'd to hear a Prince of Wales is born:
> Whose brows his boastful laurels shall adorn ...
> While in his aweful little eyes we find
> He's of the brave, and the forgiving kind.

The anti-William-of-Orange feeling is very strong but the end
is again uneasy. Did she feel James needed to be reminded that
a King should be forgiving? Exhilarated by the imminent birth
he had, only two days before, clapped the Archbishop of
Canterbury and six other bishops in the Tower for publishing a
seditious libel against him. They had refused to read James's
latest proclamation for liberty of conscience from the pulpit
and had then petitioned the King against having to read it.
They were confined until June 15th and then set free on bail
after applying for writs of habeas corpus. Their release was a
triumphal progress with crowds falling on their knees to ask the
bishops' blessing as they passed.

The end of Aphra Behn's poem on the birth falls completely
apart into apologies that her transports are too great for 'scanty
verse', and too vast for 'narrow numbers to contain'. She who
had recently versified twenty years of every mingled emotion
now felt unable to cope with this. Why did she try? I think
because it would have been too noticeable if she hadn't and
probably, as usual, because she needed the money. Bad as the
verses are, nothing she wrote of this kind could fail. They also
went to two editions and then to a third bound up with the
first set on the Queen's pregnancy. Fortunately they weren't
her last state poem, as they were Dryden's. It would have been
a bad note to end on.

At the end of them was a notice announcing the publication
of the 'most ingenious and long expected History of Oroonoko'
on Wednesday next. Dryden's *Britannia Rediviva* appeared about

June 23rd. 'England's Happiness or a Health to the Young Prince of Wales', which must have been one of the earliest of the nativity poems, was in the Stationers' Register by June 13th. I imagine Aphra Behn's came somewhere between those dates, which gives an approximate date of publication for *Oroonoko* of the last ten days in June.

Southerne, when he adapted *Oroonoko* for the stage, said a friend had told him that she always told the story more feelingly than she wrote it. The comment was made with more approval of the telling because, I suspect, it seemed closer to his own version. No doubt she did tell the story well, but oral and written are two quite different techniques and designed for different ends. What she was after in the writing wasn't merely to play on the emotions. The written *Oroonoko* is more complex than this and than Southerne's version, which for my money owes as much to *The Widow Ranter*[3] as to *Oroonoko* and isn't as good as either. She who had been and continued to be accused so often of plagiarism had herself become source material for other dramatists.

Oroonoko had been 'long expected' and she had told it many times. What other psychological impetus than the very deep one of solidifying her life for eternity in art could have prompted it? The answer is quite simple. Emotionally Oroonoko, Imoinda and their unborn child are James, Mary and the unborn, while she was writing it, prince. Trefry, Marten and her family are the loyalists; Byam and Banister and their rabble are the opposition. I don't think she was aware of this herself but it's undoubtedly so. Even Oroonoko's 'blackness' was a characteristic of the Stuarts. She was preparing herself for tragedy, even though she didn't know it, and for the heroic deaths of the royal family.

That said, there remains the surface cloak in which the fable is wrapped and which is what the reader first takes in. It has been argued both that this is the first emancipation novel and that it isn't. What must be pointed out, to establish the historical perspective, is that it's a book written by someone who couldn't conceive the philosophical lengths to which the supporters of slavery would go, any more than she could foresee the future degradation of women or the factory system. The situation was also made very different from the later phase of slavery by the fact that there were white as well as black slaves at this time.

There's no difference because of his colour between Oroonoko and any white King. There are acknowledged cultural and religious differences, in which she represents his viewpoint with more approval than she does that of the Christian Europeanized settlers. Oroonoko's religion is that of Buckingham's natural man. In Buckingham's *A Conference*, 1685, he tells a story of his young negro servant whom he finds one day looking, as he thinks, ill. When Buckingham asks him if he doesn't feel well and tells him to go to the housekeeper for something to make him better, the boy says he's quite well but very astounded by something he has seen, which turns out to be Christians at a communion eating their god. One of Buckingham's opponents in replying to his *Reason and Religion* had remarked that the duke's view would have let in Mohammedanism and other Eastern religions as tolerable. Aphra Behn's position in *Oroonoko* is very close to Buckingham's and for this reason too I think she supported James in his moves towards liberty of conscience.

Oroonoko himself isn't just a noble savage. That strand is supplied by the Indians. He is a civilized, both in his native and in European terms, and educated prince. The blacks who betray him are no worse than the Christians who deceive and torture him, slightly less so since they are weakened by concern for their frightened women and children. What Aphra Behn describes is a situation of total equality which has been upset by the thing she despised: the concept of property. The slaves have become property, as women purchased in the marriage market were property. The later concept of them as animals or less than human is completely alien to her. They are never less than men and may sometimes be gods. Gods in this human context must be translated as supermen or heroes in modern terminology. Even Tuscan, Oroonoko's lieutenant, who betrays him in the end, is behaving only like those Englishmen who changed sides in the Civil War.

Some people, among them the quaker George Fox and Thomas Tryon, for whom she had written her poem in praise of his dietary proposals, were already advocating better treatment for the slaves but there was also a growing movement to christianize them, and the Indians, which Oroonoko rejects, although Imoinda is a little more susceptible to 'stories of nuns'.

Aphra Behn's concept of a hierarchy, which is an entirely fluid structure allowing men to move either up or down from the position of their birth by virtue of intelligence, courage, charm and so on, also allows her to be racially egalitarian. Southerne was much more worried by the property element and gives Oroonoko a speech in which he defends this concept and says the owners are not to be blamed since they have paid for their slaves like any other goods.

Southerne also makes Imoinda white, presumably because no actress could be asked to black up. This adds an interesting touch of miscegenation in the style of *Othello* but destroys Imoinda as a black beauty whose tribal scarrings Aphra Behn details with seventeenth-century scientific interest and in terms that make them as cross-culturally acceptable as possible.

Aphra Behn used George Warren's book to refresh her mind, probably her own journal observations, Neville Payne's experiences and those of other acquaintances with West Indian backgrounds. There were many other books she could have read which had come out since her return, including Governor Lynch's *A Description of Jamaica*, Tryon's own *Friendly Advice to Gentlemen Planters*[4] and, for the African part, *The Coasts of Afric Called Guinnee*.[5] Europeans had been trading to Africa now for long enough for there to be a considerable body of knowledge about African affairs. Her description of the sophisticated and intriguing Coramantien court transfers to Africa that exotic fascination felt by Europeans for the Turkish world.

The differences between Southerne's version and Aphra Behn's are enormous. Hers is both harsher and cooler. Oroonoko doesn't die with dignity by his own hand; he is hacked to bits by a lynch mob. When Imoinda is taken away from him and shut up, it isn't to be sexually assaulted by the governor who is in love with her but so that she shan't be so distressed as to endanger her life and her child's, 'not in kindness to her but for fear she should die with the sight or miscarry, and then they should lose a young slave, and perhaps the mother'. The sharpness of perception which so enlivens *The Fair Jilt* and which Aphra Behn had increased through satire and the thrusts of her dramatic dialogue are here used to make the work convey the tragedy without sentimentality but with a kind of fierce precision. It's a measure of the book's currency that Oroonoko

became a slang term for a smoker, since it's by concentrating
on his pipe that Oroonoko himself endures his last torments. It
was also the kind of courage she expected from James II *in
extremis* and I wonder if there was an echo in her mind of the
reverse situation, Montrose tormented by the foul pipes of his
jailers on the night before his execution.

Oroonoko is dedicated to the son of the Earl of Lauderdale,
sometime member of the cabal and old enemy of Burnet.
Richard Maitland, the son, was a protestant married to the
daughter of the extreme presbyterian Earl of Argyll. Both Maitland and his wife are praised in the dedication for their devotion
to their religion and he for his learning and loyalty. In speaking
of the truth of the story she says: 'If there be anything that
seems romantic I beseech your lordship to consider these
contries do, in all things, so far differ from ours that they produce unconceivable wonders, at least, so they appear to us,
because new and strange.' It's an observation few people were
capable of making but it's allied to contemporary scientific
thought and it allowed her to see the character of Oroonoko
from both sides at once.

A protestant dedicatee must have seemed to her necessary at
this time. Her only certain previous Scottish dedication had
been of *Lycidus* to James's appointee and Catholic convert, the
Earl of Melford, just after James had revived the Order of the
Thistle and conferred one of the first honours on him. It was his
job to secure Scotland for James against the covenanters and he
and his brother were at this time its virtual rulers. Some time
this year she made another Scottish dedication to William
Douglas, son of the Duke of Queensberry who had been sacked
by James in Melford's favour. In it she acknowledges the great
veneration she must have for some of the great men of that
nation among whom, presumably, she included the King.

This dedication is to her translation of Fontenelle's *A Discovery of New Worlds* together with her essay on translated prose.
It was the second translation of a work by him that she had
produced in a few months. The first was *The History of Oracles
and Cheats of the Pagan Priests* and it was dedicated to a figure
who has himself become a part of English folk culture: the now
notorious Judge Jeffreys. In his own day, as the modern edition
of *Poems on Affairs of State* points out, he was nothing of the sort.

Though he was largely disliked and ridiculed for being jumped-up, his bloody assizes were only what the seventeenth century expected in the wake of a rebellion. He was a great theatre-goer and on one occasion saved a play by Shadwell by his frequent attendance.[6] Aphra Behn was quite sincere when she said that she was less discouraged by the grandeur of his titles (he was now Lord Chancellor) than by his wit. She describes the work as 'a discourse of religion in a time when we have scarce any other theme' but one that deals only with the pagan religion. She is still in this dedication keeping her moderate position, refusing, like the Kentish gentry, to become embroiled in matters of religion until forced.

She makes one important remark in this dedication that, by echoing a feeling she expresses in the poem on the pregnancy of the Queen, helps to date publication of *The History of Oracles* to the beginning of 1688. She says that she would have offered Jeffreys panegyrics 'but oh! the muses have all taken wings' and she is 'necessitated servilely to creep after the sense of foreign authors stinting the generous fancy to another's thought'. In the poem to Queen Mary on her pregnancy the muses have fled from England but may come back with the boy's birth.

In spite of his birth, however, the muses were still absent from her, although they managed to brush Dryden with a wing or two. This stated loss of poetic drive I've tried to account for above. It makes the dating of the Cowley translation more difficult unless she is including that under 'another's thought'. If not, it must be that the Cowley translation followed *The History of the Oracles* and the entry in the Stationers' Register doesn't include her part of the book.[7]

This first translation of Fontenelle is over two hundred pages. Those who were reading carefully might have remarked that there was very little difference between pagan and Catholic priests when it came to superstitious cheats. If there is a hint of this in her choice of a book to translate, it has hardened by the time she translates the next work by Fontenelle as *A Discovery of New Worlds*, for the title page goes on: 'To which is affixed a preface by way of an essay on translated prose wherein the arguments of Father Taquet and others against the system of Copernicus (as to the motion of the earth) are likewise considered and answered.' Father Taquet was a Jesuit who had argued against the Copernican theory that the earth and other planets went round the sun instead of everything going round the earth as the older Ptolemaic system had taught, on the grounds that it was contrary to scripture.

In the dedication to William Douglas, whose wife, one of the Yorkshire Boyles, she praises in passing, Aphra Behn makes the required modest bow: 'If it is not done with that exactness it merits I hope your Lordship will pardon it in a *woman* who is not supposed to be well versed in the terms of philosophy, being but a new beginner in that science.' She is however already 'so much a philosopher as to despise what the world says of it'.

In many ways the introductory essay is one of the most daring things she ever wrote. It defined her religious position unequivocally, it defied St Paul's law about women preaching even though it wasn't done in a pulpit, and the world's law that the new sciences were for men. Her excuse for all this is that Fontenelle had introduced a woman as one of the speakers in his five discourses. She thought an English woman might adventure to translate anything a French woman may be supposed to have spoken. Then she found it wasn't so easy. This is her excuse for a disquisition on comparative philology but before she embarks on it she, by omission, parts company with Dryden. 'As for the translation of verse nothing can be added to that incomparable essay of the late Earl of Roscommon.' This, for her, is a terrible slap in the face, without even a nod in the direction of Dryden and the essay which had prefaced the volume of Ovid's *Epistles* to which she herself had contributed. It's made even more so by Dryden's publication in July of a translation from French of the life of St Francis Xavier.

Whether there's some personal reason for this it's hard to tell. The deterioration in the political situation with the imprisonment of the bishops might in itself be enough to account for it. There's no licensing date on the translation, so it could belong to any part of 1688, but I think all the indications in it suggest the middle of the year, before the collapse of James had excited her sympathy and loyalty.

She bases her comments about the relative difficulties of translation between different European languages on a history of the descent of those languages both from Latin and from a Teutonic parent by way of invasions and movements of peoples.

From this she finds reasons for the comparative ease of movement between English and Italian and the converse difficulty
between English and French. Some, indeed a lot, of her history,
has been modified by a further two centuries of study. What's
remarkable is that she should take this scientific line of approach
and that much should still be acceptable today. It's amusing to
see her comments on the vast change in the French language
since Froissart. At this point she has an excuse for beating the
English drum a little while deriding our tendency to 'chop and
change our languages as we do our clothes at the pleasure of
every French tailor'. French has the better sound, English the
better 'signification'.

Her comments on the musicalness of French, its use of
elision and gender changes to avoid an 'ill sound' are still valid
and show the craftsman in her very much at work. She sums up
the problem succinctly: 'If one endeavours to make it English
standard it is no translation. If one follows their flourishes and
embroideries it is worse than French tinsel.' Then she hastens
to correct any too harsh impression of setting the genius of one
language against another by explaining that both appear the
more beautiful to their native speakers 'as the negroes of
Guinney think us as ugly as we think them', which links this
work with the double vision I mentioned before in *Oroonoko*.
Her philological excursion ends with a glossary of three terms
with her reason for translating them in the way she has.

All this is daring enough and would in itself have got her the
reputation of a savante. Worse was to come for she now began
on a criticism of the book and a defence of Copernicus. She
criticizes Fontenelle for making his lady Marquise say either
very many silly things or observations so learned that the
greatest philosophers in Europe couldn't make better. The book
is also very uneven. Further he 'ascribes all to Nature and says
not a word of God Almighty' so that he appears almost 'a pagan'.
If he had stuck to his idea of the vastness of the universe, which
he proves by the appearance and distances of the planets and
fixed stars, he would have done very well but his ideas of
inhabitants even in the Milky Way are the height of extrav-
agance.

However, and here it becomes clear that she has only been
flexing her muscles so far, as for the system of Copernicus 'I can-

not but take his part as far as a woman's reasoning will go'. She won't bother with arguments from mathematical astronomy but as for other arguments she will certainly take on Father Taquet and others. She then proceeds, under the headings of geometry, chronology and astronomy, to examine various passages from scripture and to point out the anomalies between them to prove that the Bible is meant to be understood allegorically and in any case doesn't preclude the Copernican theory. In passing she judges the best edition of the English Bible to be that by Buck in Cambridge, quotes St Jerome's letters to Vitalis, touches on the geography of the Holy Land and concludes that religion and faith are matters for the church and that the sciences are best left to learned men, not to General Councils, Decrees of the Church and so on. She has corrected an error in the height of the earth's atmosphere which appears in the book, since Descartes and Rohalt both make it three leagues, not the thirty which is given and must be a printer's error.

It's hard for us today to understand the boldness of what she has done. After it follow over a hundred and fifty pages of agile, lucid, balanced prose which she shrugs off by saying that she had to decide whether to do a strict translation 'or to give you the subject quite changed and made my own,' but she hasn't either the health or the leisure for the last so she offers the first 'such as it is'.

Aphra Behn was very pleased with her essay. She had greatly enjoyed doing it and thought that she might even 'venture to publish somewhat more useful to the public' along the same lines. As for making so much use of scripture on such an occasion she hopes no one will think her too bold. She has 'a precedent, much esteemed by all ingenious men, that is Mr Burnet's Book of Paradise and antediluvian world'.

This isn't Gilbert Burnet but another cleric of the same surname, Thomas Burnet, whose *Telluris Theoria Sacra* had been published in 1681. He was yet another Yorkshireman, a pupil of Tillotson, and at one time tipped for an archbishopric. In 1685 he had been made master of Charterhouse and had come into conflict with James II over the admission of a Roman Catholic as a pensioner. His views were extremely unorthodox, including the concept of a universe like a great egg crushed at the Flood.

That she should cite him shows her own basic unorthodoxy and also her willingness at this point to side publicly with someone as out of royal favour as he was.

The other Burnet, Gilbert, had now become possibly the person most disliked by James II who had been trying to have him sent home from The Hague. Burnet had been forced to become a naturalized Dutch citizen to save William the embarrassment of having to extradite him, and sentence of outlawry had been passed on him in August 1687.

Some of the views which Aphra Behn expressed in this preface were the pre-conversion views of Rochester, in particular the view that Burnet himself reported in *Some Passages of the Life and Death of ... the Earl of Rochester*, that 'for the story of creation how far some things in it may be parabolical, and how far historical has been much disputed', and the whole probing philosophical, rational, scientific approach smacks of her philosopher prince Buckingham. The conclusions she comes to still owe much to her Kentish upbringing, that passion for moderation, non-aggression, and allowing as much freedom of conscience among neighbours as possible. The sphere of the church is strictly limited and this gives fewer areas for people to quarrel seriously in. The rest can be left to reason and knowledge and may be taken or left without making it cause for civil war.

XXVII

Burnet

Unknown to her and Gilbert Burnet on opposite sides of the Channel, and seemingly of the political fence, the moves were already being made that would bring them to a meeting. The night after the acquittal of the bishops Admiral Arthur Herbert left London disguised as a sailor for The Hague, carrying an invitation from several English lords and one bishop for William to come over. Perhaps the most significant and double-dealing among those appearing on a list of William's friends was the Earl of Bath, George Grenville's uncle and Sir Thomas Gower's kinsman by marriage. Burnet kept up his stream of pamphlets and had already published a dozen in 1688 before he sat down to compose his meditation on his forthcoming voyage for England in case the expedition should prove 'disastrous'.

James meanwhile had taken fright at the obvious temper of the country which had shown itself in bonfires and rejoicings at the release of the bishops and he had decided to summon a new parliament. The appointment of Catholics to official positions was slowed down but the King issued instructions for men he thought were loyal to stand for the new Parliament, among whom was Aphra Behn's friend Thomas Condon, who also seems to have been a Yorkshireman, since he was to stand for Scarborough and had been made deputy lieutenant of the East Riding earlier in the year.

The business of earning a living still had to go on and Aphra Behn produced another short translation but this time of a work of fiction, the romantic story of Inez de Castro and Pedro the Cruel, which she translated as *Agnes de Castro*. Two more stories, I believe, followed this, one certainly which was called

The History of the Nun or the Fair Vow-breaker, which was licensed on October 22nd, and *The Nun or the Perjur'd Beauty*, which wasn't published until after her death but is so like the other in its high Catholic baroque setting that I date it about this time.

The first of these two was dedicated to Hortense Mancini, the wandering duchess. As usual the story has been chosen as appropriate to the person to whom it is dedicated. There's no hint of the political situation in the dedication but a new version of Aphra Behn's sadness at being kept from court. It was a year since Nell Gwyn's death and now she had looked at 'the whole tour of ladies at court' and singled out the duchess to tell her 'how infinitely one of your own sex ador'd you'. She wouldn't have done this while Nell Gwyn was alive but once she was dead the bisexual, cultured and romantic Mazarine was the obvious choice. Permission for the dedication was probably brought about by the combination of George Grenville, St Evremond and her acquaintance with Waller who had been a great friend and frequent visitor to the duchess. Mazarine also had the added advantage of being apolitical. She had kept her pension from Charles even after his death and she spent most of her time at her house in Chelsea. Aphra Behn uses her to lament her own station that prevents her having the 'satisfaction of being ever near Your Grace'. Aphra Behn's sexual ambiguity seems to have grown stronger as she got older, either because she was less attractive to young men or because of the whole John Hoyle complex. In Gildon's *Miscellany* of 1692 there's a poem which is undoubtedly hers, though it might have been written in a male persona, which Gildon entitles 'Verses design'd by Mrs A Behn to be sent to a fair lady, that desir'd she would absent herself to cure her Love. Left unfinish'd'. It describes a useless visit to the country to try to cure herself of love for 'the lovely charmer' who has made her 'a wretched conquest to your wit'. Taken with the *Lycidus* poem 'To the Fair Clarinda who made love to me' of a year before it is, I think, clear evidence of a strong homosexual interest at least in the last few years of her life, and her dedication of *The History of the Nun* reflects this. The story itself also shows an increased pity for women who are 'by nature more constant and just, than men, and did not their first lovers teach them the trick of change, they would be doves, that would never quit their mate, and, like Indian wives, would leap alive into the graves of their deceased lovers, and be buried quick with 'em'. The pity is partly self-pity. She would have liked a lover to whom she could have been so passionately faithful.

Seven days after *The History of the Nun* was licensed William's new armada set sail from Holland, but because of the discrepancy between old and new style, it was not until November 5th that the Dutch actually landed. James II had in the meantime issued a general pardon and the loyalist gentry had flocked to offer their services in raising troops. Among these young George Grenville tried desperately to be, writing to his father to beg him to let him fight for the King who, although he had been badly advised, was still the King, since he had been too young to fight for him in the Monmouth rebellion. The attitude of many loyal Anglicans was that the church taught obedience to the sovereign who was its head. Charles Hatton wrote from Plymouth in November: 'We have had some deserters, and I am told it hath been reported that I was one; but ... knowing how firmly I have imbibed the principles of the Church of England, you will be secure I can never depart from my allegiance to my prince.'

Burnet had accompanied the expedition and now had William's declaration of intent read in Exeter Cathedral. James had belatedly held an extraordinary council on October 22nd to provide formal testimony about the birth of the Prince of Wales, which was one of the matters which William had announced that he was coming to enquire into. Burnet in his reflections on William's declaration satirized this attempt by James to establish the child's legitimacy. The loyalists began slowly to crumble. James's other son-in-law, Prince George, and his favourite Lord Churchill were two of the first to join William's army, which began to move slowly east towards Salisbury.

James seems to have been entirely shattered by what had happened and this is hardly surprising. In personal terms it was a tragedy of Lear-like proportions. Mary and Anne had become 'pelican daughters' allowing their ambitious husbands to combine to drive their father from his throne and possibly endangering his life. History, of course, has seen the episode from a quite different angle but contemporaries didn't miss the tragic implications. James's protestant mistress Catherine Sedley,

Countess of Dorchester, was reported to have said to Mary: 'If I have broke one commandment you have another: and what I did was more natural.'[1] The accounts of James when he went to Salisbury in November to lead the army are of insomnia, nose bleeds and a terrible restlessness that made him unwilling to delegate even the smallest details. On December 2nd Anne sent to William by the Earl of Devonshire that she wished to join him. Sir Robert Howard also wrote on the same day urging him to take the throne. James returned to London from Salisbury and a commission was set up to treat with William. On December 9th the Queen and the baby prince went down the Thames by barge and crossed to France. Two days later and without any warning James followed them in secret, accompanied by Lord Jeffreys. On December 12th he was stopped in a boat off the coast of Kent and brought back eventually to London. William had reached Windsor and for a few days there was a stalemate until William ordered James out of the city and he retired to Rochester. On the day before Christmas Eve he took ship for France. He had therefore deserted the kingdom and his crown was forfeit.

I have had to tell this story at length because of its effect on Aphra Behn. It was a situation which she had somehow to absorb and make her own personal decision about and she must have been as confused and divided within herself as were others of her political position. But her case was further complicated by her personal loyalty to James. She was also ill and in need of money. Some time about now she wrote and dedicated to George Grenville the story *The Lucky Mistake* which was published in 1689. It's a story with a French setting as a compliment to him as he had been educated here. The dedication begins with reference to national affairs. 'At this critical juncture, I find the authors will have need of a protector as well as the nation, we having peculiar laws and liberties to be defended as well as that … Let the heroes toyl for crowns and kingdoms and with what pretences they please.' This must put the dedication after James's flight, perhaps after Sir Roger L'Estrange had been committed to Newgate on December 16th and Dryden had been stripped of the laureateship[2] but before the arrival of Queen Mary on February 12th.

The story in honour of George Grenville is one of love which ends happily. Her flirtation with glory is over and she acknowledges the springs of her own poetry in a compliment to him on his: 'sure the muses who have so divinely inspir'd you with poetic fires, have furnish't you with that necessary material (Love) to maintain it'. The story isn't a translation but 'an original' and based on fact. His many favours to her deserve more than this little piece 'but my increasing indisposition makes me fear I shall not have many more opportunities of this kind, and shou'd be loath to leave this ungrateful world, without acknowledging my gratitude more signally than barely by word of mouth'. She is paying her debts so that she can come home without shame again.

In the new year Robert Gould published his poems with among them several vicious attacks on Aphra Behn.

> Ephelia! poor Ephelia ragged jilt,
> And Sappho famous for her gout and guilt
> Either of these, tho' both debauch't and vile,
> Had answered me in a more decent style:
> Yet hackney writers, when their verse did fail
> To get 'em brandy, bread and cheese, and ale,
> Their wants by prostitution were supplied;
> Show but a tester you might up and ride:
> For punk and poetess agree so pat
> You cannot well be this, and not be that.

Gould is railing here against a mistress to whom he had addressed *Love given over*. *Against Silvia*. Silvia, who was herself a poet, replied and in return he has written *The Poetess, a Satyr*. In case there should be any doubt about whom he meant by Sappho he identifies her in another poem:

> Farces and songs obscene, remote from wit
> (Such as our Sappho to Lysander writ)
> Employs their time; so far th' abuse prevails,
> Their verses are as vitious as their tails;
> Both are exposed alike to public view,
> And both of 'em have their admirers too.

The poems compare her unfavourably with 'the chaste Orinda' and to complete the tirade he includes Aphra Behn in his long satire *The Playhouse*, begun in 1685 but revised for this new edition, with references to *The City Heiress* 'by chaste Sappho writ', that 'clean piece of wit', and *The Emperor of the Moon*, "twill never tire', which he objects to because it's a farce. Gould was to complain that Betterton and Elizabeth Barry prevented his play from being put on because of his remarks about them in this satire. It was certainly a bad time for it to come out from Aphra Behn's point of view and perhaps this is another thing to which she is alluding when she speaks of the poets' need of a protector.

Among the ungrateful world and the heroes who toiled for crowns and kingdoms under the pretence of religion, she must have been particularly hurt by the ultimate disloyalty of Henry Howard, who had eventually swung the Eastern counties over to William. The defection of the Gowers she must have grown used to. What now should her own position be? She must have longed again to be able to fight and to join the King in exile but she was ill and growing poorer. How was she to make a living and what in any case was the right attitude to take? All this must have gone through her mind. The country was without a King but James had forfeited the right to rule by flight. I believe she accepted this. The next rightful heir was his eldest daughter and to her now the crown must legally pass.

During January discussion had been hot on the question of the succession. At first it had seemed clear that either there must be a regent or the crown must go to Mary, but it soon began to appear that a faction headed by Halifax and William's favourite Bentinck wanted it for William himself. Gilbert Burnet says that he argued strongly against this with Bentinck on one occasion for many hours far into the morning. 'Such a step', he told him, 'would engage the one sex generally against the Prince; and in time they might feel the effects of that very sensibly.' Against this background Aphra Behn's last two poems were written.

The first is very soon after the proclamation of William and Mary on February 13th. Mary had arrived at Whitehall by river the day before. The poem is called 'A Congratulatory Poem to Her Sacred Majesty Queen Mary Upon Her Arrival in England'. It begins with the poet mourning in a thickly shaded grove beside the Thames. This may be metaphorical but it's also probable that Aphra Behn had left London during this troubled period and was staying somewhere in the country just outside. While she is resolved in this 'long retreat' to 'tune no more her songs on Britain's faithless shore', she hears the trumpets of the river nymphs proclaiming Mary's arrival. For three stanzas the poem seems like a deliberate echo of the baroque mode of the coronation pindaric with 'blue locks and shelly trumpets' and the 'brooding Spring' begins to produce flowers before her time.

Then the mood changes. All the muses adore except hers: 'Sullen with stubborn loyalty she lay.' But Mary herself begins to change her and she finds herself wishing to join the adoring crowds and 'from every thought a newborn reason came'. The next stanza is addressed directly to James and is marked in the margin 'J R' which I take to be a reaffirmation of her conviction that he is still in her mind 'rex'. She calls him 'Great Lord of all my vows' and asks his permission for 'my muse who never fail'd obedience yet' to pay tribute to Mary since she is part of him. 'Let me be just – but just with honour too.'

The conflict in her shouldn't be obscured by the baroque surface. She certainly expected anyone whose opinion she valued to understand. She goes on to describe Mary, and the reasons for Aphra Behn's decision to accept her are gradually made clear. There need be no more bloodshed, none of that renewal of civil war she feared and order can be re-established.

> The murmering world till now divided lay,
> Vainly debating whom they should obey,
> Till you great Caesar's offspring blessed our isle,
> The differing multitudes to reconcile.

Once again she was forced to defend. Mary aroused instant dislike in almost every quarter by her seemingly light-hearted behaviour in the middle of what even James's enemies saw was a tragic situation. She, and her sister, were accused of light-heartedly triumphing over their father's misery. Burnet, apparently realizing the unfortunate impression she was making, spoke to her a few days after the proclamation. She gave him an immediate explanation. She was only too well aware of the tragedy but William had warned her that a glum face would be interpreted as chagrin at having to share the crown with him. Her levity was merely overacting.

Aphra Behn describes her manner as if she had seen Mary.

Her sister Anne had gone to the theatre with Lady Churchill, both decorated with orange ribbons. Was Aphra Behn herself able to go out? She had presumably returned to London and was back in her lodgings in or near Dorset Street. If she hadn't seen Mary herself, she had had a description of her, and of William too, for as the lines are a commendation of Mary they strike at William's coldness.

> Through all no formal nicety is seen,
> But free and generous your majestic mien,
> In every motion, every part a queen.

Burnet, realizing also the unfortunate impression that William was now making, and 'encouraged by many' tried to speak to the new King 'to change his cold way' and when he was cut off wrote 'a very plain letter' to warn him what the nation thought of this, with the result that the King didn't speak to him for several months. This however didn't deter Burnet from his duty towards William nor from what some people thought of as his meddling in state affairs, and as part of this he went to see Aphra Behn.

He must have been encouraged to do so by her poem to Queen Mary and by her known Anglicanism. Perhaps he hoped for another spectacular deathbed conversion. What he tried to get, I believe, was a pindaric for the forthcoming coronation like that she had written for James and another Mary but celebrating William's achievements. In both he failed. She had nothing to repent that she hadn't already made provision for in her paraphrase of the Lord's Prayer. What he did get was her last, and one of her best, poems, which was published in broadsheet. Her publisher was no longer Tonson but William Canning, who was arrested later in 1689 for publishing Jacobite material. He was very close by in the Temple Cloisters and this, apart from his politics, would have made him a popular choice for her as it grew more difficult for her to walk. The move from Tonson may also be involved with her falling out with Dryden.

This last is called 'A Pindaric Poem to the Reverend Doctor Burnet on the honour he did me of enquiring after me and my muse'. The 'Dr' dates it before his consecration as Bishop of Salisbury on March 31st.[3] He has come to her and given her the honour of his choice and preference for a great work. He reasons with her for a long time and she feels him beginning to conquer against her will. His arguments remain in her mind 'And please, and charm, even while they grieve and pain'. At this point she brings in his previous opinion of her.

> But yet how well this praise can recompense
> For all the welcome wounds (before) you'd given.

Anne Wharton had either shown her Burnet's letter or told her its contents and she hasn't forgotten. She called them 'welcome wounds' because one must always be ready to accept criticism, at least she usually was, without resentment. The rest of the poem can be read in two quite separate ways and I'm not at all sure if she knew herself which one she intended.

She says that Burnet is offering her an immortality and greatness that she has never had before, since she has only sung of 'shepherds and their humble love' but never of heroes and kings. This is a lie which would be so obvious to everyone, and that included thousands who knew she had written the state poems and in particular the coronation ode, that it's either the hyperbole of modesty or a piece of deep irony. The next few lines, an image of coins made current by their stamp even though made out of inferior metal, does nothing to clear up the problem. The poem is at once simple truth and sharp satire.

In the fourth stanza she apologizes for having to refuse his offer because of her loyalty to James II.

> The breeze that wafts the crowding nations o'er,
> Leaves me unpity'd far behind
> On the forsaken barren shore,
> To sigh with echo and the murmuring wind.

This is the forsaken Dido mourning alone as Aeneas' ship fades from sight. She goes on, seeming to praise him, but the praise has a double edge. It's his writing, she says, that has brought about the revolution, not the sword, and even though she calls it a 'seraphick quill' she describes it as being able to change 'every notion, every principle / To any form, its great dictator please' which is a very back-handed compliment. The specific reference is to the publication in January of several of Burnet's papers mainly from 1688, and in particular to that one in which he justified rebellion.[4] Among them had been an answer to

Henry Neville Payne on his justification of James's moves towards toleration. Troy was won by 'nobler strategem', not by
force of arms. The pen is mightier.

The last stanza contains her final autobiographical statement

> Tho I the wondrous change deplore,
> That makes me useless and forlorn,
> Yet I the great design adore,
> Tho ruin'd in the universal turn.
> Nor can my indigence and lost repose,
> Those meager furies that surround me close,
> Convert my sense and reason more
> To this unprecedented enterprize
> Than that a man so great, so learn'd, and wise,
> The brave achievement owns and nobly justifies.

Burnet, she says, must and will write the story of 'Great Nassau',
as she calls King William, and his pen will make William's
name more immortal than even his own 'renown'd and celebrated fame'.

The whole poem is fraught with her own feelings of ambiguity.
She had refused a commission. Whether it had come from the
new court or was just Burnet's idea I don't know. But although
she was dying his visit had done her a great deal of good. The
muse had come back. She had betrayed nothing but had acted
with total dignity. William was a usurper and unnecessary.
England had been governed by a woman alone before and
could be now. She would recognize Mary and her right to
succeed but not William's. On April 11th the joint coronation
took place without her blessing. Burnet preached the sermon.
Five days later on the 16th, the anniversary of Buckingham's
death two years before, she died.

The memoir says it was through an 'unskilful physician' but
this seems unlikely. She had been 'dying' since the loss of John
Hoyle and the onset of her illness in 1686. Now she had nothing
to live for and no prospect of anything to live on. However
much she had praised Mary, she must have recognized in her
the submissive woman who would never be the protector or
patron of an Aphra Behn.

Who was there when she died? Perhaps George Jenkins, that
longtime friend, to whom she entrusted the bringing out of one

of her posthumous children, *The Widow Ranter*. Perhaps Eliza and Gloriana, either of whom might be that 'one of the fair sex' who wrote her memoir. Perhaps Ravenscroft or young George Grenville. Neville Payne was probably in hiding and was soon to be in prison. Who attended her? Not, I think, Burnet, or word would somehow have come down. If it was anyone other than her local vicar I think it was probably Thomas Sprat, the 'learned Thyrsis', Buckingham's old chaplain, who was Dean of Westminster and had assisted at the coronation. Thyrsis too, I believe, was responsible for her burial in Westminster Abbey on April 20th, no doubt backed by Burnet and by those of sufficient wit and position not to mind the odium or satire that might accrue to them from such an act. She lies in the cloister and not among the 'trading poets' in poets' corner but with the Bettertons and Anne Bracegirdle.

Did John Hoyle pay for the black marble stone for which One of the Fair Sex says he wrote the words? They are, I think, an epitaph she would have approved of.

> Here lies a proof that wit can never be
> Defence enough against mortality.

XXVIII

Epilogue

There were at least two more epitaphs: Nat Lee's extremely
moving one in which he speaks of his unexpressed love for her,
and Dryden's epilogue to *The History of Bacon in Virginia*, which
was performed, when the theatre got going again after the
political upheaval, in autumn 1689. The play was a failure
partly because Aphra Behn wasn't there to cast it and oversee
the production and partly because she was out of favour with the
triumphant party. The prefatory dedication by George Jenkins
says quite specifically that the play is one of her last (but not the
last) works and that she charged him with producing it. Unless
she had creditors whom she wanted paid off, her motive must
have been simply the writer's parental care that didn't want it
stillborn. The dedication also speaks of a very bad production
indeed. Significantly Elizabeth Barry, whom Betterton describes
as a perfectionist in her art,[1] didn't play the Indian queen as
would have been expected although the part was probably
written for her. It was played by her young rival Anne Bracegirdle.

Dryden called the play a farce but this is untrue. It's a tragi-
comedy and provides the structure for Southerne's *Oroonoko*. It
doesn't precisely follow historical events but then she would
have argued drama isn't meant to. This was why she had told
Oroonoko's story in prose which Southerne had described in his
preface as 'burying her hero in a novel' when with her theatrical
experience she could have made a play around him. *The History
of Bacon in Virginia* draws on her earlier colonial experiences for
its description of the white settlers. The tragic love of Bacon and
the Indian queen provides the dramatic meat while the high

comedy comes from the last of her spirited women, the Widow Ranter who is successful in getting a new husband. Her name comes from the radical sect which Christopher Hill has anatomized so well in *The World Turned Upside Down*. She is the ultimate in Aphra Behn's pleas for equality.

Whatever had been the cause or the extent of the cooling in the relationship between Aphra Behn and Dryden, she too had been a good Tory and he was prepared to speak up for her and the play. She is the only woman, he alleges, of whom you can say she gave you pleasure when she was dead and he pleads for the play as for a posthumous child.

> This is an orphan child; a bouncing boy,
> Tis late to lay him out or to destroy.
> Leave your dog-tricks, to lie and to forswear,
> Pay you for nursing and we'll keep him here.

In June 1690 Betterton produced *The Prophetess or The History of Dioclesian* with music by Henry Purcell. Now that the political excitements were over it was time to turn back to the important things of life. The masque which is the *pièce de résistance* of the work is a triumph of love, a reiteration of sentiments in a pastoral setting which must surely have reminded many among the audience of Aphra Behn's own work. I can't believe but that at one point she must have seemed to be actually referred to.

> Let monarchs fight for power and fame,
> With noise and arms mankind alarm ...
> Greatness shall ne'er my soul enthral,
> Give me content and I have all.
> Hear mighty love to thee I call;
> Give me Astrea and I have all;
> That soft, that sweet, that charming fair,
> Fate cannot hurt whilst I have her
> She's wealth and power, and only she,
> Astrea's all the world to me.

So identified was she as Astrea that this is actually the forename under which she appears in the Abbey registers. The final chorus of the masque echoes her own song 'Love in fantastic triumph sat' with its chorus line 'Triumph victorious love'.

Betterton came, as he grew older, to speak harshly of opera because the rash of foreign imports had taken the audiences from the drama. He also came to think disproportionately better of tragedy than comedy but at this time it seems to me quite possible that he was paying his own tribute to someone he had known and worked intimately with for nearly twenty years.

In 1696 Gildon produced *The Younger Brother*, the second of her posthumous plays, which also failed. Presumably it's the play she calls her 'new comedy' in *Oroonoko* since the hero is named after Colonel Marten. The play was certainly written after 1684, because of the reference I've mentioned before to the exhibition of the rhinoceros in Act II, yet for some reason it's been thought a much earlier work.[2] It has much in common with *Love Letters Between a Nobleman and His Sister* and this too would make it not earlier than 1683. Gildon altered the first act but only by completely cutting a stretch of political dialogue and putting in a chunk of his own which is very easily identified. He also made more cuts because it was too long for the audience of the 'nineties. Nothing could save it, however, but this seems to have been more because of a clique against Gildon than one against Aphra Behn whose other plays were now being performed and reprinted, along with her novels and poems which included half a dozen new publications, and her own reputation seemed assured. Gildon dedicated it to the literary son of one of the great colonial families, Christopher Codrington.

Of those who had known her, the most emotionally important, John Hoyle, was stabbed to death in 1692. Luttrell records:

> Saturday 28th May. Mr Hoil of the Temple on Thursday night was at a tavern with other gentlemen, and quarrelling with Mr Pitt's [*sic*] eldest son, a gentleman, about drinking a health as they came out Mr Hoil was stabbed in the belly and fell down dead, and thereon Pitts fled; and the next morning was taken in a disguise and is committed to Newgate.

Later in June Luttrell reported that the jury had found Pitts guilty of manslaughter but that 'the next heir is appealing'. John Hoyle was buried in the vault of the Temple Church. Sir Charles Sedley, the last of the wits since Etherege had died in 1691, wrote a poem on the occasion. Apparently Hoyle had a

cane which he raised to Pitts[3] who then drew and ran him
through, as the jury judged, in self-defence. What's particularly
interesting about Sedley's poem is that he strongly suggests that
Hoyle was a republican.

> A learned lawyer, at the last,
> No Tory, as I'm told,
> Began to talk of tyrants past,
> In words both sharp and bold.
>
> He touched a little on our times,
> Defin'd the power of Kings,
> What were their virtues, what their crimes,
> And many dangerous things.

Sedley also suggests that Hoyle was given to drinking too much
and was by this time 'ancient'. This piece of hindsight on their
relationship opens up a whole extra area for conflict between
them and yet one which she never mentions. On the other hand
in several places in her work she writes of kings as a necessary
evil, while presumably exempting the reigning Stuart, and unknown in her Golden Age, and this sounds like something they
would have agreed on.

Creech, young Daphnis, committed suicide in 1701 on being
given a country living by the college of All Souls where he had
been for nearly twenty years. John Howard, Silvio, fled the
country, together with Richard Maitland[4] and, for a time,
George Grenville. Henry Neville Payne turned to his old voca-
tion, of plotting, this time for James's return, and was arrested
and brutally tortured but, adept survivor, was finally released
to join the other exiles at James's court at St Germain. Dryden,
mighty Dion, lived to write the century's epitaph. Elizabeth
Barry, Amoret, who was renowned for her meanness continued
to act for many years and even led a revolt of the players against
Betterton, who nevertheless forgave her.

Oroonoko was translated into French and German during the
eighteenth century and must have contributed to the pool of
ideas that became the anti-slavery movement. It's a work that
should be part of the canon of English literature and could
easily be read in secondary schools even if none of her other
work is thought suitable. For in many ways emancipation

hasn't yet completely caught up with her in her guiltless celebration of the erotic, the quality for which she was most famed in her own day and most abused after, but perhaps our society has at last reached the point where it can echo Dryden in the epilogue to *The History of Bacon in Virginia*:

> She who so well cou'd love's kind passion paint,
> We piously believe, must be a saint.

Notes

Where no publisher or place of publication is listed, all books referred to were published in London.

CHAPTER I APHRA JOHNSON

1 I exclude Marie de France, the other possible claimant, simply on the grounds that we don't know enough about her life to judge.

2 William Cameron, *New Light on Aprha Behn* (Univ. of Auckland Press, 1961).

3 'The Circuit of Apollo', in Anne Finch, *Poems*, ed. M. Reynolds (Univ. of Chicago Press, 1903).

4 Whether the Thomas Beane whom she married in 1632 was a barber I've not been able to find out. In his marriage licence he's described as 'yeoman'. By her will, proved by Aphra Amis, May 20, 1651 (PCC Grey 1103 f77), she left most of her property to her daughter Aphra. She also had a son Peter, and, since the infant Aphra Amis who died so young was survived by a twin, Peter, it is clearly probable that they were all related.

5 Mundy, *Notes and Queries*, NS I 1954 and II 1955, and Society of Generalogists.

6 Alfery Giles married William Beane, 1647, and Afery Welsmith married George Bean, 1659, both in Canterbury Cathedral. See registers.

7 There are five in the *Visition of Kent 1663* among the local gentry and well over twenty of all classes among the Canterbury marriage licences 1619–60.

8 Dryden, *Letters* (? 1699).

9 'A Letter to Mr Thomas Creech . . ', *Miscellany* (1685).

10 So of course did some of the aristocracy. See for example the female letters in the Hatton correspondence. Not all were Dorothy Osbornes.

11 See *Visitation of Kent 1619* and *Canterbury Marriage Licences*, ed Cowper (Canterbury, 1894). There's another Johnson of Tunbridge Wells who is listed in the *Visitation* but the family is neither properly Kentish nor gentry.

12 B.L., Harley MS., 7587–605, vol. 2.B.

13 D.N.B. and register of St Stephen's, Hackington.

14 Will of Dame Barbara Culpepper proved August 19, 1643, Commissary Court of Canterbury.

15 From Sir John Manwood. E. Hasted, *Kent* (4 vols, Canterbury, 1778) III.

16 *Canterbury Marriage Licences*, 1619–60, and register of St Paul's.

17 The vicar, the Rev. Cyril Munt, kindly allowed me to check the entry in the original register of which there is also a printed copy to 1800.

18 *Canterbury Marriage Licences*, 1568–1618. The marriage took place at Preston and appears in the register.

19 Hasted, *Kent,* III.

20 Richard Culmer seems to have been acting 'Minister in charge' in the prolonged absence of the vicar Robert Austen. He was apparently known as Blue Dick and was an extreme Puritan and largely responsible for the 'utter demolishing of all monuments of superstition' in Canterbury Cathedral including the stained glass windows and sculptures.

21 There may indeed by an even older connection between the Denhams and the family Dame Barbara first married into, the Smyths, since the village of Sturry was also part of the Strangford estates and a Francis Dynham, gentleman of Sturry, was bondsman for the marriage of Jane Dynham in 1601 (*Canterbury Marriage Licences*).

22 Oddly enough a Thomas Thurston and a John Aucher kept a J.P.'s accounts book in the 1690s to early 1700s, now in the Maidstone Record Office.

23 'An Account Book of the Committee of Kent', in Kent Archaeological Soc., *Seventeenth Century Miscellany* (Ashford, 1960), *Kent Records*, vol. XVII.

24 Parish register of St Alphage.

25 They were a branch of the Thanet family through Silas Johnson, whose son Thomas and his siblings inherited his father's lands in Sturry and with whom Culpepper had dealings much later in his life. (He appears in the *Adversaria*, B.L., Harley MS., 7587–605, 'J' volume with other Johnsons. Unfortunately many of the entries are indecipherable.) In his will Silas Johnson is described as 'of the cathedral precinct' in Canterbury. He had married a

Priscilla Bix, widow, of a good Kent family, in 1639 in Fordwich. The status of this family gives us some idea of Culpepper's estimate of Aphra Johnson's family status at birth.

26 Thomas Culpepper's father refers to 'my brother Henry Crispe' in his will. He had married Culpepper senior's sister. Aphra Behn's Henry Crispe was his great-grandson.

CHAPTER II KENT IN THE INTERREGNUM

1 Whether or not we accept Eaffry Johnson as Aphra, the date of 1640 for her birth, which has been the traditional one, must be about right because of the date of birth of Thomas Culpepper. An exception is the *Gentleman's Magazine* 1817 which in a Compendium of County History gives 1642 Canterbury for Aphra Behn but without any substantiation.

2 More study among Kent documents for the period might turn up extra information. There is no mention of Bartholomew Johnson among the Kent sequestration papers and account books which make up S.P. 28, 110, in the P.R.O. though there is a reference to Mr Johnson steward to Lord Strangford while the latter was a tenant of the Earl of Northampton in 1645. This could of course be a relative of Aphra Behn, even her father. There's another tantalizing reference to a Thomas Denham, tenant of Mr Richard Thornhill who later married Joanna, daughter of Sir Beville Grenville and therefore a member of a family closely associated with Aphra Behn in later life (see later chapters). Thomas Denham is also said to have lands of the Earl of Northampton (Accounts of Daniel Shetterden to 1651).

3 *The Compton Census 1676*, in Kent Archaeological Soc., *Seventeenth Century Miscellany* (Ashford, 1960), *Kent Records*, vol. xvii. The figures are probably only of adults over 16.

4 See Everitt, *Community of Kent* (Leicester Univ. Press, 1966), for figures to back these generalizations which I have abstracted.

5 Ibid., p. 153.

6 Aubrey, *Brief Lives*, ed. Oliver Lawson Dick (1950).

7 Henry Fitzroy, Duke of Grafton, was the son of Charles II and Barbara, Countess of Castlemaine.

CHAPTER III SURINAM

1 Sloane MS. 3662. *The Discription of Guyana* by a Major Scott, reprinted in Hakluyt Soc. Series II, vol. lvi, West Indies & Guiana 1623–67.

2 This may be a false etymology but is an often quoted one. There was also a Parham in Antigua.

3 The best account of this is still N. D. Davis, *Cavaliers & Roundheads in Barbados* (Demerara, 1883).

4 For all this see C.S.P. Col. 5 America & West Indies 1661–8. The commission for Barbados in Portland MSS. is dated June 5, 1663.

5 Sloane MS. 159. Reprinted in Hakluyt Soc., op.cit.

6 The likelihood is that by 1688 she was disguising her age.

7 Calendared in H.M.C., Portland MSS. in the British Library and the University of Nottingham. Some transcribed in Hakluyt Soc., op.cit.

8 The actual appointment was June 5, 1663 but Harley was already in Dover by Oct. 31, 1662, waiting to embark.

9 It's interesting to watch the rapid deterioration from Sept. 11, 1663: 'My lord is very kind to me … '

10 First Provost Marshal of Surinam and then of Antigua. C.S.P. Col. 1669–74.

11 C.S.P. Col. 1661–8.

12 S.P. LR 263aa 4.

13 Trefry could be spelt with a double 'f'.

14 H.M.C., Bouverie MSS.

15 *Discription of Guyana*, op.cit. Willoughby lost two fingers and was wounded in the head. His assailant, James Allen, poisoned himself.

16 Dedication, *All the Histories and Novels* … , ed. Charles Gildon (1696).

17 B.L., Portland MSS.

18 His and his sister's wills were proved in the same year. He died unmarried, leaving his property to her.

19 A list of his majesty's subjects transferred from Surinam to Jamaica in H.M.S. *Hercules* in 1675 includes a William Johnson with forty-four slaves. Hand-written note by V. L. Oliver at the Society of Genealogists. He is a possible 'kinsman'.

CHAPTER IV SCOT

1 George Bate, *The Lives of the Regicides* (1661).

2 Pepys mentions his arrest on June 1, 1663.

3 Letter to Daniel Searle, 1659, the Letterbook of Thomas Povey, B.L., Add. MS. 11411.

4 MSS. note in the handwriting of V. L. Oliver at the Society of Genealogists. The note is unfortunately incomplete but Oliver gives the reference for the memorial as Brooks MSS. Medley 690 vol. II.

5 V. L. Oliver, *Caribbeana* (1910), VOL. I.
6 C.S.P. Dom. (?) 1663.
7 H. Platt, *Astrea and Celadon: an untouched portrait of Aphra Behn* (Modern Language Association of America 49, 1934).
8 The description suggests a possible relationship to the Gorges family.
9 Will of Francis Willoughby dated July 17, 1666.
10 *The Genealogist*, NS vol. XXIII, pp. 204–5.
11 *Orinooko.*

CHAPTER V SIR THOMAS GOWER

1 'Above all, the Hanse – Towns of Hamburgh, Lubeck, Bremen .. had the worst luck for none of them could ever be distinguished from the Dutch.' Clarendon, *The Continuation of the Life* (Oxford, 1760).
2 *Returns of Aliens in London*, Huguenot Soc. (Aberdeen, 1902), vol. II.
3 Society of Genealogists. Boyd, however, warns about the incompleteness of his lists.
4 According to the tombstone of his father in High Hutton church.
5 H.M.C., Sutherland MSS., Appendix to 5th Report, and for most of the following material on the Gowers, Levesons, Temples and Grenvilles.
6 There is a possibility that she wasn't his wife but his father's since they were both Sir Thomas Gower, Bart. See C.A.M. 1652–5 and Grey 1651 f159.
7 C.C.C. Dec. 4, 1646.
8 H.M.C., Sutherland MSS., 5th Report.
9 Yorkshire Marriage Licences, Society of Genealogists, Boyd Index.
10 *Visitation of Bucks 1634.*
11 See Cobham wills, *Kentish Archaeology*, ed. W. A. Scott Robertson (1877), vol. II, which give the detail of all this.

CHAPTER VI THE FIRST DUTCH WAR

1 C.S.P. Dom. 1663–4 and J. Walker, 'The Yorkshire Plot', in *Yorkshire Archaeological Journal*, 1934, vol. XXXI. Also Clarendon, *The Continuation of the Life* (Oxford, 1760).
2 C.S.P. Dom. May 15, 1664.
3 *Clarendon State Papers*, vol. 5 (1970).
4 Clarendon, op. cit., where he attributes the advice to Coventry.
5 C.S.P. Dom. 1641 when Villiers was President of the Council of York.

6 Sir Charles Littleton, Hatton Correspondence, Camden Soc., N 522 (1878), Aug. 7, 1665.

7 Clarendon, op. cit.

8 His brother Thomas Noel died in Surinam in 1666. A niece of Thomas Povey, Sara, married into the Leveson family. The Harleys too were connected, by marriage to the Newports, with the Levesons.

CHAPTER VII THE SPIES

1 'The House out of Doors', 1653, in *The Rump* (1660).

2 J. Bampfield, *The Apology of Colonel Bampfield* (1685).

3 Charles's clemency to Anne Scot, recorded in the Sutherland MSS., backs up Oliver's suggestion that she was a sister of the royalist Sir Ralph Baesh.

4 *London Gazette.*

5 Honeywood is a Kent name.

6 Though there had been a payment for secret service to Henry Killegrew his son in Nov. 1664 of £2,000.

7 So described in a letter to Sir William Temple.

8 *London Gazette*, April 20, May 4, May 10. The Portuguese ambassador was stripped and robbed, etc.

9 Arlington, *Letters to Sir William Temple etc*, ed. Babington (1701).

CHAPTER VIII ANTWERP

1 Preface to C.S.P. Dom. 1666–7 written in 1864

2 The letters are S.P. 29: 167, 60; 169, 38, 39, 117, 118; 170, 75; 171, 65, 120; 172, 14, 66, 81; 173, 3, 4; 177, 42; 182, 143.

3 All the figures fluctuate slightly in the different accounts in the State Papers.

4 C.S.P. Dom. Aug. 31, 1666.

5 I have put this letter here because that is its place in C.S.P. Dom. but the photostat shows a date of Sept. 22 new style, which 'came to my hands the 22 our style'. It could be that the first 22 is a slip of the pen for 12. Robert Luson was at Ipswich just before the restoration.

6 In this context 'hope' has the same force as in an expression like 'I hope I know my duty', implying 'I am sure'.

CHAPTER IX TO PRISON

1 C.S.P. Col. The Dutch fleet anchored on Feb. 16 new style. Surinam fell the next day.

2 C.S.P. Col. 'Some of the English enlisted with them and promised to show them every corner of the country.' Sir William Temple mentions in a letter of 1668 that the English who decided to stay took an oath of allegiance to the Dutch.

3 Letter to Arlington to Sir William Temple, June 3. The State Papers give a full account. The *London Gazette* not surprisingly tried to play it down. There was a panic run on the goldsmiths.

4 National Library of Ireland MSS. 2324, 2332, 2348.

5 All these are numbered S.P. 29, 251.

6 Part of the story of Prince Tarquin was told her by Franciscan Fathers.

7 They were later reconciled.

8 For this and other comments see Van Lennep's *The London Stage 1660–1700* (Southern Illinois Univ. Press, 1965).

9 Van Lennep has? May 69 as the date of the letter but they were waiting for Dryden's next play which must be *Tyrannic Love* produced in June by Van Lennep's dating. This would give more time for rehearsal if the letter was written in January.

CHAPTER X FIRST PLAYS

1 A Colette–Willy-like situation? Van Lennep attributes it to William Cavendish.

2 *The Country Captain* appears in the Stationer's Register, Jan. 30, 1673, as by *Lady* Newcastle.

3 'A Discourse Upon Comedy', in Farquhar, *Works* (1742).

4 J. Downes, *Roscius Anglicanus* (1789).

5 From a letter printed in the preface to the 1667 edition of her works.

6 Willard Thorp, 'Henry Nevil Payne, Dramatist and Jacobite Conspirator', in *The Parrott Presentation Volume*, ed. Craig (Princeton, 1935).

7 Christopher Hill, *The World Turned Upside Down* (1972) *passim*.

8 Based on Van Lennep, *The London Stage 1660–1700* (Southern Illinois Univ. Press, 1965). I may have missed a writer or even two but that wouldn't affect the overall picture.

CHAPTER XI EARLY POEMS

1 A. Hamilton, *Memoirs of Count Grammont*, ed. Fea (1906).

CHAPTER XII THE DUTCH LOVER

1 Shadwell's *The Miser* according to his preface was written in a month.

2 Willard Thorp, 'Henry Nevil Payne, Dramatist and Jacobite Conspirator', in *The Parrott Presentation Volume*, ed. Craig (Princeton, 1935).
3 Essex Papers (Camden Soc. NS 47, 1890).
4 Otherwise called *Mamamouchi*.
5 He appears in the cast list of Ravenscroft's *The Careless Lovers* in March 1673 but not again.

CHAPTER XIII ABDELAZER

1 'To my Lord Lisle, Aug. 1666', in J. Swift (ed.), *Letters Written by Sir William Temple* (1700).
2 Or Bradstreet. Hero of John Berryman's fine poem.
3 Possibly a son of the Captain Edward Bedford who ran the Nursery under Killegrew, 1667–9.
4 The Works of John Dennis quoted in Van Lennep, *The London Stage 1660–1700* (Southern Illinois Univ. Press, 1965).
5 *The Rover*, Part One.

CHAPTER XIV JOHN HOYLE

1 Camden Soc., 44, 1849.
2 Middlesex Sessions Rolls. S.P.R. Apr. 27. 15 Charles II.
3 Middlesex Sessions Rolls G.D.R. 15 Charles II.
4 See for instance the duels of 1675 in Hatton Correspondence, Camden Soc., NS 22 (1878), Ossory against Gerard and Armstrong against Scroope.
5 However, in a set of elegiac verses published after Henry Purcell's death he appears as Damon.
6 Even heterosexual sodomy. Buckingham was framed and tried on such a charge.
7 Watch rate books of St Bride's.
8 Radcliffe was himself a lawyer.
9 'A Letter to Mr Creech at Oxford, Written in the last great frost', *Miscellany* (1685).

CHAPTER XV THE PLAGIARY

1 Wilson (ed.), *Rochester–Savile Letters* (Ohio State Univ. Press, 1941).
2 Essex Papers (Camden Soc., NS 47, 1880).
3 Van Lennep, *The London Stage 1660–1700* (Southern Illinois Univ. Press, 1965).

CHAPTER XVI THE CALM

1 *Modesty triumphing over impudence*, a pamphlet of 1680.
2 C.S.P. Dom. and Col. 1676.
3 Or *Tamoran*.
4 *The Lover's Watch*, in *The Works of Aphra Behn*, ed. Summers (6 vols, New York, reprinted 1967), vol. VI.
5 The elegy on Buckingham, for instance, in Villiers, *The Dramatick Works*, ed. Brown (1715).
6 Since my writing this, Mr Selby Whittingham, who is at work on a monograph of Greenhill, has informed me that a descendant of Greenhill's, Robert Benson, owned a portrait said to be of Aphra Behn by Greenhill now, alas, lost.
7 I suspect this should be a comma, not a full stop.
8 See George de F. Lord (ed.), *Poems on State Affairs 1660–78* (Yale Univ. Press, 1963).
9 'Like her that missed her name in a lampoon/And griev'd to see herself decayed so soon.'

CHAPTER XVII SIR PATIENT FANCY

1 J. Downes, *Roscius Angelicanus* (1789).
2 *The Functions and Disorders of the Reproductive System.*
3 Algernon Sydney, for example, was paid by the French ambassador, while at the same time Louis was paying Charles.
4 H.M.C. Appendix to 14th Report, Part II, 1894.

CHAPTER XVIII THE POPISH PLOT

1 *Moneys Received and Paid for the Secret Services of Charles II and James II 1679–88* (Camden Soc., 52, 1851).
2 Register of the Privy Council 1678–9, P.R.O.
3 'Cully', a dupe or fool but meant affectionately here.
4 Fillamour in *The Feign'd Curtezans*: 'I'll convince you of that error that persuades you harmless pictures are idolatrous.'

CHAPTER XIX THE MEAL-TUB PLOT

1 Schless in his *Poems on Affairs of State 1682–5* (Yale Univ. Press, 1968) says the 'highly popular Whig ballad "Young Jemmy"' appeared in 1681 which could mean these two poems are later but Aphra Behn had already written a Jemmy Scots poem in 1672. Perhaps the 'Captain —— ' of *The Muses Mercury* was really

Monmouth. The first, which begins 'Young Jemmy was a fine lad', was certainly written by 1682 when it was pirated; see later. It exists in a broadsheet in the B.L. as 'The Princely Shepherd'.

2 Smith, *Current Intelligence*, March 23-7.

3 Though Payne's patron Sir Ellis Leighton already knew Buckingham.

4 There's a poem called 'To the Author of Sodom' by John Oldham, his friend and protégé, who would surely have known if the play was by Rochester and would not have addressed him as the author of *Sodom* in the terms the poem uses.

5 I have failed to find him in any of the Inns of Court registers. A John Fishbourne, son of Richard, of Windsor Berks, gent., matriculated at Trinity, Oxford, Dec. 16, 1664, aged 16. He seems a likely candidate.

6 David Vieth in *Attribution in Restoration Poetry* (Yale Univ. Press, 1963) accepts this date.

7 He was one of the witnesses to a codicil to Rochester's will where his name is given as B de Belle-fasse. In the will itself he inherited Rochester's clothes, linen and other items as John Baptist Bell Dosse.

8 Swift indeed called her 'Afra the Amazon light of foot', referring to what he thought her inability to write pindarics, along with most of the rest of her generation.

9 The fight between Cleomena and Thersander is based on that between Tancredi and Clorinda. Even the initials are the same. Aphra Behn had read Spenser's *The Faerie Queen* for she uses the Bower of Bliss in a later work.

CHAPTER XX THE DEATH OF ROCHESTER

1 Psychologically there must also have been a hope of avoiding death by repentance borne out by one occasion when he felt briefly better and hoped to live to lead an amended life. See Burnet's *Some Passages* ... (1724).

2 Lee calls Flatman her 'mate'. He also lived in St Bride's parish. He died a little before her.

3 J. Granger, *Letters*, ed. Malcolm (1805). I take it this is the reference Oldys means, in his MS. note to the B.L. copy of Langbaine on Burnet's 'character' of her in his character of Mrs Wharton 'Burnet Vol. 10'.

4 For a quick check compare Arber's *Milton* Anthology (1638-74) with his *Dryden* (1675-1700). The first has 3 women poets; the second 9. E. Arber (ed.), *British Anthologies* (1899).

CHAPTER XXI THE ROVER'S RETURN

1 *Odes, Songs and Satires of the Reign of Charles II*, MS. in Dyce Collection, V. & A. Library.
2 Dec. 14, 1681, Army Lists. Sir Charles Littleton wrote to Christopher Hatton that he had 'got £6,000 by it' so he could have spared something for a dedication.

CHAPTER XXII DAPHNIS

1 The poem is called 'The Tory Poets' and is attributed to Shadwell and dated Sept. 1682. I may therefore be misreading the dating in these lines or the poem may have been written over a period or the expression may be imprecise.
2 These lines are so like a passage in Robert Gould's satire *The Playhouse* that I incline to give him their authorship too.
3 The payment for a prologue or epilogue was about £10, depending of course on the reputation of the writer. References in the prologue to *The Jealous Lovers* date it from about the same time as the epilogue to *Like Father, Like Son* of which it seems to be a close version. Perhaps this last play is a rewrite of Randolph's play which was very successful in 1682 according to Langbaine. In which case instead of its being unpublished because it was unsuccessful she might have thought it too close to the original to justify reprinting.
4 I.e. 1683 new style.
5 *Newdigate newsletters*, July 29, 1682. Lee's *Lucius Junius Brutus* had been banned in 1680.
6 In 1685. It's been suggested by Wilson, *All The King's Ladies* (Univ. of Chicago Press, 1958), that she was married to a Kentish Knight, Sir Charles Slingsby of Patricksbourne.
7 Sir Thomas Gower's granddaughter Melior married a Gentleman of the Chapel Royal, Thomas Richardson.

CHAPTER XXIII LOVE LETTERS

1 Grammont mentions his liking for her even when she was a child.
2 A third edition of the *Epistles* was advertised in the *Gazette* in June. It was probably this that provoked Prior, though he seems not to have known it was a third edition but thought it was a new work undertaken because of the union of the companies and Betterton's new policy.
3 A very full account is in *Cobbett's Complete Collection of State Trials* (1811), vol. IX.

4 Burnet alleged that Sir Ellis Leighton, Payne's patron, was himself a creature of Buckingham.

5 She thought well of it and included it among her poems in 1684. This broadside publication may have been a pirated version and she therefore laid claim to it the following year. An alternative is a reference to *The Wavering Nymph*, a version of *Mad Amyntas* again by Thomas Randolph for which she had written two songs by 1684 when she included them in her collection.

6 The verse letter written in the 'last great frost'. See below.

7 Dryden, *Letters*, ed. Ward (Duke Univ. Press, 1942).

8 Dryden had praised her in an epilogue to *Tamerlane the Great* by Charles Saunders in 1681: 'A woman wit has often graced the stage.'

9 She had similarly dated her poem to Creech, Jan. 25, 1682. Dryden's poem to Creech, which is the first of the series, is also dated Jan. 25. Like the one I believe may be his on Aphra Behn, it's anonymous. Everyone was expected to know the master's hand.

10 See Levey, *Burlington Magazine* (May 1961).

11 B.L., Harley MS. 7317.

CHAPTER XXIV JAMES II

1 The young Pope was a protégé of Lansdowne.

2 Richard Ames?

3 Her tombstone shows no date of birth, I suspect because she concealed it.

4 I'm not suggesting there hadn't been novels before but the success of this made the whole genre more commercially attractive.

5 Thomas Wilkes, *A General View of the Stage* (1759).

CHAPTER XXV FAREWELL TO LOVE

1 Tom Brown notes with glee how Collier would have castigated her had she been alive then.

2 The alternative seems to be that the poem is by George Jenkins; if so it's an almost unbelievable flash in the pan.

3 'An Epistle to Julian', B.L., Harley MS. 7317.

4 It was one of only two new plays that year, so low had the theatre fallen.

5 An image based on his own epitaph for himself in his commonplace book: 'Fortune filled him too full, and he run over.'

6 Among the records in the Corporation Record Office, Guildhall, London.

7 Sir John Cotton was a relative of Sir Thomas Gower through his first Howard marriage and also connected by the Eures.

8 Tom Brown called him 'cormorant Higden for devouring known'.

CHAPTER XXVI OROONOKO

1 Jackson (ed.), *Diary of Abraham de la Pryme* (Surtees Soc., 1869).

2 It could have been through Tate that she met Creech since, according to his commendatory verses, Tate was already Creech's friend when he published *Lucretius*.

3 Southerne must have seen or read it before he did his Oroonoko which wasn't until 1696.

4 The links with Tryon's book are further explored by R. Sheefey, *Studies in Philology* (1962).

5 Possibly a translation from the French of De Bellefond (Paris, 1669). Stationers' Register, March 1669.

6 Even though hated by the opposition. He incurred Whig odium by, among other things, giving judgment for Thomas Culpepper in 1687 against Lord Devonshire who had caned him in public.

7 There's some justification for this in the wording of the *London Gazette* advertisement of July 1689 which specifically mentions Book Six, hers, as if it hadn't been there before.

CHAPTER XXVII BURNET

1 Hatton Correspondence, Camden Soc., NS 22 (1878).

2 The date for this varies from Dec. 1688 to Feb. 1689.

3 Reresby, *Memoirs*, ed. Browning (Glasgow, 1936), calls him 'Bishop of Salisbury (the late Dr Burnet)' in the account of the coronation.

4 An enquiry into the measures of submission to the Supreme Authority, and of the grounds upon which it may be lawful or necessary for subjects to defend their religion, lives and liberties 1688.' Included in *Eighteen Papers*, 1689.

CHAPTER XXVIII EPILOGUE

1 Betterton, *The Life of Thomas Betterton*, ed. Gildon (1710).

2 Giles Jacob thought it was written ten years before her death.

3 Sedley says Pitts was the son of a usurer.

4 Lord Maitland's library was advertised for sale in the *Gazette* in March 1689.

Books most often cited
or consulted

Where no publisher or place of publication is listed, all books referred to were published in London.

Acts and Ordinances of the Interregnum
Arlington, Lord, *Letters to Sir William Temple etc*, ed. Babington, 1701
Ashley, M., *England in the Seventeenth Century*, Penguin, Harmondsworth, 1971
Bampfield, J., *The Apology of Colonel Bampfield*, 1685
Bate, G., *The Lives of the Regicides*, 1661
Behn, A., *Miscellany*, 1685
—*Aesop's Fables*, with Francis Barlow, 1687
—*History of the Oracles*, 1688
—*A Theory of New Inhabited Worlds*, 1688
—*Love Letters Between a Nobleman and His Sister*, 1694
—*All the Histories and Novels Written by the Late Ingenious Mrs Behn Together with the Life and Memoirs of Mrs Behn*, ed. Gildon, sixth edn. 1718
—*Covent Garden Drolery*, ed. Summers, 1927
—*The Works of Aphra Behn*, 6 vols, ed. Summers, New York, reprinted 1967
Betterton, T., *The Life of Thomas Betterton*, ed. Gildon, 1710
Brown, T., *Works*, 1760
Burnet, G., *Some Passages of the Life and Death of the Right Honourable John Wilmot Earl of Rochester*, 1724
—*History of His Own Time*, ed. Airy, Oxford, 1897
Calendar of the Clarendon State Papers, ed. F. J. Routledge, 5 vols
Calendar of the Committee for Compounding (C.C.C.)
Calendar of State Papers Colonial, America and the West Indies (C.S.P. Col.)

Calendar of State Papers Domestic (C.S.P. Dom.)
Cameron, W. J., *New Light on Aphra Behn*, Univ. of Auckland, 1961
Canterbury Marriage Licences, ed. Cowper, Canterbury, 1894
Cary, H., *Memorials of the Great Civil War*, 1842
Chapman, H., *Great Villiers Second Duke of Buckingham*, 1949
Clarendon, *Life and Continuation of the Life*, Oxford, 1760
Clarke and Foxcroft, *Gilbert Burnet, A Life*, Cambridge, 1907
Committee for the Advance of Money (C.A.M.)
Correspondence of the Family of Hatton 1601–1704, Camden Society, NS 22, 1878
Cowley, A., *Six Books of Plants*, 1693
Creech, T., *Lucretius, Of the Nature of Things*, 1715
De Sola Pinto, V., *Enthusiast in Wit, A Portrait of John Wilmot Earl of Rochester*, 1962
Downes, J., *Roscius Anglicanus*, 1789
Dryden, J., *Letters*, ed. Ward, Duke Univ. Press, 1942
Ephelia, *Female Poems*, 1682
Etherege, Sir George, *Letters*, ed. Bracher, Univ. of California Press, 1974
Everitt, A., *The Community of Kent in the Great Rebellion 1640–60*, Leicester Univ. Press, 1966
Gould, R., *Works*, 1709
Granger, J., *Letters*, ed. Malcolm, 1805
Great News from the Barbadoes, 1676
Grenville, G., *Works*, 1736
Hamilton, A., *Memoirs of Count Grammont*, ed. Fea, 1906
Harbage, A., *Thomas Killigrew*, 1930
Hasted, E., *Kent*, Canterbury, 4 vols, 1778
Jacob, G., *The Poetical Register*, 1723
Kent Archaeological Society, *Seventeenth-century Miscellany*, Ashford, (Kent Records, vol. XVII), 1960
Kentish Archaeology, ed. W. A. Scott Robertson, vol. II, 1877
Killegrew, T., *Comedies and Tragedies*, 1664
Langbaine, G., *English Dramatick Poets*, Oxford, 1691
Melville, L., *Society at Royal Tunbridge Wells*, 1912
Oliver, H., *Sir Robert Howard, A Critical Biography*, Duke Univ. Press, 1963
Oliver, V., *A History of Antigua*, 1894
—*Caribbeana*, 1910
Otway, T., *Works*, ed. Summers, 1926
Parrott Presentation Volume, The, ed. Craig, Princeton, 1935
Penguin Book of Restoration Verse, The, ed. Love, 1968
Philips, K., *Works*, 1669

Phillips, E., *Theatrum Poetarum*, 1675
Poems on Affairs of State 1660–1714, ed. Schless, Yale Univ. Press, 1968
Reresby, Sir John, *Memoirs*, ed. Browning, Glasgow, 1936
Returns of Aliens in London, Huguenot Society Publications, Aberdeen, 1902
Rochester–Savile Letters, The, ed. Wilson, Ohio State Univ. Press, 1941
Rodway and Watt, *A Chronicle History of Guiana*, 1888
Rogers, P., *The Dutch in the Medway*, Oxford, 1970
Rump, The, 1660
Summers, M., *The Restoration Theatre*, 1934
Tatham, J., *The Rump*, 1661
Temple of Death, The, 1695
Thoresby, R., *Diary and Letters*, 1830
Thurloe State Papers
Tixall Letters, ed. Clifford, 1815
Underdown, D., *Royalist Conspiracy*, Yale Univ. Press, 1963
Van Lennep, W., *The London Stage 1660–1700*, Southern Illinois Univ. Press, 1965
Vieth, D., *Attribution in Restoration Poetry*, Yale Univ. Press, 1963
Villiers, G., *Works*, ed. Brown, 1715
Voyages Imaginaires, vol. 26, Amsterdam, 1788
Warren, G., *Description of Surinam*, 1667
West Indies and Guiana 1623–1667, Hakluyt Society, 2, vol. 51
Wiley, A., *Rare Prologues and Epilogues*, 1940
Wilkins, G., *The Miseries of Inforst Marriage*, Students' Facsimile Edition, 1913
Williamson, J. A., *English Colonies in Guiana etc 1604–68*, Oxford, 1923
—*The Caribee Islands Under the Proprietary Patents*, Oxford, 1926
Wilson, J., *All the King's Ladies*, Univ. of Chicago Press, 1958
Woodcock, G., *The Incomparable Aphra*, 1948
Yorkshire Archaeological Society Journal, 1934

Index